D1243685

CHURCH GROWTH
AND THE
WHOLE GOSPEL

BY C. PETER WAGNER

Our Kind of People: The Ethical Dimensions of Church Growth in America
Stop the World, I Want to Get On
What Are We Missing?
Your Church Can Grow
Your Spiritual Gifts Can Help Your Church Grow
The Protestant Movement in Bolivia
Your Church Can Be Healthy

CHURCH GROWTH
AND THE
WHOLE GOSPEL

A Biblical Mandate

C. Peter Wagner

1817

HARPER & ROW, PUBLISHERS, SAN FRANCISCO

Cambridge, Hagerstown, New York, Philadelphia
London, Mexico City, São Paulo, Sydney

To Doris
for thirty years
a wife, a companion, a lover,
a partner in ministry

Unless otherwise indicated, all Bible quotations are from the King James Version.

FIRST EDITION

Designer: Jim Mennick

Library of Congress Cataloging in Publication Data

Wagner, C. Peter.
    CHURCH GROWTH AND THE WHOLE GOSPEL.

    Includes index.
    1. Church growth. 2. Church and social problems. 3. Evangelistic work.
BV652.25.W32   254'.5   81-47433
ISBN 0-06-068942-0   AACR2

81 82 83 84 85   10 9 8   7 6 5 4 3 2 1

Contents

Contents   ix

Introduction

"It comes as no surprise to discover that Church Growth Principles give little attention to any serious notion of Christian social action."[1] These words come from the pastor of St. Andrew Lutheran Church in Hurst, Texas, Rev. Amanda Grimmer, a friend of church growth. She recently studied the movement thoroughly with the purpose of introducing it to her colleagues in the Lutheran Church in America. But while positive and appreciative of what the Church Growth Movement has contributed, Grimmer is not uncritical. She fears the possibility of "a denial of the Gospel through the adoption of lifestyles and behavior patterns that oppose its plain meaning."[2]

Is Pastor Grimmer's assessment accurate? This book attempts to answer her questions in detail. Its purpose is to show, more clearly than previous writings, how the Church Growth Movement does support the whole Gospel.

The Church Growth Movement

In 1980 the Church Growth Movement celebrated its twenty-fifth anniversary. The historical event now regarded as the beginning of the movement was Donald McGavran's publication of *The Bridges of God* in 1955. Subsequent activities by McGavran, including the founding of the Fuller Theological Seminary School of World Mission and Institute of Church Growth in Pasadena, California, in 1965, the recruiting of the nation's largest missiological faculty, and the publication of his major work, *Understanding Church Growth,* in 1970, laid solid foundations for the subsequent development of the movement.

While the early years were lonely ones for McGavran, his circle of colleagues and supporters has steadily broadened, first among leaders in the worldwide field of missiology and more recently among church leaders in North America and Europe. Lyle Schaller, for example, now characterizes the emergence of the Church Growth Movement as "the most influential development of the 1970s" on the American religious scene.[3]

Scores of books have been published applying McGavran's principles to virtually every area of the free world.[4] At least twenty independent periodicals have devoted an issue of their publication to a discussion of the Church Growth Movement.[5] Specialized periodicals such as *Church Growth: America*, the Canadian *His Dominion*, and the British *Church Growth Digest* have appeared, besides the *Global Church Growth Bulletin* edited by McGavran himself and now in its eighteenth year of publication.[6] Numbers of seminaries and Bible schools have introduced courses in church growth into their curriculum. The Fuller Seminary School of Theology offers a Doctor of Ministry program with a concentration in church growth. More recently, Ph.D. work is being done in the field.

Over a period of twenty-five years the Church Growth Movement has been refined as well as expanded. The large quantity of research (including over 350 theses and dissertations at the Fuller School of World Mission alone) has brought to light new principles of growth and modified old ones. The critics of the movement, some quite outspoken, have been extremely helpful in directing the attention of church growth advocates to areas where a closer look at certain theological and social issues needs to be taken. More than anything else, critics focus on the social implications of Christian teaching and accuse church growth of being deficient. While this book is not intended primarily as an answer to critics, it does take the agenda that they have developed with considerable seriousness. Matters having to do with the poor and oppressed, with justice and peace, with brotherhood and liberation, with wealth and lifestyle, with discipleship and the kingdom of God are all part of the concerns of biblical Christians, church growth advocates included.

It is necessary to recognize that social issues have not been entirely absent from church growth oriented literature. Two notable chapters in *Understanding Church Growth* reflect McGavran's concern for the needs of the poor. In one, "The Masses, the Classes and Church

Growth," McGavran applauds "the revolution which seethes in every land" and rejoices that "the masses are learning that they do not have to live in perpetual poverty." He supports "educated men who inform [the poor] that they have a right to plenty, and organize and arm them to wrest a large share of this world's goods from the privileged."[7]

Other faculty members of the Fuller School of World Mission have joined McGavran in commenting on social issues. The most prolific has been Arthur F. Glasser, whose development of the relationship of the cultural mandate to the evangelistic mandate will be mentioned frequently in the text of this book. Paul G. Hiebert, in listing crucial concerns for the evangelical missiological agenda, suggests that churches and missions "desperately need a theology of power and of resources" as well as a "theology of politics and economics," and a "theology of power and wealth."[8] While admittedly not enough has been done, the desire for improvement in the way that social issues are addressed is characteristic of church growth people.

How My Mind Has Changed

I myself made an attempt to address social concerns from the church growth perspective over a decade ago in a book called *Latin American Theology.*[9] As I reread the book now, I feel like a candidate for the "how my mind has changed" series. Not that I have taken a complete 180° turn. In fact I am reasonably sure that some readers of this new book will say that the leopard has not changed his spots. But today I could no longer argue as I did then that "one searches the Scriptures in vain to find a commandment that would have Christians move into the world" with a mission designed to create peace and order, justice and liberty, dignity and community.[10] No wonder Samuel Escobar would write that the church growth school of thought "eliminates from missionary action all intentions in the direction of social justice."[11] No wonder René Padilla would complain of "the superficiality that is shown throughout the whole study."[12] No wonder Mortimer Arias, who maintained an admirable level of gentleness and charity in his critique of *Latin American Theology,* would ask, "Is Wagner conscious of the contradictions of his own theology?"[13]

After studying the criticisms I have become much more aware of potential theological contradictions than I was when I wrote the book. Now, ten years later, I confess I take a much more relaxed view of myself. I realize that I am still not free from theological contradictions, although I hope to show before the first chapter is finished that I have resolved some of the old ones. Some new inconsistencies that I am not yet aware of have undoubtedly crept in, and I would hope I recognize them within ten more years.

Theological Assumptions

Although I will not develop them in detail, I think it will be helpful to list what seem to be a set of five basic theological assumptions of church growth writings. These assumptions are not always explicit, but they are almost invariably deeply imbedded in the thinking and lifestyle of those who advocate church growth principles.

The Glory of God as the Chief End of Humans. Who can argue with the Westminster Confession at this point? Church growth people want to affirm that their theological starting point is God the Father almighty, maker of heaven and earth.

The Lordship of Jesus Christ. Church growth people have been born by the Holy Spirit into the Kingdom of God. Jesus Christ is Lord. Their disposition is to obey him. None of his commandments is optional for Christians.

The Normative Authority of the Scriptures. I like the way Arthur Glasser puts it: "Church growth theology is based on the fundamental principle that Scripture alone is the only infallible rule of faith and practice. The biblical record and biblical interpretation of redemptive history is alone normative for mankind."[14]

The Ultimate Eschatological Reality of Sin, Salvation, and Eternal Death. This is a conviction that decisions made by men and women in this life bear eternal consequences. "Whoever has the Son has [eternal] life; whoever does not have the Son of God does not have life" (1 John 5:12, GNB). Universalism, or the doctrine that everyone will ultimately be saved, does not receive the support of church growth people. To be saved, people must hear and receive the gospel.

The Personal Ministry of the Holy Spirit. The Holy Spirit himself is at work in the lives of believers in all cultures. He fills them, he gives them extraordinary power, he distributes gifts, he guides them into theological and ethical development, he calls them to service.

While most church growth people feel comfortable with the designation "evangelical" or "conservative evangelical," a helpful refinement of this category has been suggested by Paul G. Hiebert and Charles H. Kraft. They have developed a two-dimensional model as follows:[15]

Most church growth people, I think, would see themselves in the "open conservative" category. I would not consider that positioning nonnegotiable, but years of experience have shown that the church growth paradigm does not usually appeal to many in the other three categories as an identity source.

Looking Ahead

Chapters 1 and 2 attempt to bring into focus the biblical teachings on social concerns. They affirm the cultural mandate as incumbent on all Christians. Chapters 3 and 4 do a similar thing with the evangelistic mandate and show how the church growth emphasis on consecrated pragmatism fits into the picture. Chapters 5 and 6 bring the two together and argue that while both the evangelistic and the cultural mandates are essential, the evangelistic mandate has priority. Chapter 7 deals with conversion, the content of the gospel, and how to avoid "cheap grace." Chapter 8 discusses the sociological and theological methodologies underlying the Church Growth Movement and stresses that meaningful social ethics need to be contextualized. Chapter 9 takes up some objections that have been raised concerning the most controversial teaching of the Church Growth Movement: the homogeneous unit principle. Chapter 10 addresses the question of the most appropriate structures for Christian involvement in social ministries.

As I consider the content, it seems to me that, of all the concepts, two stand out in their importance for joining a vigorous social outreach in the name of Christ with the kind of evangelism that brings people to Christ, folds them into Christian churches, and thereby helps churches grow. First is the need to maintain the priority of evangelism within the total mission of the church. Losing this priority almost invariably carries serious negative consequences for church growth. Second is the matter of structure. Certain social issues can be addressed effectively by the local congregation and they will enhance growth. Other issues should be avoided in the local congregation; Christians should become involved with them through other structures which equally represent the church or the people of God. The other topics in the book are important, but not, I think, as important as these two.

Notes

1. N. Amanda Grimmer, "The Church Growth Movement: An Appraisal," *LCA Partners* 2, no. 4 (August 1980), p. 11.
2. Ibid.
3. Lyle E. Schaller, "Foreword" to Donald McGavran and George G. Hunter III, *Church Growth Strategies That Work* (Nashville: Abingdon, 1980), p. 7.
4. For an annotated bibliography of books relating to church growth in America by C. Peter Wagner, send $2.00 for postage and handling to C. Peter Wagner, Fuller Theological Seminary, 135 North Oakland Ave., Pasadena, CA 91101.
5. These periodicals include *International Review of Missions* (July 1968), *Christianity Today* (January 19 1973), *United Evangelical Action* (Spring 1975), *Eternity* (June 1975), *Christian Life* (October 1975), *The Covenant Quarterly* (November 1975), *Lutheran Pastors Bulletin* (October 1976–March 1977), *Home Missions Alert* (Church of the Nazarene) (June/August and September/November 1977), *Home Missions* (Southern Baptists) (December 1977), *The Standard* (Baptist General Conference) (January 15, 1978), *Conservative Baptist* (Spring 1978), *The Asbury Seminarian* (October 1978), *The Living Church* (Episcopal) (January 14, 1979), *The Christian Ministry* (January 1979), *Vine Life* (March 1979), *Church Administration* (Southern Baptist) (April 1979), *Church Leader* (North Carolina Baptists) (May/June 1979), *IDEA* (British Evangelical Alliance) (Summer 1979), *LCA Partners* (August 1980), *Review and Expositor* (Fall 1980), *Leadership* (Winter 1981).

6. For subscription information write: *Church Growth: America*, 150 S. Los Robles, Suite 600, Pasadena, CA 91101; *His Dominion*, 4400 4th Ave., Regina, Sask. S4T OH8, Canada; *Church Growth Digest*, Roanfield Road, Cheltenham, Glos., England; *Global Church Growth Bulletin*, P.O. Box 66, Santa Clara, CA 95052.

7. Donald A. McGavran, *Understanding Church Growth*, rev. ed., (Grand Rapids: Eerdmans, 1980), p. 276.

8. Paul G. Hiebert, "Holism and the Integrated Christian Life," in *Crucial Dimensions in World Evangelization*, ed. Arthur F. Glasser, et. al. (Pasadena: Wm. Carey Library, 1976), p. 85.

9. C. Peter Wagner, *Latin American Theology: Radical or Evangelical?* (Grand Rapids: Eerdmans, 1970).

10. Ibid., p. 30.

11. Samuel Escobar, "The Need for Historical Awareness," in Samuel Escobar and John Driver, *Christian Mission and Social Justice* (Scottdale, PA: Herald Press, 1978), p. 23.

12. C. René Padilla, "A Steep Climb Ahead for Theology in Latin America," *Evangelical Missions Quarterly* 7, no. 2 (Winter 1971), p. 101.

13. Mortimer Arias, "Polemics and Restatement," *Christian Century* 88, no. 22 (June 2, 1971), p. 700.

14. Arthur F. Glasser, "Church Growth Theology," in *Church Growth Movement*, Proceedings of Eleventh Biennial Meeting, Association of Professors of Missions (June 12–14, 1972), p. 17.

15. For a development of this model see Charles H. Kraft, *Christianity in Culture: A Study in Dynamic Theologizing in Cross-Cultural Perspective*, (Maryknoll, NY: Orbis, 1979), pp. 39–41.

CHAPTER 1

The Church, the Kingdom, and the Cultural Mandate

John the Baptist, the person God sent to "prepare the way of the Lord," preached the kingdom of God. Matthew summarizes John's message as, "Repent ye: for the kingdom of heaven is at hand" (Matt. 3:2). When the proper time had come, Jesus received baptism from John, resisted the devil's temptation in the wilderness, went to Capernaum, and began his three years of public ministry. What was his initial message? "From that time," Matthew reports, "Jesus began to preach, and to say, Repent: for the kingdom of heaven is at hand" (Matt. 4:17). He taught his disciples to pray, "Thy kingdom come" (Matt. 6:10). He explained the kingdom in a series of parables, likening it to a sower, a grain of mustard seed, leaven, a hidden treasure, a pearl of great price, a dragnet, and a householder (Matt. 13). When he sent the twelve apostles on their first mission, he instructed them to "preach, saying The kingdom of heaven is at hand" (Matt. 10:7). When he later sent out seventy, he told them to heal the sick and say, "the kingdom of God is come nigh unto you" (Luke 10:9).

The kingdom was a prominent theme both before and after the resurrection. During the forty days between the time Jesus was raised from the dead and his ascension, he spoke to his apostles of "the things pertaining to the kingdom of God" (Acts 1:3). When Philip evangelized Samaria he was "preaching the things concerning the kingdom of God" (Acts 8:12). Paul preached the kingdom of God in Ephesus (Acts 19:8), and the very last thing we know about him is that he was in Rome "preaching the kingdom of God" (Acts 28:31). Paul, James, Peter, and the author of Hebrews all mention the kingdom in their epistles.

The Evangelical Resurrection of the Kingdom Idea

George Eldon Ladd says, "Modern scholarship is quite unanimous in the opinion that the kingdom of God was the central message of Jesus."[1] If this is true, and I know of no reason to dispute it, I cannot help wondering out loud why I haven't heard more about it in the thirty years that I have been a Christian? I certainly have read about it enough in the Bible. Matthew mentions the kingdom 52 times, Mark 19, Luke 44, and John 4. But I honestly cannot remember any pastor whose ministry I have been under actually preaching a sermon on the kingdom of God. As I rummage through my own sermon barrel, I now realize that I myself have never preached a sermon on it. Where has the kingdom been?

Many observers, among them critics of the Church Growth Movement, have raised the same question. For example, Justice C. Anderson of Southwestern Baptist Theological Seminary says, "Perhaps the Church Growth School needs a stronger emphasis on the kingdom concept." Although he admits that "Southern Baptists have much to learn from Dr. McGavran and his disciples," he nevertheless is worried about their methodology and has objections "in the light of Christian theology in general."[2] Renowned Dutch missiologist Johannes Verkuyl asks, "Can McGavran be charged with ecclesiocentrism in failing to understand that the church must be paired with the kingdom?"[3] I myself was brought up short when Raymond J. Bakke of Northern Baptist Seminary commented in a review of one of my recent books, "It's been a long time since I read a significant work on ecclesiology or missiology that never once mentioned the kingdom. . . ."[4]

I became a Christian in 1950, during what is now being called the "Great Reversal." When I was converted in university and joined Inter-Varsity Christian Fellowship, I became identified with the evangelical wing of Protestantism, and I have been an evangelical ever since. I soon learned that our group was engaged in serious theological warfare and that mostly we were on the losing side. We were battling against liberalism, against postmillennialism, against evolution, against Freudian psychology, against naturalism, against humanism—all of which could be more or less summed up in the term "the social gospel." What did this imply?

The origins of the social gospel have been traced back to the latter part of the 1800s.[5] Its principal advocate in America was Walter

Rauschenbusch, who used the kingdom of God motif as a major integrating element in his theological development. "The social gospel," Rauschenbusch says, "tries to see the progress of the kingdom of God in the flow of history. . . . Its chief interest is the Kingdom of God."[6] By association, then, the kingdom of God became an enemy of evangelicals. Feelings were so strong that some went to the extreme of opposing any sort of Christian activity designed to heal the hurts of society.

The social gospel was not the only misuse of the kingdom of God idea during the Great Reversal. Dispensational charts put the kingdom of God in the future, so that, while it was real, it had little direct bearing on how Christians were to live today. Some, such as William Miller, set dates for the arrival of the kingdom. The dates came but the kingdom didn't. Jehovah's Witnesses called their churches "Kingdom Halls" and thereby did not enhance its appeal to evangelicals. Appearing among all of this was the theme that the kingdom of God had already begun in America. As H. R. Niebuhr tells us, "The kingdom of the Lord was a human possession . . . in particular the kingdom of the Anglo-Saxon race, which is destined to bring light to the gentiles by means of lamps manufactured in America."[7]

Against that background, evangelicals during most of the twentieth century chose to concentrate largely on soul saving. Wes Michaelson is correct in his observation that the evangelical heritage has been "dominant individualism," with its great emphasis on "converting," while assigning a peripheral status to "questions of discipleship, justice and the shape of the church."[8] The Church Growth Movement, firmly located in the evangelical camp, uncritically, and somewhat innocently, participated in this ethos.

But while the kingdom of God theme had been virtually buried by American evangelicals, its gradual resurrection began shortly after World War II. Most observers list Carl F. H. Henry's *The Uneasy Conscience of Modern Fundamentalism,* published in 1947, as the first stirring. Fuller Theological Seminary, which was founded that same year and where Henry himself taught, was given a mandate by its president, Harold John Ockenga, to spearhead a neo-evangelical movement in which concern for justice, peace, oppression, racial equality, and other major social issues would be restored to the evangelical agenda. Through the 1950s it was a lonely road, but during the 1960s the group Richard Quebedeaux calls the "young evangelicals" joined the movement and energetically proclaimed, with considerable success, the need to restore evangelical social concern. They may have swung the pendulum back a little too far, but that could be expected. When the decade of the 1960s had concluded, David Moberg could observe that, overall, evangelicals were "awakening to their inconsistencies" and "returning to the totality of the Christian Gospel."[9]

The Kingdom of God in the Bible

Evangelicals may have buried the kingdom of God concept, but they never buried the Bible. The absolute trustworthiness and authority of the Scriptures is a banner they have always held high. The fact that the kingdom of God is such a prominent biblical teaching has been stressed convincingly in recent years by evangelical scholars such as Fuller's George Eldon Ladd[10] and the American "radical discipleship" group,[11] and in the writings of Howard A. Snyder,[12] Latin Americans Orlando Costas, René Padilla, and Samuel Escobar,[13] and the South African David Bosch,[14] among others. Because it is biblical, evangelicals are prone to listen.

Naturally, it will take time to assimilate what we are learning from such brethren into church growth thinking. It took time to unwrap the grave clothes from Lazarus. But as I review the literature, three characteristics of the kingdom of God seem especially important for the more specialized interests of church growth thinking: the Christocentric nature of the kingdom, the future reality of the kingdom, and the present reality of the kingdom.

The Christocentric Nature of the Kingdom. While the Greek word *basileia* (kingdom) can mean both the geographical area over which a king reigns and the exercise of kingly sovereignty, it is in the latter sense that the word is used in the New Testament teaching on the kingdom of God. As Edmund P. Clowney says, it signifies royal power and describes "his dominion rather than his domain."[15] The king, of course, is none other than Jesus Christ, although he himself refused to make this claim, because he knew it would be misunderstood as a domain rather than a dominion. The common Christian affirmation that Jesus is Lord is at once an acknowledgment that Jesus is God and that he is the ruler of the kingdom of God. Those who have not yet confessed Jesus as Lord cannot be part of the kingdom. The Bible also warns that those who do confess Jesus as Lord with their mouths, but not in their hearts, and by their deeds, will also not enter the kingdom of God (Matt. 7:21–23). It is important to recognize that only where Jesus Christ is openly and consciously declared to be Lord is the kingdom of God present. In a cosmic sense Christ reigns over all creation, but this reign is not actualized until persons have submitted to it in faith, trust, and obedience. No one can even see the kingdom of God unless he or she has been "born again" (John 3:3). In the kingdom the individual becomes a new person, belongs to a new humanity, and joins a new community. "Old things are passed away; behold, all things are become new" (2 Cor. 5:17). Personal submission to the king, Jesus Christ, is the chief characteristic of the kingdom of God.

The Future Reality of the Kingdom.   The Bible teaches that time can be divided into two significant periods. Jesus speaks of "this world" and "the world to come" (Matt. 12:32). The Apostle Paul uses similar terminology when he says that Christ is exalted above all principalities and powers "not only in this world, but also in that which is to come" (Eph. 1:21). The event which separates the two ages is the second coming of Jesus Christ.

Details of how the rapture and the millennium might fit into the sequence of events do not alter the fact that the kingdom in a real sense is eschatological. A time will come when Jesus "shall have delivered up the kingdom to God, even the Father" but until that time Jesus will reign as king (1 Cor. 15:24). He will be supreme until all enemies of the kingdom are conquered, the last enemy being death. In the age to come there will be no more sorrow, sickness, oppression, injustice, war, discrimination, poverty, murder, idolatry, exploitation, greed, imprisonment, corruption, or death. When this happens, the kingdom will once again become Theocentric rather than Christocentric, for "the Son will place himself under God, who placed all things under him; and God will rule completely over all" (1 Cor. 15:28, GNB). The whole creation will be delivered from the bondage of corruption at that time, but until then it "groaneth and travaileth in pain" (Rom. 8:22).

The Present Reality of the Kingdom.   Since we do not live in the future, but in the present, we live in an age when corruption, death, sickness, mud, and filth are very much a part of our world, as they will continue to be until Jesus comes. But still, with all the power that the devil exercises as the "god of this world" (2 Cor. 4:4), the kingdom of God is not completely postponed for the age to come—it has entered into this very present age. Arthur Glasser says, "We must keep in mind the fact that the presence of the kingdom of God in this age should be seen as God's dynamic reign invading the here and now."[16] If the kingdom is present, it follows that those for whom the kingdom is a reality, those who have been born again and who obey the king, must live lives more characteristic of the age to come than the present age. Jesus' kingdom is not *of* this world, but it is *in* this world.

Since the devil still has a great deal of power, the most evident and visible sign of the kingdom's presence in this age is confrontation with and victory over Satan. One of Jesus' key statements about the kingdom came when the Pharisees accused him of casting out demons by the power of Beelzebub, the prince of the demons. After Jesus pointed out that Satan's kingdom itself could not endure if Satan cast out Satan, he said this: "If I cast out devils by the Spirit of God, then the kingdom of God is come unto you" (Matt. 12:28). While not denying that Satan has been given vast control of global affairs in this present age, Jesus announces that victory over Satan is a sign of the kingdom in the present, and that this victory is chiefly displayed by the casting out of demons. Ladd argues that this is the "essential theology of the kingdom of God." While at the end of this age Jesus will *destroy* Satan, in this age he releases the power to *bind* Satan so that "men may be delivered from his power."[17]

Old Testament Ideals

The phrase "kingdom of God" does not appear in the Old Testament. It is the consensus of biblical scholars, however, that the idea of the kingdom is very much present there. It is implicit in the rule of God over the events of history in general and over the nation of Israel in particular. It is also implicit in the messianic prophecies of hope which looked forward to their fulfillment in Jesus Christ. The people of Israel did not always live up to the standards of Jehovah God their king. Frequently God had to send prophets to call the people back, and sometimes he allowed their enemies to conquer them as a punishment for not living kingdom lives.

Throughout the Old Testament, God's ideal for the lifestyle of all human beings is clear. They were first to relate to him as the one and only God through worship and sacrifices. The sin of idolatry is condemned in the first of the ten commandments and stands out as the most blatant characteristic of the disobedience of God's people until the Babylonian captivity. They were also commanded to obey his law which gave specific details of how to live out the righteousness of the kingdom in their particular cultural setting. Israel was supposed to be an example of this kind of kingdom living to all other nations.

God promised he would reward obedience with *shalom*, that wonderful Hebrew ideal of harmony with God and peace with oneself, material prosperity, happy family life, social righteousness, protection from enemies, and whatever else makes up the good life of the Semitic culture. "I make peace [*shalom*]," says God (Isa. 45:7). "I will give peace [*shalom*] in the land" (Lev. 26:6). The Messiah was to be called the "Prince of Peace [*shalom*]" (Isa. 9:6). When Jesus, the Prince of Peace, came, there ensued what Arthur Glasser describes as "nothing less than the beginning of an era marked by the fulfillment of the great Messianic promises of the Old Testament."[18] God's kingdom ideals for his people in the Old Testament continue as ideals for those of us who today claim to be in the kingdom and submitted to the reign of Jesus the Messiah and king.

Pitfalls to Avoid in Kingdom Thinking

In making practical applications of the teaching of the kingdom of God, two pitfalls in particular need to be avoided. Because so many well-intentioned people have fallen into these traps in their enthusiastic efforts to apply kingdom principles, they need to be highlighted here.

Identifying the Kingdom of God with a Kingdom of This World.

Advocates of certain social designs are tempted to become so enthusiastic about their design that they think the kingdom of God can be identified with it. Societies that appear to be approaching their design are said to be approaching the kingdom of God. Jesus himself ran into this problem during his ministry. The kingdom of God was conceived by some first-century Jews to be freedom from Roman rule, the political restoration of the kingdom of David. The Messiah they expected was a person who would lead the struggle to throw off the yoke of oppression, subjugation, exploitation, and injustice epitomized by Rome. But Jesus staunchly refused to be used politically by any group of people. When he was brought before Pilate, Pilate asked him if he was king of the Jews —meaning the political sense. Jesus clearly said, "My kingdom is not of this world." He did not deny that he was a king in a cosmic sense, but he refused to be identified with a political cause. Pilate had no problem with that kind of a king, so he acquitted Jesus (John 18:33–38).

As an example, consider Maoist China. Some Christian China-watchers through the years have evaluated the Maoist revolution in millennial terms. They have seen there what they interpret as the rising up of the "new man" and "signs of the kingdom." Now, there is no denying that much social progress has been made in China over the past thirty years. I recall meeting my friend Philip Hogan, head of the Assemblies of God Foreign Mission Department and former missionary to China, on the day he returned to the U.S. after his first visit to mainland China in 30 years. He told with amazement of the clean streets, the orderly people, the ample food supply, the provision of medical care, and the abolition of prostitution. He mentioned that theft was so minor a problem that he was given no key to his hotel room. Hogan, however, did not think he was in the kingdom of God. Arthur F. Glasser calls the association of Maoist China with the kingdom of God "unmitigated nonsense" that has betrayed the whole theologizing process. He mentions the damage done by reducing "the good news of the kingdom to radical politics," "downplaying the inveteracy of human evil," and "resisting the biblical priority of preaching the redemptive gospel and calling men and women to repentance and faith." Glasser is indignant against those who see signs of the kingdom of God in a society, however radically transformed, in which Maoist philosophy deliberately, openly, and aggressively rejects Jesus Christ the king.[19]

If, as we have argued previously, the kingdom of God is Christocentric, any attempt to identify it with contemporary socio-political movements is misguided. As Lewis Smedes of the Fuller Seminary School of Theology says:

History should be clear enough for us, if the Bible is not, that whatever snippets of the kingdom order are present in human affairs, they are mixed up with human ignorance, pretension, and sin. Only God himself, sometime, not now, not in the most promising human action, will make the earthly order identical with his heavenly kingdom."[20]

Identifying the Kingdom of God with the Church.   In his new book, *I Believe in Church Growth,* Eddie Gibbs of the British Bible Society says, "The writings of Donald McGavran do not make clear the relationship he sees between the church and the kingdom."[21] This is probably a fair observation. To my recollection, a theoretical discussion of the relationship between the two has not yet appeared in church growth literature.

The nature of the relationship between the church and the kingdom has not enjoyed total consensus among biblical scholars. As Andrew Kirk pointed out in an address at the Lausanne Congress on World Evangelization, a few authors make a complete identification, a large number make a partial identification, and a smaller group makes a radical separation between the two.[22]

Without arguing the point here, I follow the views of those scholars who see a partial identification of the church with the kingdom of God. I agree with George Ladd, who says, "If the dynamic concept of the kingdom is correct, it is never to be identified with the church. . . . The kingdom is the rule of God; the church is a society of men."[23] The church should totally reflect the lifestyle of the kingdom, but, as we are all painfully aware, it does not. While most Christians I know do acknowledge Jesus as their Lord and seriously try to live lives that would be a credit to the kingdom of God, few if any fully accomplish it, and they are embarrassed by their failure. The church even includes on its rolls some extremely nominal members who do not attend worship services, who use the Lord's name in vain, who do not tithe their income, who succumb to the lust of the flesh, the lust of the eyes, and the pride of life, who get drunk, who have little concern for the poor, and who, if it were legal, would keep slaves. No, the church cannot be identified with the kingdom of God one-on-one.

But this same church is described in the Bible as the bride of Christ, the household of God. Its members are called to be saints (Rom. 1:1). It is a "chosen race, a royal priesthood, a holy nation, God's own people" (1 Pet. 2:9, RSV). This is kingdom language. It would be a mistake to divorce the church entirely from the kingdom. Ladd argues that those who received Jesus' preaching of the kingdom were viewed as inheritors of the future kingdom but also "as the people of the kingdom in the present, and therefore, in some sense of the word, a church."[24] I like the way Howard Snyder describes the church as "a charismatic community and God's pilgrim people, his kingdom of priests . . . the community of the king."[25] The kingdom creates the church, not vice versa. But the church bears witness to the kingdom and is an instrument of the kingdom. The church needs to balance its present witness that the kingdom has come near in Jesus Christ and that salvation, peace *(shalom)*, love, and justice are all available, with the reality that these blessings are now incomplete and not yet in the final, perfect form they will take in the age to come. The church is not perfect; however, there is no other agency in the world that has been designated by God as the interpreter of the kingdom to this present generation.

Church Growth and Kingdom Growth

Some church growth is kingdom growth, and some isn't. Suppose that First Methodist Church, for example, grows from 500 members to 1000 members in ten years. Statistically that is good church growth. But suppose further analysis shows that a nearby Methodist church of 150 members closed its doors and 100 of them joined First Methodist. Then a Church of the Nazarene split and 200 of its members came in. Another 100 moved into town and brought letters of transfer with them. The final 100 were men and women who had no previous church affiliation and who were led to Christ through the witness of the members of First Methodist. How much of the growth was kingdom growth? Obviously only the 100 who were converted from the world, or 20 percent. Eighty percent was nothing more than what one author has called "the circulation of the saints."

Of course, behind the affirmation that the 20 percent was kingdom growth is a crucial assumption: that those 100 people truly, by word and deed, submit to Jesus as Lord. If they do, they are not only Methodists, but also members of what Snyder would call the community of the king. They have become part of the fellowship of "those who have experienced God's reign and entered into the enjoyment of its blessings."[26] Thus, church growth is not to be confused with denominational self-aggrandizement or the preservation of a human institution. Behind growth statistics in general is the need for discernment as to what kind of growth is taking place. Church growth has taught that new people come into the church three ways: by biological, transfer, and conversion growth.[27] The major burden of the Church Growth Movement has been to assist new conversion growth, the kind of church growth that most nearly parallels true kingdom growth. It is in this sense that Clowney affirms that "church growth is kingdom growth by the power of the Holy Spirit, the life of the New Creation."[28]

Preaching the Kingdom

In its effort to be faithful to the kingdom, the church must preach the Gospel. If the church does not preach the gospel of the kingdom, who will? The king has told us to preach the gospel to every creature (Mark 16:15). When will Jesus return and begin the age to come? "This gospel of the kingdom will be preached throughout the whole world, as a testimony to all nations; and then the end will come" (Matt. 24:14, RSV). Kingdom behavior is gospel-preaching behavior. At least 16,000 distinct people groups, presently comprising over two billion individuals, have not yet received a satisfactory witness of the kingdom. If they are not only to hear of the kingdom of God, but to be born again into it and enjoy its blessings, cross-cultural missionaries must be sent to them with the gospel. If this is not a high-priority item for a Christian person, a local church, a denomination, or a council of churches, their kingdom behavior is suspect, to say the least.

The intent of the kingdom style of gospel preaching is to make disciples for the king. He commanded it in the Great Commission (Matt. 28:19–20). Part of the commitment of becoming a true disciple is a commitment to the body of Christ. This is why Peter Beyerhaus stresses, in his Lausanne plenary address on the kingdom, that "the goal of evangelism is not only to make individual believers" but "to persuade these believers to be incorporated as responsible members into the church as God's Messianic community."[29] If true kingdom preaching, by the power of the Holy Spirit, makes disciples who become responsible church members, then the growth of the church is very intimately connected with the growth of the kingdom of God. This view avoids, I hope, the danger that J. G. Davies warns against when he says that "to define the goal of mission as church growth is to indulge in an ecclesiastical narrowing of the concept of the kingdom of God."[30] Certainly no church growth advocate that I know would want to be guilty of narrowing either the concept of the kingdom of God or the command for its extension.

As the kingdom of God is preached and more and more people submit themselves to the reign of the king, the wider blessings of the kingdom of God will be more evident. God's people are people who are committed to the promotion of justice and peace. They oppose those in the kingdom of Satan. Since the kingdom of Satan, as Orlando Costas says, "stands for what oppresses, dehumanizes, and enslaves man, the kingdom of God must stand for what humanizes, liberates, and enriches man."[31] Churches full of people who serve Satan rather than God are not the kind of churches that the Church Growth Movement has ever recommended. Church growth teaching advocates people living the kingdom lifestyle. I like the way Ronald J. Sider puts it: "In the power of Christ, Christians can begin now to live in Christ's new kingdom even through it will come in its fullness only at the eschaton."[32]

The Cultural Mandate

I first came across the term "cultural mandate" many years ago when reading an essay by Arthur Glasser, written before he joined the faculty of the Fuller School of World Mission.[33] His call to succeed Donald McGavran as Dean symbolized to me the incorporation of a strong social emphasis into the Church Growth Movement. Some have said that they do not like the term "cultural mandate."[34] Their reasons seem to me unconvincing. Balanced by the parallel "evangelistic mandate," the terms furnish helpful thought categories for understanding with precision the central dimensions of the mission of the church.

As I ponder the cultural mandate and what it means for the growth of the church, three aspects stand out: its origin, its demands and its scope.

The Origin of the Cultural Mandate.   As with any significant kingdom concept, the cultural mandate has its origin in God. It was first given before the fall, when only Adam and Eve comprised the human race. As the creation narrative unfolds, God says, "And now we will make human beings; they will be like us and resemble us. They will have power over the fish, the birds, and all animals, domestic and wild, large and small" (Gen. 1:26, GNB). It was done, and Adam and Eve were ready to receive their first recorded divine commandment: "Have many children, so that your descendants will live all over the earth and bring it under their control. I am putting you in charge of the fish, the birds, and all the wild animals . . ." (Gen. 1:28, GNB). These first human beings were given what Robert Webber calls "delegated sovereignty" over God's earthly creation.[35] They were to treat creation as God himself would treat it. That was the cultural mandate.

In New Testament times Jesus not only exemplified the cultural mandate in his own life and ministry, he summed up the entire teaching of the law and the prophets by saying, "Love the Lord your God with all your heart, with all your soul, and with all your mind. This is the greatest and most important commandment. The second most important commandment is like it: Love your neighbor as you love yourself" (Matt. 22:37–39, GNB). No one can be a kingdom person without loving one's neighbor. No Christian can please God without fulfilling the cultural mandate.

The Demands of the Cultural Mandate.   The specific content of the cultural mandate is awesome. God expects a great deal of those to whom he has entrusted the earth and all of its goodness. Distribution of wealth, the balance of nature, marriage and the family, human government, keeping the peace, cultural integrity, liberation of the oppressed—these and other global responsibilities rightly fall within the cultural mandate. Since it is God's will that the human race live in *shalom,* those among them who have been born again into the kingdom and who purport to live under the Lordship of Jesus Christ are required to live lives that will promote *shalom* to the greatest extent possible. Psalm 144 lists some of the blessings of God on his people: they have victory over their enemies, their sons grow up like strong plants, their daughters are like stately columns, their barns are filled with crops of every kind, sheep bear young by the tens of thousands, cattle reproduce plentifully, no cries of distress are heard in the streets, and their God is the Lord. While it must be kept in mind that such an ideal situation will not occur until the age to come, it is God's desire that the people he has called out reflect and promote such blessings to the best of their potential.

Some specific demands of the cultural mandate were set forth by John the Baptist when he said that those who had affluence should share with the less fortunate, that tax collectors should not overcharge, that soldiers should not be brutal or accuse falsely, and they should be content with their wages (Luke 3:11–14). This is only a sampling of the requirements of the cultural mandate; the Sermon on the Mount and numerous other biblical passages add significantly to the list of God's expectations.

The Scope of the Cultural Mandate.   The cultural mandate has never been rescinded. It was given at creation and will be in effect until Jesus returns. Christian people are God's chosen agents for doing what they can to make it happen. Every Christian and every church must contribute in some way to the effective fulfillment of the cultural mandate. It is not enough to think and theologize about it. It takes doing. It is not enough even to pray about it. It takes energy and involvement. Changed persons do not automatically move out to change society. They need to be taught, they need to be encouraged, they need to see exemplary models that they will desire to imitate.

For most Christians who have committed their lives to Jesus as Lord, this is not new information. One of the most influential books among American Christians in recent years has been Billy Graham's *Peace with God*. In it, Graham acknowledges evangelical criticisms of the social gospel. "But," he argues, "Jesus taught that we are to take regeneration in one hand and a cup of cold water in the other. Christians, above all others, should be concerned with social problems and social injustices. . . . The Christian is to take his place in society with moral courage and stand up for that which is right, just and honorable."[36] Few evangelical Christians would take exception to Graham's statement.

More apropos of the Church Growth Movement, Donald McGavran has united his voice with those of other evangelicals who recognize the binding nature of the cultural mandate. He says:

Today the sinfulness of the social order offends thoughtful Christians everywhere. . . . The great inequalities of wealth and poverty among the haves and have-nots, and the revolting treatment meted out to oppressed minorities, are clearly contrary to the will of God and Father of our Lord Jesus Christ. Christians of all shades of theological opinion recognize this and, in varying measure, work to rectify it in the areas of their responsibility.[37]

Perhaps the most representative evangelical statement in our generation, the Lausanne Covenant, puts it this way: "The message of salvation implies also a message of judgment upon every form of alienation, oppression and discrimination, and we should not be afraid to denounce evil and injustice wherever they exist. When people receive Christ they are born again into his kingdom and must seek not only to exhibit but also to spread its righteousness in the midst of an unrighteous world" (Art. 5).

Incarnational Growth

Orlando Costas sees four major areas in which church growth takes place: numerical growth, organic growth, conceptual growth, and incarnational growth. The latter, incarnational growth, has directly to do with the cultural mandate. Incarnational growth, Costas says, means "the degree of involvement of a community of faith in the life and problems of her social environment."[38] Most Christians would agree that incarnational growth is an important part of service to God. Most, I think, would also admit that neither they nor their churches are satisfactorily involved in it.

Measuring instruments have yet to be developed that can help us monitor our progress toward incarnational growth. As an ideal, Costas argues that "the church is faithful to her witnessing vocation when she becomes a catalyst for God's liberating action in the world of poverty, exploitation, hunger, guilt and despair. . . ."[39] He suggests that Christians do three specific things: they "stand in solidarity with the people," they "show with concrete actions that God cares" and "they help them understand" their situation. If these ideas are to become practical, and I hope they soon will, measurable guidelines will have to be drawn up so that a given local congregation will be able to know whether it has grown incarnationally from year to year, or how it compares with similar churches in similar cultural settings. Perhaps one could begin by measuring the percentage of total church income given to causes outside the local parish. This is a challenge for future research.

The Signs of the Kingdom

When Matthew describes the beginning of Jesus' public ministry he says, "From that time Jesus began to preach, and to say, 'Repent: for the kingdom of heaven is at hand' " (Matt. 4:17). Luke provides more detail. He says that Jesus had been preaching around Galilee, he was becoming famous, and then he went into the synagogue at Nazareth, his home town. He opened the book of Isaiah and read the following passage from Isaiah 61:1–2:

The Spirit of the Lord is upon me,
because he has anointed me to preach the good news to the poor.
He has sent me to proclaim release to the captives
and recovering of sight to the blind,
to set at liberty those who are oppressed,
to proclaim the acceptable year of the Lord (Luke 4:18–19, RSV).

When he finished, Jesus said that this prophecy was fulfilled in himself and thereby caused such a commotion that they drove him out of the town and tried to kill him (Luke 4:21–30).

This portion of Scripture needs some special attention because of the prominent place it occupies in the writings of those who are attempting to stimulate the church toward greater fulfillment of the cultural mandate. It appears as consistently in the writings of the radical discipleship school and in the Geneva-based theology of the World Council of

Churches as does the Great Commission in church growth writings. As I study these writings, however, I detect what I consider an exegesis and application of the text that may do only partial justice to the lifestyle of the kingdom of God that the Scripture demands. It seems to me a case of selective obedience to the commands of God.

Why do I say "selective obedience?"

As Ronald Sider points out, "Many people spiritualize these words either by simplistically assuming that [Jesus] was talking about healing blinded hearts in captivity to sin or by appealing to the later Old Testament and intertestamental idea of 'the poor of Yahweh.' "[40] I agree with Sider that spiritualizing the passage will not do justice to it. There is very important literal meaning here, and I am prepared to take it somewhat more literally even than Sider and other authors have been inclined to do.

Before explaining this, I want to expand the list of the signs of the kingdom found in the Luke 4 passage. John the Baptist sent his disciples to Jesus to ask if he was really the one for whom John the Baptist had been preparing the way. John's disciples, when they arrived, saw Jesus' deeds: he healed sick people, cast out evil spirits, and restored sight to blind people (Luke 7:21). Then they heard his words: "The blind see, the lame walk, lepers are cleansed, deaf hear, the dead are raised, and the gospel is preached to the poor" (Luke 7:22). This was to indicate to John the Baptist that Jesus indeed was the person bringing the kingdom of God.

These two lists give us two general categories of signs of the kingdom:

Category A: Social signs or signs applied to a general class of people. These include (1) preaching good news to the poor, (2) proclaiming release to the captives, (3) liberating the oppressed, and (4) instituting the Year of Jubilee ("acceptable year of the Lord").

Category B: Personal signs or signs applied to specific individuals. These include (1) restoring sight to blind people, (2) casting out demons and evil spirits, (3) healing sick people, (4) making lame people walk, (5) cleansing lepers, (6) restoring hearing to deaf people, and (7) raising the dead.

These two lists, of course, do not exhaust the New Testament signs of the kingdom, but they do sum up the two major lists that Jesus himself gave. When Jesus later sent his disciples out to preach the message of the kingdom of God, he added other signs to Category B, such as (8) speaking in new tongues, (9) taking up serpents, and (10) drinking deadly poison with no ill effects (Mark 16:17–18).

There are some interesting and, I think, important differences between Category A signs of the kingdom and Category B signs. While they both have to do with the cultural mandate, Category A signs are usually fulfilled somewhat gradually while Category B signs are usually miraculous or supernatural. Category A signs may have a more permanent effect on society over a longer term, while Category B signs may have a temporary effect, mostly on individuals. Category A signs are somewhat more ambiguous than the rather straightforward Category B signs.

Category B signs are what is generally meant by the word "miracles." It is what the Bible refers to when it records the prayer of the believers in Jerusalem, "that *signs* and *wonders* may be done by the name of thy holy child Jesus" (Acts 4:30), or the account that Stephen, full of faith and power, "did great *wonders* and *miracles* among the people" (Acts 6:8), or the testimony of the Apostle Paul: "Truly the signs of an apostle were wrought among you in all patience, in *signs,* and *wonders,* and *mighty deeds*" (2 Cor. 12:12, italics added). But it is Category A signs —providing free hearing aids for the poor, shipping tons of rice to Cambodia, picketing for free labor unions in Czechoslovakia, agitating for land reform in Peru—that change social structures. It seems that the main function of Category B signs is to draw public attention to the power of God in order to open unsaved people's hearts to the message of the gospel.

The Signs in Jesus' Ministry

Since Jesus contended that the signs were fulfilled in his own ministry, let us consider how they were fulfilled. Jesus preached good news to the poor. Society might exploit and exclude poor people, but the kingdom of God did not. "Blessed are you poor," he said, "for yours is the kingdom of God" (Luke 6:20, RSV). Jesus spent a great deal of time with the poor peasants of Galilee. His good news was not that they would get rich in material goods if they only followed him. He was no first-century Rev. Ike. I suspect that the socio-economic class profile of Galilee was about the same at the end of Jesus' three year ministry as at the beginning.

I hope I am not unduly spiritualizing this sign when I observe that Jesus was telling the literal poor of Galilee (not just the "poor in spirit") that they need to look beyond their present unfortunate material condition to the riches of the kingdom of God. The presence or absence of a bank account does not indicate human well-being. "Man shall not live by bread alone," said Jesus, "but by every word that proceeds out of the mouth of God" (Matt. 4:4, RSV). He said that true treasures are found not on earth, where moth and rust corrupt them, but in heaven, where thieves do not break in and steal (Matt. 6:19–20). He told them not to be concerned about lack of food or clothing because in the kingdom of God their heavenly father would provide those things for them (Matt. 6:25–26). So what was the sign of the kingdom? It was telling the poor the good news that in the kingdom of God they could find a happiness, blessedness, and fulfillment that they could not find outside of it. This is my view, but since it is a Category A sign, undoubtedly many people will disagree and interpret it in other ways.

The second and third Category A signs are similar in their complexity to the first. There is a consensus of scholarship that the "captives" to be released were slaves. Without spiritualizing, it is hard to find any explicit words or deeds of Jesus that had to do with the problem of slavery in the Roman Empire or in Israel. Orlando Costas argues that Jesus "is announcing a future hope that is not yet within his power to fulfill."[41] This is similar to the above interpretation of preaching good news to the poor.

And liberating the oppressed? Is it spiritualizing too much to ask whether the chief oppression might have been that of Satan, demons, and evil spirits? Of course socio-political oppression was rampant in that day as well. But again, very little in Jesus' overt ministry actually succeeded in producing socio-political liberation, although interpreters such as John Howard Yoder find a great deal of implicit socio-political content in Jesus' teachings.[42]

When Jesus preached in the synagogue at Nazareth, he said that the year of Jubilee was beginning. The year of Jubilee is somewhat more concrete than the other three Category A signs of the kingdom. It is set forth in detail in Leviticus 25 as a literal 12-month period of time when slaves were to be freed and all land was to be returned to its original owner. Because it is so concrete, it is hard not to spiritualize the year of Jubilee. This did not literally happen during the three years of Jesus' ministry, nor has it happened since. I think that the best way to understand it may be the way we understand the kingdom of God itself. The year of Jubilee will literally be fulfilled in the age to come, but in this present age the spirit of the year of Jubilee should be reflected in the lifestyle of God's people, particularly in their special concern for stewardship of property and equitable distribution of wealth.

It is interesting that the four Category A signs of the kingdom occupy almost the totality of the literature currently produced by the major authors who have been drawing the attention of the evangelical community to the demands of the kingdom of God and the cultural mandate. Once in a while there is a passing mention of healing or of casting out of demons or of restoring sight to the blind, but rarely is there even a paragraph which develops the literal meaning of Category B signs of the kingdom. If we agree on a hermeneutic which attempts to spiritualize the signs as little as possible, it is hard to accept an interpretation of restoring sight to the blind in Luke 4:18–19 that says "But Christ's miraculous restoration of sight was a sign that he was the light of the world; it can hardly be taken as an instruction to us to perform similar miraculous cures today,"[43] or an extension of blindness to "letter blindness" meaning "illiteracy and lack of education in general."[44]

Selective Obedience

As I read through the works of those from whom I have been learning a great deal about the kingdom of God and notice what is, to me, a glaring omission of Category B signs, I feel I must raise the warning flag of selective obedience. I assert that true members of the community of the king need to reflect in word and deed the Category A signs of the kingdom. But I cannot help wondering if those who restrict their kingdom activities to Category A are not using the parts of the Bible which seem to support a predetermined socio-political ideology without taking the whole gospel of the kingdom seriously. I, of course, am not free from a similar tendency. I admit that I read the Scriptures with "church growth eyes," and this makes me to see some things that others don't see and also to filter out some things I do not feel are of the utmost importance. For years I filtered out the kingdom of God theme, and now I am grateful to those who have helped me see a vitally important dimension to the Christian life. I suspect that some others read the Scriptures with "socio-political eyes" and thereby are coming short in some aspects of kingdom living. In a sense, are we not all selective in our obedience at times, though we don't want to be?

The Disciples and the Signs

When Jesus sent his disciples out, he generally commissioned them with Category B, not Category A signs. The first time he sent out the twelve, Jesus gave them power to cast out demons and heal sickness (Matt. 10:1). When he later sent out the seventy, he did so with these orders: "Heal the sick that are therein, and say unto them, 'The kingdom of God is come nigh'" (Luke 10:9). When he gave the Great Commission for world evangelization, as recorded in Mark, he said that signs would follow the disciples' preaching, such as casting out demons, speaking in tongues, taking up serpents, drinking poison with no harm, and healing the sick by laying on hands (Mark 16:15–18). It is not that the more ambiguous Category A signs were absent—not at all. My point is that Jesus much more specifically emphasized Category B signs.

And when the disciples came back and reported, they were delighted by the results of the Category B signs because through them they felt they were participating firsthand in the cosmic dimensions of the coming of the kingdom. They rejoiced, saying, "Lord, even the demons are subject to us in your name" (Luke 10:17, RSV). At that moment one of the most dramatic events of Jesus' ministry is recorded: "He said unto them, I beheld Satan as lightning fall from heaven" (Luke 10:18). The most direct cosmic signs of the kingdom are the Category B signs. George Ladd points out that "the role that demon exorcism plays in the ministry of our Lord has been a stumbling block to modern interpreters," but Ladd cannot avoid the conclusion that "Jesus' message of the coming of the kingdom of God involved a fundamental struggle with and conquest of this spiritual realm of evil."[45] The amazing thing about the exorcism of demons is that it is so instantaneous. People were amazed, Ladd says, "because Jesus spoke words of command and men were at once delivered from satanic bondage."[46]

After Jesus had left the earth, the ministry of his followers continued to be characterized by Category B signs. The great and amazing sign of the kingdom on Pentecost was speaking in tongues (Acts 2:4). Likewise with Peter when he first took the gospel of the kingdom to the Gentiles in the house of Cornelius (Acts 10:46). The people around Jerusalem brought sick and demon-possessed folk to the believers "and they were healed every one" (Acts 5:16). When Philip went to Samaria demons were cast out, lame and paralyzed walked (Acts 8:7). Paul's breakthrough in Lystra came when he said to a cripple, "Stand up and walk." And the cripple did (Acts 14:8–11). At Malta, Paul was bitten by a poisonous snake with no ill effects (Acts 28:3–5), and he healed the father of Publius (Acts 28:8). Examples of Category B signs of the kingdom could be multiplied over and over from biblical descriptions.

An authentic kingdom lifestyle must be balanced. The cultural mandate has much to do with a Christian ministry to the poor and oppressed, the victims of social injustice. It also has to do with serving as a channel for the supernatural working of the Holy Spirit in amazing, miraculous works of healing, casting out of demons, raising the dead, and speaking in tongues. A key biblical passage that seems to balance them is Paul's teaching that we battle not "against flesh and blood, but against the principalities, against the powers, against the world rulers of this present darkness, against the spiritual hosts of wickedness in the heavenly places" (Eph. 6:12, RSV), for which we need the whole armor of God and the sword of the Spirit. I agree with Ronald Sider that this includes "both the sociopolitical structures of human society and the unseen spiritual forces."[47] It includes Category A and Category B signs. To choose to participate in one group of signs to the exclusion of the other is selective obedience.

The Signs and Church Growth

This chapter concludes with a note on how the signs of the kingdom relate to church growth. It seems to me that one reason why Jesus sent out his disciples on preaching tours with explicit Category B instructions (Category A signs were, of course, implicit) was that Category B signs would have the most direct effect in aiding the stated goal of making disciples. Category A signs are important, but they do not have nearly the immediate and dramatic effect in attracting people to the person of Jesus Christ and to the kingdom of God. I mentioned several biblical examples of how this happened; let me mention one more.

Acts 3 relates an experience of Peter and John shortly after Pentecost. As they went to the temple they stopped and talked to a beggar. They had undoubtedly seen the beggar on many previous occasions, because his regular begging place for years had been the gate of the temple. Jesus would have passed him on a number of occasions. But this time the disciples stopped. Why? Because they had something in mind. The Holy Spirit had led them to use a Category B sign to draw attention to the public preaching of the gospel. Some may object to the thought that they had premeditated using a miracle to draw attention, but I know of nothing in the text to sustain the objection. After a brief dialogue, Peter said, "In the name of Jesus Christ of Nazareth, rise up and walk." And the man, who had been lame for forty years and who was familiar to practically every citizen of Jerusalem, got up, jumped around, ran into the temple, and told everyone what had happened. A crowd immediately gathered on Solomon's porch and Peter preached them a gospel sermon. The healing of the lame man was the lead paragraph of his sermon.

What happened? The church grew.

On Pentecost, a sign of the kingdom, speaking with other tongues, drew the crowd, and the church grew from 120 to 3,120 (Acts 2:41). Three months later a sign of the kingdom, instantaneous healing of a lame man, drew the crowd, and the church grew from 3,120 to 5,000 (Acts 4:4).

As I have researched the growth of the church in many areas of the world, I have found that the most spectacular church growth is frequently accompanied by Category B signs of the kingdom—signs like restoring sight to the blind. I do not mean restoring sight indirectly, through research into glaucoma or by fitting eyeglasses, much less teaching illiterates how to read, good as these things are. I mean that people who woke up in the morning and could see nothing could see the world around them before they went to bed because of a miracle done in the name of Jesus. A few weeks ago, for example, my family and I went to a nearby church called Christian Chapel. In the Sunday morning service, a man got up and walked to the platform. He told how, for five months, he could not see the food on his plate and how his wife had to lead him wherever he went. But that previous Friday night some believers had put mud on his eyes, prayed for him, and when he washed the mud off he looked up and for the first time in months could see the stars! I took this as a sign of the kingdom in that church.

I recently talked to Caesar Molebatsi, a black South African leader who lives in Soweto. He had been imprisoned there because he took a public stand against some of the racist and oppressive apartheid policies of his government. As he described this, I took it as a Category A sign of the kingdom. A few weeks later I talked to my good friend John Wimber, who had gone to South Africa on a preaching tour. He described a family whose two-year-old child had not slept for more than forty-five minutes at a time in his life. John laid hands on him and prayed in Jesus' name that the boy would be healed. He slept the night through and has been doing so ever since—a Category B sign of the kingdom. And both signs took place in the same country.

The last two times I was in Georgia, I made my way into the hills of the northeastern part to a town called Kingston, population 714. There, on Saturday nights, I attended a white frame church called The Church of the Lord Jesus Christ. I met a fine group of brothers and sisters who loved the Lord. None of them was rich. None was a college graduate. The preacher, in fact, was a fascinating combination of eloquent and illiterate (by his own testimony). In the services I saw fervent singing, joyous clapping of hands, dancing in the Spirit, speaking in tongues, testimonies, prophecies, preaching of the Word, and as a climax the handling of deadly poisonous snakes and drinking of strychnine. I discussed this with several members of the congregation. When I asked why they handled snakes they replied, simply, "Because Jesus told us to do it as a sign." Another sign of the kingdom.

Some time ago I was fascinated by the extraordinary growth of the Pentecostal movement in Latin America. As I researched the causes, I found that one of the major factors in that growth was faith healing. Churches that do not practice faith healing tend to grow at a much slower pace in Latin America. Although there are some exceptions, the churches most involved in Category A signs to the exclusion of Category B do not seem to be growing as well. It does seem that where the blind see, the lame walk, the deaf hear, the demons are cast out, that there the victory over Satan is plain and simple for all to see, and men and women are attracted to Jesus and to his kingdom.[48]

Churches seem to grow most vigorously where the signs of the kingdom, especially the Category B signs, are operating with freedom and power.

Notes

1. George Eldon Ladd, *A Theology of the New Testament* (Grand Rapids: Eerdmans, 1974), p. 57.
2. Justice C. Anderson, "The Nature of Churches," in *The Birth of Churches: A Biblical Basis for Church Planting*, ed. Talmadge R. Amberson (Nashville: Broadman, 1979), p. 61.
3. J. Verkuyl, *Contemporary Missiology: An Introduction* (Grand Rapids: Eerdmans, 1978), p. 68.

4. Raymond J. Bakke, "Our Kind of People," *Evangelical Missions Quarterly* 16, no. 2 (April 1980), p. 127.

5. For a contemporary analysis of the Great Reversal and its origins in the social gospel, see David O. Moberg, *The Great Reversal: Evangelism Versus Social Concern* (Philadelphia: Lippincott, 1972); and John D. Woodbridge, Mark A. Noll, and Nathan O. Hatch, *The Gospel in America: Themes in the Story of America's Evangelicals* (Grand Rapids: Zondervan, 1979), pp. 240–247. An earlier history of Christian attitudes toward the kingdom of God is found in David J. Bosch, *Witness to the World: The Christian Mission in Theological Perspective* (Atlanta: John Knox Press, 1980), pp. 140–158.

6. Walter Rauschenbusch, *A Theology for the Social Gospel* (New York: Abingdon, 1917), p. 146. Although Rauschenbusch himself maintained a place for personal salvation in his theology, his followers in another generation did not. Christianizing the social order was their idea of the mission of the church.

7. H. Richard Niebuhr, *The Kingdom of God in America* (New York: Harper & Brothers, 1937), p. 179.

8. Wes Michaelson, "Evangelicalism and Radical Discipleship," in *Evangelicalism and Anabaptism*, ed. C. Norman Kraus (Scottdale, PA: Herald Press, 1979), p. 66.

9. Moberg, *The Great Reversal*, p. 177.

10. In all probability, George Eldon Ladd has advanced evangelicalism's understanding of the kingdom of God more than any other scholar. For his more mature thought, see especially *Jesus and the Kingdom: The Eschatology of Biblical Realism* (Grand Rapids: Eerdmans, 1964) and *A Theology of the New Testament*.

11. See, especially the periodicals, *Sojourners* and *The Other Side*, and Jim Wallis, *Agenda for Biblical People* (San Francisco: Harper & Row, 1976), and Michaelson, "Evangelicalism and Radical Discipleship."

12. Howard A. Snyder, *The Problem of Wineskins: Church Structure in a Technological Age* (Downers Grove, IL: InterVarsity Press, 1975); *The Community of the King* (Downers Grove, IL: InterVarsity Press, 1977); and *The Radical Wesley and Patterns for Church Renewal* (Downers Grove, IL: InterVarsity Press, 1980).

13. Representative recent works include Orlando E. Costas, *The Integrity of Mission: The Inner Life and Outreach of the Church* (San Francisco: Harper & Row, 1979); Samuel Escobar and John Driver,

Christian Mission and Social Justice (Scottdale, PA: Herald Press, 1978); C. René Padilla, ed., *The New Face of Evangelicalism: An International Symposium on the Lausanne Covenant* (Downers Grove, IL: InterVarsity Press, 1976).

14. David J. Bosch, *Witness to the World: The Christian Mission in Theological Perspective* (Atlanta: John Knox Press, 1980).
15. Edmund P. Clowney, "The Missionary Flame of Reformed Theology," in *Theological Perspectives on Church Growth*, ed. Harvie M. Conn (Nutley, NJ: Presbyterian & Reformed, 1976), p. 141.
16. Arthur Glasser, "Salvation Today and the Kingdom," in *Crucial Issues in Missions Tomorrow*, ed. Donald McGavran (Chicago: Moody Press, 1972), p. 43.
17. Ladd, *Theology of the New Testament*, p. 66.
18. Glasser, "Salvation Today and the Kingdom," p. 42.
19. Arthur F. Glasser, "China Today and the Christian Movement: An Evangelical Perspective," p. 4. This unpublished paper was presented at an unofficial high-level meeting of evangelical, ecumenical, and Roman Catholic missiologists specializing in China, held at the Overseas Ministries Study Center, Ventnor, N.J., April 15–17, 1980.
20. Lewis Smedes, "From Hartford to Boston," *The Reformed Journal* 26, no. 4 (April 1976), p. 21.
21. Eddie Gibbs, *I Believe in Church Growth* (London: Hodder & Stoughton). The quotation was taken from the prepublication manuscript, Chapter 2.
22. J. Andrew Kirk, "The Kingdom of God in Contemporary Protestantism and Catholicism," in *Let The Earth Hear His Voice*, ed. J. D. Douglas (Minneapolis: World Wide Publications, 1975), p. 1073.
23. Ladd, *A Theology of the New Testament*, p. 111.
24. Ibid., p. 106.
25. Snyder, *The Community of the King*, p. 41.
26. Ladd, *A Theology of the New Testament*, p. 119.
27. Donald A. McGavran, *Understanding Church Growth*, rev. ed. (Grand Rapids: Eerdmans, 1980), pp. 98–100.
28. Clowney, "The Missionary Flame . . .," p. 143.
29. Peter Beyerhaus, "World Evangelization and the Kingdom of God," in *Let The Earth Hear His Voice*, ed. Douglas, p. 288.
30. J. D. Davies, "Church Growth: A Critique," *International Review of Missions* 57, no. 267 (July 1968), p. 293.

31. Orlando E. Costas, *The Church and Its Mission: A Shattering Critique from the Third World* (Wheaton, IL: Tyndale, 1974), p. 66.
32. Ronald J. Sider, "Resurrection and Liberation: An Evangelical Approach to Social Justice," in *The Recovery of Spirit in Higher Education: Christian and Jewish Ministries in Campus Life,* ed. Robert Rankin (New York: Seabury, 1980), p. 156.
33. Arthur F. Glasser, "Confession, Church Growth, and Authentic Unity in Missionary Strategy," in *Protestant Crosscurrents in Mission,* ed. Norman A. Horner (Nashville: Abingdon, 1968), pp. 178–221.
34. Robert E. Webber traces the concept back to John Calvin, although Calvin does not mention the term itself. See Robert E. Webber, *The Secular Saint: A Case for Evangelical Social Responsibility* (Grand Rapids: Zondervan, 1979), pp. 144–153. Glasser denies that he originated the term "cultural mandate"; nevertheless, it is he who has popularized the slogan as a rallying point for evangelical social ministry.
35. Ibid., p. 37.
36. Quoted in Arthur Johnston, *The Battle for World Evangelism* (Wheaton, IL: Tyndale, 1978), p. 138.
37. McGavran, *Understanding Church Growth,* p. 25.
38. Costas, *The Church and Its Mission,* pp. 89–90.
39. Orlando E. Costas, "Evangelism and the Gospel of Salvation," *International Review of Mission* 63, no. 249 (January 1974), p. 33.
40. Sider, "Resurrection and Liberation," p. 160.
41. Costas, *The Integrity of Mission,* p. 72.
42. See John Howard Yoder, *The Politics of Jesus* (Grand Rapids: Eerdmans, 1972).
43. John R. W. Stott, *Christian Mission in the Modern World* (Downers Grove, IL: InterVarsity Press, 1975), p. 98.
44. Costas, *The Integrity of Mission,* p. 71.
45. Ladd, *A Theology of the New Testament,* p. 52.
46. Ibid., p. 65.
47. Ronald J. Sider, *Christ and Violence* (Scottdale, PA: Herald Press, 1979), p. 50.
48. See C. Peter Wagner, *What Are We Missing?* (formerly *Look Out, The Pentecostals Are Coming*) (Carol Stream, IL: Creation House, 1973, 1978).

CHAPTER 2

Christian Social Ministry
in Perspective

Living a life worthy of the kingdom of God involves participation in fulfilling the cultural mandate. Involvement in social ministries is not optional for either Christians or Christian churches. If the church is the community of the king, it must reflect kingdom values.

It is not enough to state these convictions accurately. Faithful Christians must show their faith by their works (James 2:18). Many Christians are doing it well, but probably a much larger number need a great deal of improvement. One way to start this improvement is by gaining an accurate and realistic view of the world in which we live. I will not attempt to describe or catalog the major social needs of our world, but a brief glance at the condition of the poor and the hungry may prepare out minds to consider some of the major implications of Christian social ministry.

The Poor and the Hungry

The end of the "Great Reversal" has awakened the conscience of evangelicals to the depressing, massive, growing tragedy of world poverty and hunger in our generation.[1] The poor have been with us always, as Jesus said they would be, but the recent fantastic population explosion on earth has also exploded the dimensions of human poverty beyond comprehension. I do not think any of us who live in affluence can grasp the full scope of the plight of the world's poor with our minds—it can only be partially felt in our hearts. Some of this feeling is reflected in W. Stanley Mooneyham's words about the life of poverty that he has personally observed on all six continents: "What can you and I know about it—about a life where each day is a nightmare because it puts you further behind and each night is only an empty link connecting emptier days?"[2]

Ronald Sider estimates that about a half-billion persons in our world are malnourished, and another half-billion actually are starving.[3] Over twice the population of the United States, most of them in Third World nations, will go to bed hungry tonight. It seems unreal to hear of a seven-year-old girl in Brazil who pleads with her mother to sell her to a neighbor because the neighbor has food; or of a father, mother, and three small children in India committing a family suicide rather than face death by starvation; or of a small city in South America where twelve hundred girls from 11 to 17 are working as prostitutes as the only source of income for their families. It is hard for us to imagine a person seriously ill with no access to any medical attention at all; a twelve-year-old boy who hasn't been to school for three years because he can't afford the pencils, paper, and books; or children who are mentally retarded because their mothers could not produce enough milk for them as infants to prevent permanent brain damage. These are not isolated cases, but solemn, tragic, repulsive, spine-chilling conditions under which almost one-quarter of the human race lives.

Poverty, starvation, disease, brain damage, hopelessness, and despair are signs of the kingdom of Satan. They are the exact opposite of the *shalom* described in the last chapter as the ideal of the kingdom of God. Christians who have been born again into the kingdom of God cannot be indifferent to the gruesome reality of world poverty, particularly those Christians who live in affluent situations. Some restaurants in America throw away more food in one night than whole families in Bangladesh see in one year. On a global basis, the one-third of the world that is most affluent consumes 87 percent of global production, leaving only 13 percent for the remaining two-thirds. And, despite large-scale efforts to reverse the trend, the gap is widening each year. The average American consumes more than 300 times the energy consumed by the average Ethiopian.

The Biblical Bias Toward the Poor

Little wonder that the Bible teaches that God is biased toward the poor. Jim Wallis says, "The sheer bulk of the biblical teaching about the rich and poor is overwhelming."[4] I like the way Howard Snyder puts it:

"The teaching is clear, and both consistent and persistent: Of all peoples and classes, God especially has compassion on the poor, and his acts in history confirm this."[5] Ronald Sider poignantly adds: "The Bible clearly and repeatedly teaches that God is at work in history casting down the rich and exalting the poor because frequently the rich are wealthy precisely because they have oppressed the poor or have neglected to aid the needy."[6] The evangelical community in general, and the Church Growth Movement in particular, is grateful to leaders like Wallis, Snyder, Sider, and others who have brought these biblical themes to our attention.

By saying this, I would not want to give the impression that the Church Growth Movement has been oblivious to the condition of the poor and to the Christian responsibility for them. In the foundation textbook of the movement, Donald McGavran speaks of the "biblical insistence that God is a God of righteousness and *will not have the poor oppressed.*" He brings out Jesus' "marked emphasis on God's will for the masses" and mentions as a sign of the kingdom that "the poor have good news preached to them" (Matt. 11:5, RSV). "God sent his prophets," McGavran argues, "to plead the cause of the poor and to demand justice for the common man."[7] One of the most touching literary passages on the poor that I have come across is McGavran's "missionary prayer" for the poor. Here are some excerpts:

O Lord Jesus Christ, we remember that Thou wast born of a peasant mother in a poor carpenter's home. . . . Thou didst tell men that a sign of the coming of thy kingdom was that the Gospel was proclaimed to the poor. . . .

O Holy Christ, we lift up before Thee the poor of the earth, the masses of mankind, the rural multitudes whose backs are bent with toil, the urban proletariat who live in tenements, and shacks, and favellas, and barrios and zongoes, the illiterate, the oppressed, the disinherited, the fishermen and the carpenters, the landless labor, the unskilled, the poor, Lord, the poor for whom Thou didst shed Thy precious blood and on whom Thou didst look with compassion, for they are sheep without a shepherd. Grant us, Lord, Thy compassion, that we too may see the great masses of mankind as Thy lost children, and like Thee spend ourselves for them. In Thy blessed name, Amen.[8]

The Poor Receive the Good News

Studies of the growth of the church worldwide reveal the fact that, of the new Christian churches and denominations planted in this century, a large majority have been among the poor of the world. The good news has been proclaimed to poor people, and they have received it gladly. No longer are missions and missionaries postulating that civilization must precede Christianization. While some Christian leaders might still hold on to what Howard Snyder calls "the idea that solid, self-supporting churches cannot be planted among the poor, at least not without heavy subsidies and leadership from richer churches,"[9] up-to-date missiology has discarded such an approach. It has recognized that God does not wait for people to move into the middle class to be in a position to know him. On the contrary. Most Christians in the churches of Africa, Asia, and Latin America have less than six grades of schooling. Most of them live on diets of rice, bread, and beans, and never see red meat or ice cream. Most of them have dirt under their fingernails and callouses on their palms.

I recall that at the Consultation on World Evangelization held in 1980 in Pattaya, Thailand, a speaker made a rather impassioned plea that the church must identify with the poor. The implication was that Christians were affluent while non-Christians were poor. Then a sister from Guatemala took the microphone and said, "I do not understand this appeal to identify with the poor. In my country, the church *is* the poor." Samuel Escobar recognizes the fact that "in a literal sense the gospel is announced to the poor and the church grows more among the poor."[10] In his plenary address at the Second Latin American Congress on Evangelization (CLADE II), Escobar says:

In many parts of Latin America the evangelicals do not have to "identify with the poor" as the intellectuals and Marxist theologians plead. They do not have to do it simply because they already are poor and they live like Christians in the midst of the poor. One of the glories of the Gospel, ever since it arrived in Latin America, was precisely its ability to bring hope to the hearts of the poor.[11]

Escobar goes on to chide Marxist social critics and Catholic liberation theologians who continue to insist that popular Protestantism and evangelical missions are the "opium of the Latin American masses." Rather, argues Escobar, "We evangelicals of the new generation need to understand afresh how the Gospel has been a message of hope that has delivered our poor from the nightmare of religious-political-social oppression in Latin America."[12]

Summing up the research done in the Church Growth Movement, Donald McGavran reports that in the Third World, whether the churches are Lutheran, Baptist, Anglican, Methodist, Presbyterian, or Pentecostal, they are churches of the masses. "Their members are poor (peasants, landless labor, urban proletariat) and commonly illiterate. Having many members and small mission resources, they remain Churches of the masses."[13] The biblical emphasis on God's favor toward the poor shows up empirically in the way the gospel most commonly spreads around the world.

Facing the Problems of Poverty

It is much easier to describe the problem of world poverty than suggest remedies for it. Some eschatological passages in the Bible, such as 1 Timothy 3:1–5, indicate that world conditions will probably get worse "in the last days" and that selfishness, greed, corruption, and oppression will increase. Such prophecies, it seems, are being fulfilled before our very eyes. It would be easy to conclude from this that nothing can be done anyway, so why attempt it? The answer is simple. Godly people must obey the cultural mandate. It is not optional. Just because we can't do everything does not excuse us from doing something.

The causes of poverty are complex. Let's face it: some people are poor because they are lazy, and the Bible condemns that kind of poverty. "A farmer too lazy to plow his fields at the right time will have nothing to harvest" (Prov. 20:4, GNB). "If you spend your time sleeping, you will be poor" (Prov. 20:13, GNB). Some, like the prodigal son, are poor because they spend what they have foolishly. "Drunkards and gluttons will be reduced to poverty" (Prov. 23:21). Worldwide, however, these are not generally the basic root of the problem. As Stanley Mooneyham says, "You can blame lack of resources, overpopulation, colonial oppression, insufficient capital, inverted value systems, and class exploitation —and be both right and wrong."[14] All these things contribute to the stark reality of world hunger.

I think that is why I sometimes react negatively to a kind of statement often made by Christian leaders in the orbit of the World Council of Churches. The concern for the poor that was so prominent, for example, at the W.C.C. Melbourne Conference in 1980 was certainly a biblical concern. But the problem was addressed largely from the assumption that poverty is a socio-political phenomenon. There is no question that a major cause of world poverty is international injustice, exploitation, and oppression. This needs to be remedied. But some have become so preoccupied with the need for establishing what are called "centrally planned economies" (a euphemism for Marxist socialism) that they neglect or sometimes oppose short-term relief and development, which can feed hungry people and prevent death by starvation *now*, on the grounds that it may entrench the status quo and postpone the revolution. This kind of reductionism might be expected from those outside the kingdom of God. But, rather than promoting socio-political systems, a greater measure of love and compassion for people would be expected from those who profess to acknowledge Jesus as Lord. Theirs seems to be an unintended form of dehumanization.

Does God Love the Rich?

If it is true that the bias of the Bible is toward the poor, does it follow that it is also biased against the rich? This may be too strong a way to put it, but nevertheless it is clear that riches are more of a stumbling block on the road to the kingdom of God than poverty. Jesus mentioned this on several occasions. "It is easier for a camel to go through the eye of a needle than for a rich man to enter the kingdom of God" (Matt. 19:24, RSV). "Woe to you that are rich" (Luke 6:24, RSV). And the Apostle Paul adds: "Those who desire to be rich fall into temptation, into a snare . . . for the love of money is the root of all evils" (1 Tim. 6:9–10, RSV).

Riches are not a problem for God. God loves all people. The "whosoever" of John 3:16 includes the rich as well as the poor. Riches cause a problem for the person who has them. Rather than satisfy, riches produce greed and carnal ambition. Everyone wishes for a little more of this world's goods, but rich people tend to find that desire more intense than poor people. Wealth becomes an idol that many are not willing to turn from in order to serve the living and true God, as the Rich Young Ruler discovered.

But riches can be a blessing if God is present with them. In fact, God desires that some people be rich. I think that Jim Wallis is somewhat overenthusiastic in his rhetoric when he states that "nowhere in Scripture is wealth praised or admired." He is more balanced when he adds, "The danger of riches in the Old Testament is in the misuse of wealth and power in the oppression and exploitation of the poor."[15] I point this out because God does delight in rewarding people with wealth and prosperity. The whole content of *shalom* means full wombs and full tables and full wine vats and fullness of life. Numerous passages in the Old Testament, particularly in the Pentateuch, detail what God wishes to do for his people when they obey him. "If you listen to these commandments and obey them faithfully" says the law, "he will love you and bless you." Bless you with what? With what we call riches: many children, grain, wine, olive oil, many cattle and sheep. "No people in the world will be as richly blessed as you" (Deut. 7:12–16, GNB). Of course part of obeying God's command was not to exploit the poor. When Israel did, God's blessings were diminished.

I agree with Paul G. Hiebert when he says that the church needs "a theology of power and wealth . . . for the powerful and affluent."[16] This needs to go considerably further than Andrew Carnegie's book, *The Gospel of Wealth,* which asserts that the concentration of wealth in the hands of a few and competition between these is "not only beneficial, but essential for the future progress of the race."[17] It may be something more akin to the late Arthur S. DeMoss' "paradox of prosperity." DeMoss, an American philanthropist who, among many other things, funded the influential Partnership in Mission organization, argues that God's way to prosperity is not "getting, accumulating or grasping" but rather "giving."[18]

Whatever form it takes, a biblical theology of wealth must recognize the extraordinary responsibility that wealthy people have in the kingdom of God. "To whom much is given, of him will much be required" (Luke 12:48, RSV). Among God's requirements is, negatively, that rich people must not exploit the poor in order to increase their riches. Positively, it involves a clear sense of stewardship. What they do have they have only as a trust from God, and they are at most God's trustees. The riches, then, should be used to forward the mission of God in the world and spread, to the extent possible, the blessings of the kingdom of God among the poor.

The Church and the Cultural Mandate

What has been said about hunger and poverty reflects only a small, though significant, part of the world challenge to Christians to fulfill the cultural mandate. Equal space could be given to land distribution, militarism, ecology, abortion, exploitation of sex, public education, racial discrimination, care of the elderly, nationalism, crime, human rights, population growth, totalitarianism, and any number of other social issues. The crucial question is: How do Christians individually and collectively make the maximum contribution toward alleviating the effects of demonic social forces? It is not easy to answer. I agree with Howard Snyder, who says, "this will never be a neat, clear-cut, triumphant road for the Church to follow. Obedience to the gospel in a world where Satan is still active means living with tension."[19] I know of no one who has the final answer, nor do I suppose any of us will have final answers in our lifetime.

In thinking through the implications of how the church can fulfill the cultural mandate, it is important to recognize that biblically there is a qualitative difference between the church and the world. Some object to anything that sounds like dichotomization, but it does seem that Jesus quite clearly drew the lines in his prayer recorded in John 17. As Jesus prayed for his disciples, he said that "just as I do not belong to the world, they do not belong to the world" (John 17:16, GNB). But while they are not *of* the world, "they are *in* the world" (John 17:11, RSV). And the climax of the prayer is Jesus' expressed desire to "send them *into* the world" (John 17:18, RSV). The Epistle of John says, "Love not the world, neither the things that are in the world" (1 John 2:15). The Apostle Paul said, "The wisdom of this world is foolishness with God" (1 Cor. 3:19).

In our day and throughout history, Christians have come to differing conclusions about how the church should relate to the world. Of the many ways this has been worked out, four, I think, are significant enough to let us see the spectrum of options.

The Church Is Separate from the World.   Those who hold and practice this view tend to form themselves into Christian counter-cultures. This has been a traditional position, for example, of some Anabaptist and Mennonite groups. The Amish and the Hutterites practice this here in America. They feel their responsibility is to set up alternative communities where they are free to show forth what they interpret to be signs of the kingdom of God.

The Church Controls the World.   This was the view of the medieval papacy, its beginnings traceable to the emperor Constantine and therefore called by some "Constantinism." Until recently some Latin American nations maintained this attitude, inherited from Spain. This position holds that the signs of the kingdom should be legislated by the governments which control the world.

The Church Is a Servant of the World.   This option has been adopted by contemporary theologians of liberation. It holds that the church should take its agenda for action from the concerns of the world and participate in movements that will best liberate and humanize the largest number of individuals. This position frequently holds that the signs of the kingdom can be seen in secular socio-political movements.

None of the options above, as I see it, is totally wrong. Each captures some important facets of the complex relationship of the church to the world. None of them, however, appeals to the Church Growth Movement has an adequate model for understanding what God expects as he sends his church into the world. I believe that a fourth model is most acceptable to church growth thinkers:

The Church and the World Are in Creative Tension. The church must go into the world, not remain aloof. Jesus commanded his disciples to do so. The church does not attempt to control the world, since it has no biblical mandate to do so. Quite the contrary. The world is said to be controlled by principalities and powers. There is spiritual wickedness in high places. Satan is the god of this present age and will remain so until the second coming of Christ inaugurates the fullness of the age to come. And because of this, the church goes forth with the agenda of the kingdom of God and announces this agenda to the world.

Creative tension exists because the church does recognize that it is separate from the world and that its lifestyle is different. It believes that it should influence governments to the degree possible. For example, to pass just legislation that will do kingdom things, such as helping the poor and oppressed and guaranteeing the freedom to preach the gospel and plant churches. It cannot ignore the world's agenda because that agenda informs the church of the needs and hurts of the world that Jesus so deeply wants to address and heal.

Social Service and Social Action

As the church moves into the world to fulfill the cultural mandate, two general avenues of potential ministry open up. Students of the social concerns of the church have called them by different names. I prefer the terms *social service* and *social action,* and will employ these in a technical and consistent way throughout this book. Though I have no quarrel with those who prefer other terms for those categories, I want to establish clearly how I am using the terms "social service" and "social action," because, as we will see (particularly in Chapter 10), the way that the church participates in each has an influence on the way the church grows in membership. Confusion on this point has been at the root of many growth problems, and it has also affected the potential of the church for fulfilling the cultural mandate.

Social service is the kind of social ministry geared to meet the needs of individuals and groups of persons in a direct and immediate way. If a famine comes, social service will provide food for starving people. If an earthquake or tidal wave devastates an area, social service will provide food, clothing, blankets, and medical supplies; also resources to rebuild homes, schools, and churches. If agricultural production is low, social service will introduce new crops, livestock, and farming methods so that food production will increase.

Within social service there is a further technical distinction of terms that has been fairly well accepted: *relief* and *development.* [20] Relief treats the symptoms. It comes after the fact. Development treats the causes. Development would include establishing medical and dental clinics and training local people how to staff them, digging wells where the water supply is inadequate, setting up cottage industries, or providing short-handled hoes in Niger. Both relief and development are social service; they are not social action.

Social action is the kind of social ministry geared toward changing social structures. Like development, it treats causes, but the scope is much broader and the effects more far-reaching. Social action, by definition, involves socio-political changes. If a government is mistreating a minority group, for example, it involves whatever is necessary to correct the injustice. It might mean picketing the legislature; it might mean organizing an electoral campaign to unseat a senator or even a president; it might mean supporting guerrilla bands that will overthrow the whole government and rewrite the constitution. Social action might or might not involve revolution, violence, or civil disobedience in some degree. The end goal of social action is to substitute just (or more just) for unjust (or less just) political structures.

Church Growth and Social Involvement

If what has been said concerning the kingdom of God and the cultural mandate is valid, the church does not have an option as to whether or not it will be involved in social ministry. The kingdom lifestyle demands it. But just how Christians individually and collectively become involved in social ministries is not set forth in the Bible, and therefore choices have to be made. One of these choices concerns the degree of involvement in social service and social action. Both potentially manifest the signs of the kingdom, although social service relates more directly to Category B signs of the kingdom and social action more to Category A signs. But, while they are both important, it should be recognized that a choice at this point will often affect the growth of the church or churches involved.

Research on the growth and decline of churches has shown that simply the degree of involvement with fulfilling the cultural mandate does not directly influence growth rates. But here is a church growth principle: *when churches are involved in social ministries, the churches which specialize in social service tend to attract more new members than the ones specializing in social action.* I have stated the principle rather simply, but I recognize that it is highly complex. Exceptions can be found, as they can to any church growth principle, but it is a principle nonetheless. I will discuss the complexities in greater detail in Chapter 10, but at this point it is important to recognize this empirical fact.

It is also important here to raise the question of why. Why do churches which engage in social service seem to grow better than those which engage in social action? I think there are three significant reasons for this:

Failure to Distinguish Between Types of Signs of the Kingdom. Category A signs of the kingdom are different from Category B signs. As we saw in the last chapter, when Jesus sent his disciples into the world, he specifically gave them Category B signs, the signs that have a close parallel with social service. The Category A signs, related to social action, while they are incumbent on Christians today, are not specifically and explicitly mandated by Jesus for his disciples.

Failure to Distinguish Between Socio-political Liberation and Salvation. The Lausanne Covenant states that "reconciliation with man is not reconciliation with God, nor is social action evangelism, nor is political liberation salvation (Art. 5). In an excellent discussion of this point, John Stott argues that to call socio-political liberation "salvation," as some are doing today, "is to be guilty of a gross theological confusion." He reminds us that, at the World Council of Churches' 1973 conference on "Salvation Today," some enthusiastic participants put Chairman Mao on a level with Jesus Christ and claimed to have been "saved by Mao" or that Mao was "God's Messiah to the Chinese." Stott comments that "it is childish to the point of blasphemy to equate this kind of 'salvation' with the saving work of our Lord Jesus Christ."[21] I agree with John Stott. While it pleases God whenever people are liberated from oppression and exploitation, churches that mistakenly believe their participation in such social action is *evangelism* and will "save" people, in the biblical sense of the word, predictably will develop growth problems.

Failure to Distinguish Primary from Secondary Functions of the Church. I repeat that the cultural mandate is obligatory for the church. But, based on what I have learned through reading, research, and experience, I have come to the conclusion that the typical Christian church is much more competent at social service than at social action. The track record of churches, denominations, and councils of churches in the field of social engineering has been much less than remarkable. A recent poll taken by *Christianity Today* and the Gallup Organization showed that clergy tend to think their political and economic pronouncements help to make Christianity relevant. But, not surprisingly, neither the general public, nor even Christians in the pew, think such statements are very important at all. Princeton's Paul Ramsey suggests that churches that harbor such notions have derived them "incestuously from the secular elites, the makers and shakers of contemporary opinion."[22] Social action is so complex that few churches are competent to make intelligent decisions concerning it. I do believe that certain kinds of social action can effectively be done by Christians, but the appropriate structure for such a ministry is usually not the local church.

Planning for Christian Social Ministry

In fulfilling the cultural mandate, especially in ministries involving social service, churches need to see clearly what should be done and why. Most Christians agree that their churches should help the poor, for example, but, in fact, less than one percent of American churches have what they themselves consider "especially successful" programs to help the poor.[23] Most American churches are far from perfect, of course, and need improvement in many areas of their life. But do they need to be *that* far from perfect? If so, they may find it embarrassingly difficult if not impossible to respond to the biblical question: "But if anyone has the world's goods and sees his brother in need, yet closes his heart against him, how does God's love abide in him?" (1 Jn. 3:17–18, RSV).

In planning for greater social involvement, it is helpful to consider three questions that are frequently raised when churches begin to develop programs for social ministry: Why? What? and Who?

Why Do We Engage in Social Ministry? Basic to the answer to this question, of course, is all we have been saying about the cultural mandate. Social ministry glorifies God because it is done in obedience to God. Beyond that, however, many Christians wonder whether to engage in social ministry can be considered a legitimate end in itself or if we should do it only as a means to the end of winning souls.

As I see it, social service can be both. One church in America, which is growing rapidly by attracting a large number of unchurched people to Christ, has as its motto for ministry, "Find a need and fill it; find a hurt and heal it." By discovering the felt needs of unchurched people and designing church programs of service that will meet those needs, the church uses social service as an evangelistic means. Hundreds of examples could be drawn from world missions which established schools, hospitals, or orphanages in order to help open people's hearts to the gospel message. In the New Testament accounts of the spread of the faith, as we have seen with the lame man at the temple in Acts 3, social service in the form of miracles and wonders (Category B signs of the kingdom) seems to have functioned as a means of preparing people for the message of salvation.

But, having said this, I do not believe it is necessary to justify all Christian social ministry on the basis of its help in saving souls. The Good Samaritan bound up the wounds of the person who was robbed and beaten with no conditions attached. When Jesus healed the ten lepers, his healing was 100 percent successful, though only 10 percent came to faith through it. Jesus healed the man at the pool of Bethesda despite the fact that (a) he didn't even know who Jesus was, (b) he didn't even thank Jesus for his healing, and (c) when Jesus later told him to stop sinning he betrayed Jesus to the Jewish authorities, who plotted to kill him (John 5:1–18). But the event is recorded as a significant part of Jesus' ministry. Carl F. H. Henry argues that "the primary reason for social involvement ought not to be an indirect evangelistic ploy"[24] but rather a straightforward demonstration of God's justice in the world. There is biblical justification for doing good whether or not men and women are brought to faith in Christ as a result of it.

What Are We Aiming for in Christian Social Ministry? If we leave aside for the moment the use of social ministry as a means toward evangelism and concentrate on the service itself, what would we like to see happen? An appealing answer might be: to help make all poor people rich. However, I doubt that this is an adequate answer for more than one reason. But before I give the reasons, let me say up front that our goals for people in crisis situations are not that ambiguous. For example, if a village in Ethiopia has been out of food for a month the goal of social service is to deliver them the food they need to restore and maintain their physical strength. Situations of emergency relief form a category of their own.

But suppose people are making it. Barely. They never have enough to eat; they have no access to modern medicine, to schools; they have no sanitary facilities or sewers, they live in cockroach-infested shacks; they seldom bathe, and if they are fortunate they have one change of clothes. Should our goal be to help these people get rich? I think most of us would say, well, perhaps not rich, but at least middle class. We would like them to be more like us.

After saying this, however, it is well to pause and ask ourselves how much of our own cultural ethnocentrism we have injected into our ideals for the rest of the world, whether within our own nation, on the Indian reservations or in the Appalachian hills, or in the Third World, where a billion or so people are living much as I have described. Our Anglo-American tendency is to equate material prosperity with happiness and well-being. One negative effect of multinational corporations is their penchant to project Anglo-American material values as "the good life." Edward Stewart points out in his analysis of American culture: "Americans consider it almost a right to be materially well off" and they "tend to project this complex of values, centering around comfort and material well-being, to other peoples. They assume that given the opportunity, everyone else would be just like themselves. Hence they are disturbed by the sight of the rich churches of Latin America standing in the midst of poverty."[25]

My own sixteen years of experience living in one of the poorest countries of the Third World has helped me to see Stewart's point. We need much more cross-cultural research on what exactly constitutes "quality of life" to each of the world's 30,000 or so distinct groups of people, and that quality of life needs to be defined from *within* rather than from *without*. This may require more cultural humility than some Americans—Christian or not—could muster, but I believe it is the approach which best respects human dignity and cultural integrity. What right do we have, for example, to tell mothers in Kenya or India how many children they should have? Some American blacks who have "made it" economically are now wondering out loud how satisfying Anglo-American values really are. One says, "The keys to the executive suite did not turn out to be the keys to the kingdom after all." He goes on:

This brings us to the heart of the black dilemma today: success in America does not mean the possession of such inward qualities as family affection, courage, pity, patience, hope, faith, self-sacrifice—qualities not unknown in the black community during its most appalling trials. Success means the ownership of things.[26]

I do not profess to know what constitutes true quality of life. But I do have ringing in my ears one of the most common statements that Latin Americans make contrasting their lifestyle with North Americans: "North Americans live to work; we work to live." When I think back on those easy-going ulcer-free days of long siestas in the hammock, guitar music on the dirt streets in the evenings, friendliness and hospitality, I wonder how important indoor plumbing is anyhow. Who is it that has their values straight? I don't know, but I am quite sure that simply handing out material goods, except for emergency relief, may not always be the best goal of Christian social service. In this light perhaps we need to reread Paul's words to Timothy: "So then, if we have food and clothes, that should be enough for us. But those who want to get rich fall into temptation and are caught in the trap of many foolish and harmful desires, which pull them down to ruin and destruction" (1 Tim. 6:8–9, GNB).

Who Should Be the Recipients of Our Social Ministry? It is helpful to think of Christian social responsibility as moving outward in three concentric circles from each Christian individual. The first people I must reach out to in Jesus' name are the members of my own family. In our American culture this generally means the nuclear family; in many other cultures it means the extended family, which may be a circle of one hundred or so people. "But if anyone does not take care of his relatives," says Paul, "especially the members of his own family, he has denied the faith and is worse than an unbeliever" (1 Tim. 5:8, GNB).

The second priority for Christian social service is our brothers and sisters in Christ. This is emphasized in Galatians 6:10: "So then, as often as we have the chance, we should do good to everyone, and *especially* to those who belong to our family in the faith." The believers in Jerusalem might have shared with the unchurched poor, but it is not recorded that they did. Their sharing was among themselves (Acts 2:44–45). They did not help widows in general, but Christian widows (Acts 6:1). Paul's collections in the Gentile churches were for the poor Christians in Jerusalem. It is not always recognized that the much-quoted "cup of cold water in Jesus' name" refers to helping Christian messengers of the Gospel, not to humanity in general (see Mark 9:38–41; Matt. 10:40–42). In all probability this also is the best interpretation of the passage about giving food to the hungry, drink to the thirsty, hospitality to the stranger, clothes to the naked, and visits to the prisoner, as recorded in Matthew 25:31–46.[27]

The third priority for Christian social service is the needy of the human race in general. Galatians 6:10 clearly says that we should "do good to everyone." Because it is a third priority it does not mean that this is optional. The poor and hungry and needy and oppressed of the whole world need to be helped by people who live a kingdom lifestyle and who take seriously the cultural mandate. Christians who use these biblical priorities to deny global responsibility, as some unfortunately have done, are disobedient to God and should repent and mend their ways.

Redemption and Lift

Because God has a special bias toward the poor, and because the gospel spreads most naturally and easily among the poor, particularly in Third World nations, a good deal of church growth research has focused on special problems of lower class churches. Donald McGavran's research shows that "as the Church is established among the masses in the world, again and again it is stopped dead in its tracks."[28] While the causes of such stoppage are complex and vary between groups of people, one of the most general causes is summed up in McGavran's chapter "Halting Due to Redemption and Lift," in *Understanding Church Growth.*[29] This chapter, a touchstone in church growth literature, describes better than anything I have seen the problem that occurs when socio-economic lift, due largely to the material blessings which accompany Christian conversion, effectively removes the Christians from meaningful contact with the social class into which they themselves were born.

The problem for the growth of the church is this: "How then can the

Church lift and redeem Christians and yet have them remain in effective contact with receptive sections of society which they *can* influence?"[30] One answer, which church growth has rejected on the grounds of obedience to the cultural mandate, is to do all possible to keep new believers poor. This would be impossible even if desirable, because in most cases part of the *shalom* that new believers find in the kingdom of God is an improved quality of life, sometimes including increased material blessings.

McGavran was not the first to notice the phenomenon. Sociologists of religion have studied it for some time. H. Richard Niebuhr, back in the 1920s, described it as follows:

. . . One phase of the history of denominationalism reveals itself as the story of the religiously neglected poor, who fashion a new type of Christianity which corresponds to their distinctive needs, who rise in the economic scale under the influence of religious discipline, and who, in the midst of a freshly acquired cultural respectability, neglect the new poor succeeding them on the lower plane.[31]

To American Christians, one of the most familiar cases of redemption and lift is the United Methodist Church, which was planted in our country as a church of the poor in 1766, but which by its 100th anniversary had already begun its inexorable move into the middle class. God then raised up the Holiness and Pentecostal movements to take their place among the poor. Now, 100 years later, leaders in the Holiness and Pentecostal churches are becoming concerned that they themselves may be abandoning the poor and becoming middle class.

John Wesley himself, the founder of Methodism, had accurately prophesied the redemption and lift of his movement. Wesley says:

Wherever riches have increased, the essence of religion has decreased in the same proportion. Therefore I do not see how it is possible in the nature of things for any revival of religion to continue long. For religion must necessarily produce both industry and frugality, and these cannot but produce riches. But as riches increase, so will pride, anger, and love of the world in all its branches. How then is it possible that Methodism, that is, a religion of the heart, though it flourished now as a green bay tree, should continue in this state? For the Methodists in every place grow diligent and frugal; consequently they increase in goods. Hence they proportionately increase in pride, in anger, in the desire of the flesh, the desire of the eyes, and the pride of life. So, although the form of religion remains, the spirit is swiftly vanishing away.[32]

Only in rare cases have redemption and lift been avoided for an extended period of time. I discovered one such case when I researched the Pentecostal movement in Chile some years ago. This is a church which started in 1907 and which has largely remained a church of the poor, laboring class of Chile. There are many reasons for this, but in my judgment the major one is the system of ministerial selection and training that has developed. Rather than following the more traditional pattern of training pastors in seminaries and Bible schools, the Pentecostals use an apprenticeship system which I have called "seminaries in the streets." Because the leadership continues to be older, mostly first generation Christians, and from the laboring class, the church in general has not suffered the kind of lift that would remove it from its origins.[33]

Vigorous Giving Prevents Redemption and Lift

Unless Christians take specific measures to prevent it, such as the Chilean Pentecostals have done, redemption and lift will soon halt the spread of the gospel among the poor in a given situation. Again, John Wesley himself recommended what may be one of the most practical ways to avoid it: *give vigorously*. He said:

Is there no way to prevent this continual decay of pure religion? We ought not to prevent people from being diligent and frugal; we must exhort all Christians to gain all they can, and to save all they can; that is in effect to grow rich. What way then can we take, that our money may not sink us into the nethermost hell? There is one way and there is no other under heaven. If those who gain all they can, will likewise give all they can, then the more they gain, the more they will grow in grace, and the more treasures they will lay up in heaven.[34]

I agree with John Wesley. Most people who read this book will be Christians who, by worldly standards, are affluent. Vigorous giving would not make them poor, but the proceeds could go a long way, in the name of Christ, to fulfill God's mandates and help alleviate the condition of the poor both spiritually and materially.

One of the most creative suggestions for Christian stewardship in recent years has been set forth by Ronald Sider. He recommends the "graduated tithe."[35] I want to identify with the graduated tithe, although I approach it in a slightly different manner. Sider's suggestion is a little more radical than mine, although I admit his is the most ideal. Sider advocates limiting the total disposable income (personal expenditures and savings) to $14,850 per family (1977 dollars). The Sider approach has built into it a commitment to a simple lifestyle. He and his family practice what they preach. They live in inner-city Philadelphia, in Germantown, where they relate to and identify with the urban poor.

While many American Christians would affirm their agreement with the Lausanne Covenant, which states: "Those of us who live in affluent circumstances accept our duty to develop a simple lifestyle in order to contribute more generously to both relief and evangelism" (Art. 9), very few, I am afraid, are going to move into Germantown to do it. I personally thank God for those of my friends who are doing it. But, as I have developed in detail elsewhere, I believe that the ability to do that stems from a spiritual gift of voluntary poverty, and relatively few members of the body of Christ have that particular gift.[36]

The stark reality of the situation is that a great majority of Christian church members in America, one of the world's most affluent nations, do not tithe even 10 percent of their income. The Internal Revenue Service figures show that Americans across the board contribute about 2 percent of their income. Median income of church members is around $16,000 per consumer unit, while church contributions per consumer unit are about $350. This figures to slightly over 2 percent, no more than the general public. America's born-again Presidents do not set much of an example. In 1975 Jimmy Carter gave only 4.9 percent, and Ronald Reagan gives a paltry 1.4 percent.

My plan for a graduated tithe has three phases. Let me say at the beginning that it does not apply to those Christians to whom God has given the spiritual gift of giving. Like voluntary poverty, there is a special gift of giving that some members of the body of Christ have and some do not.[37] My plan applies only to Christians who don't have that gift, but who are expected to exercise their roles for generous giving and living a simple lifestyle.

Phase One: Give 10 Percent of Your Income to God

I do not believe that anyone is so poor or so in debt that they cannot begin simple tithing immediately. This is nothing more than mere obedience to God. Withholding the tithe is called in the Bible robbing God (Mal. 3:7–10). In the long run, withholding the tithe hinders rather than helps the material condition of a family or an individual. Many Christians who do not tithe do not understand this. The Bible teaches that God will give back more than you give: "Give to others, and God will give to you. Indeed, you will receive a full measure, a generous helping, poured into your hands—all that you can hold. The measure you use for others is the one that God will use for you" (Luke 6:38, GNB). This applies to the poor as well as the rich. God may be biased toward the poor, but that does not give the poor a license to rob God. In some cases (not all to be sure) people could rise out of their poverty if they only began obeying God and giving him what is due.

Phase Two: Graduate Your Tithe to 25 Percent

Here, of course, I am using "tithe" loosely, since its literal meaning is 10 percent. Once you are giving 10 percent of your gross income to God, my suggestion is that over the years you raise the *percentage* you give every time your income goes up. The more you make, the higher percentage of your income you give. Aim for 25 percent as a goal. For many this will be enough. However, others will by then have learned the blessings, both spiritual and material, of cheerful giving, and they will continue the momentum over and above the 25 percent.

Phase Three: Make a Christian Will

Most Americans accumulate an estate of one size or another. It is irresponsible stewardship for a Christian not to make a will, since in that case most of the estate may go to the government. In my opinion, a Christian will should designate at least one-half the estate for God's work. This means that those who are affluent enough to have surplus income beyond what they need for the expenses of a relatively simple lifestyle, and who invest it in order to make more income, have designated not 10 percent or 25 percent, but 50 percent of that extra income to God.

These suggestions may not be universally acceptable. But I believe that something like this is necessary if we take our responsibility to live kingdom lifestyles seriously. To reiterate, vigorous giving does two things besides pleasing God: it encourages us to live a simpler lifestyle and it frees up significant resources to help meet the spiritual and material needs of the world's poor and oppressed.

Notes

1. I recommend, as a start toward fulfilling the cultural mandate, that every Christian home build a modest library of four books on world hunger: W. Stanley Mooneyham, *What Do You Say to a Hungry World?* (Waco, TX: Word Books, 1975); Ronald J. Sider, *Rich Christians in an Age of Hunger: A Biblical Study* (Downers Grove, IL: InterVarsity Press, 1977); Ronald J. Sider, ed., *Cry Justice: The Bible on Hunger and Poverty* (New York: Paulist Press 1980); and Julio de Santa Ana, *Good News to the Poor: The Challenge of the Poor in the History of the Church* (Geneva: World Council of Churches, 1977).

2. Mooneyham, *What Do You Say to a Hungry World?* p. 37.

3. Sider, *Rich Christians in an Age of Hunger,* p. 33.

4. Jim Wallis, *Agenda for Biblical People* (San Francisco: Harper & Row, 1976), p. 88.

5. Howard A. Snyder, *The Problem of Wineskins: Church Structure in a Technological Age* (Downers Grove, IL: InterVarsity Press, 1975), p. 39.

6. Sider, *Rich Christians in an Age of Hunger,* p. 84.

7. Donald A. McGavran, *Understanding Church Growth,* rev. ed. (Grand Rapids: Eerdmans, 1980), pp. 278–279.

8. Ibid., p. 281

9. Snyder, *The Problem of Wineskins,* p. 37.

10. Samuel Escobar and John Driver, *Christian Mission and Social Justice* (Scottdale, PA: Herald Press, 1978), p. 39.

11. Samuel Escobar, "Esperanza and desesperanza en la crisis continental," in *América Latina y la evangelización en los años 80* (Lima, Peru: Congreso Latinoamericano de Evangelización, 1980), p. 300.

12. Ibid., p. 301. See also Emilio Willems, *Followers of the New Faith: Culture Change and the Rise of Protestantism in Brazil and Chile* (Nashville: Vanderbilt University Press, 1967), pp. 86–93, 218.

13. McGavran, *Understanding Church Growth,* p. 283.

14. Mooneyham, *What Do You Say to a Hungry World?,* p. 43.

15. Wallis, *Agenda for Biblical People,* pp. 89, 90.

16. Paul G. Hiebert, "Holism and the Integrated Christian Life," in *Crucial Dimensions in World Evangelization,* ed. Arthur F. Glasser, et. al. (Pasadena: William Carey Library, 1976), p. 85.

17. Quoted in John D. Woodbridge, Mark A. Noll and Nathan O. Hatch, *The Gospel in America: Themes in the Story of America's Evangelicals* (Grand Rapids: Zondervan, 1979), p. 239.

18. Arthur S. DeMoss, *God's Secret of Success,* privately published pamphlet, 1980, p. 5.

19. Howard Snyder, *The Community of the King* (Downers Grove, IL: InterVarsity Press, 1977), p. 115.

20. For extended treatment of the differences between, and complexities of, relief and development, see Mooneyham's chapter "Development: People-Building vs. Nation-Building, in *What Do You Say to a Hungry World?* pp. 197–219.

21. John R. W. Stott, *Christian Mission in the Modern World* (Downers Grove, IL: Intervarsity Press, 1975), pp. 95–96.

22. Paul Ramsey, "Perils of Pronouncements," *Christianity Today* 24, no. 17 (October 10, 1980), p. 43.

23. See *Christianity Today* 24, no. 14 (August 8, 1980), p. 18.

24. Carl F. H. Henry, *A Plea for Evangelical Demonstration* (Grand Rapids: Baker, 1971), p. 112.

25. Edward C. Stewart, *American Cultural Patterns: A Cross-Cultural Perspective* (LaGrange Park, IL.: Intercultural Network, 1972), pp. 64–65.

26. Roy DeLamotte, "Can Blacks Escape the Mainstream?" *Christian Century* 97, no. 9 (March 12, 1980), p. 277.

27. See Charles C. Ryrie, "Christ's Teaching on Social Ethics," *Bibliotheca Sacra* 134, no. 535 (July/September), 1977, pp. 223–224.

28. McGavran, *Understanding Church Growth,* p. 295.

29. Ibid., pp. 295–313.

30. Ibid., p. 299.

31. H. Richard Niebuhr, *The Social Sources of Denominationalism* (New York: World Publishing, 1929), p. 28.

32. Ibid., p. 70.

33. For details on this, see my *What Are We Missing?* (formerly *Look Out! The Pentecostals Are Coming*) (Carol Stream, IL: Creation House, 1978), pp. 70–73; 89–100.

34. Quoted in Niebuhr, *Social Sources of Denominationalism*, pp. 70–71.

35. Sider, *Rich Christians in an Age of Hunger*, pp. 171–188. See also "An Evangelical Commitment to Simple Lifestyle," a helpful statement produced by the International Consultation on Simple Life-

style, Hoddeston, England, March, 1980, cosponsored by the Lausanne Committee and the World Evangelical Fellowship.

36. See my *Your Spiritual Gifts Can Help Your Church Grow* (Glendale, CA: Regal Books, 1979), pp. 96–99.

37. Ibid., pp. 92–96.

CHAPTER 3

The Church and the Evangelistic Mandate

Men and women who have been born again into the kingdom of God consistently testify how different their lives are in comparison to what they were before they became disciples of Jesus Christ. Within themselves they feel peace of mind, release from guilt, new hope, liberation from fear, increased joy, and fuller understanding of the meaning of life. They find they have a new relationship with God. They worship him and pray to him and thank him for their food. Since they are in the community of the king, they have new relationships with people they call brothers and sisters in Christ. They are able to reach out in love and fellowship, and they receive care and concern from others in the family of God. They also find themselves readjusting their goals. As they learn more about God, they increasingly want to know his will for them, and they want to obey it. They soon find themselves part of a great outreach to the world around them.

Part of God's will for the people of the kingdom is the fulfillment of the cultural mandate described in detail in the last two chapters. But God's purpose in the world is not exhausted when Christian people reach out in obedience to help heal the individual and social hurts of the poor and oppressed. Another important aspect of God's work in the world, which he calls his people to participate in, is the evangelistic mandate. This chapter describes it in some detail.

The Evangelistic Mandate

The term "evangelistic mandate" forms a pair with "cultural mandate." They are as clear and useful as any expressions I have found to describe the two major areas of human responsibility in carrying out God's program in the world. It goes without saying that implied in the word "mandate" is the concept that they are *mandatory*. True Christians, for whom Jesus is really Lord, do not have the luxury of sitting back and coolly deciding whether they will participate in carrying out one or the other. There is no such option. Serving God, the king, necessarily includes both the cultural mandate and the evangelistic mandate.

As we attempt to understand the evangelistic mandate in depth, it will be helpful to look at its origin, its urgency and its goals.

The Origin of the Evangelistic Mandate. Like the cultural mandate, the evangelistic mandate has its origin in God. It is rooted in the very nature of God. Unlike the cultural mandate, there was no evangelistic mandate before Adam and Eve fell into sin. There was no need for it. The relationship of the human race with its creator was one of openness and uninhibited fellowship. Whenever God came to the garden, there were Adam and Eve. God declared this to be "good" (Gen. 1:31).

But then Satan came along, and Adam and Eve sinned. When God came to the garden the next time, they were nowhere to be found. God's first words to human beings after the fall were the beginning of the evangelistic mandate: "Adam, where art thou?" (Gen. 3:9). These are the words of a people-seeking God, a God who cannot be content if there are human beings, made in his own image and likeness, who, because of sin, are not in fellowship with him. Every man, woman, and child in the world was created by God to enjoy fellowship with him.

The evangelistic mandate has continued down through the ages. It was given to Abraham when God chose him to be the father of his people, Israel (Gen. 12:1–3). It was repeated by Jesus. The whole history of redemption that is told in terms of covenant, sacrifice, atonement, repentance, new birth, the cross, and the resurrection sums up God's working out of the evangelistic mandate. God desires that those who should be in fellowship with him be found, loved, and brought back to the father. He is a people-seeking God.

One of the great theological mysteries of the kingdom is why God has chosen to work out his evangelistic plan through human intermediaries. Since he is omnipotent, he could do it all by himself if he so chose. But, no, he has designed the process of redemption to be dependent upon the working of his Spirit through men and women who are already part of the community of the king. Salvation comes when people call on the name of the Lord. But, Paul asks rhetorically, "How shall they call on him in whom they have not heard? And how shall they hear without a preacher?" (Rom. 10:13–14). Our people-seeking God is also a people-using God. Consequently, he has given us the evangelistic mandate.

The Urgency of the Evangelistic Mandate.   In my Introduction I mentioned that one of what I consider the five theological nonnegotiables underlying the Church Growth Movement is the ultimate eschatological reality of sin, salvation, and eternal death. The worst possible condition of human beings is to be alienated by sin from the God who created them. Yet, those who, either because they have never heard of Jesus or because they have heard and rejected, have not put their faith and trust in Jesus as Savior and Lord are now alienated and will be alienated throughout all eternity. There is no Savior other than Jesus Christ (Acts 4:12). The only opportunity any individual has to hear the Gospel and be saved is during his or her lifetime here on earth.

This is the theological reason why the evangelistic mandate is urgent. When a person dies without hearing that "God so loved the world that he sent his only begotten Son, that whosoever believes on him should not perish but have eternal life" (John 3:16, RSV), it is too late. The best thing that could possibly happen to that person has been denied.

Not only is the evangelistic mandate urgent theologically, it is also urgent demographically. Approximately 30 percent of the world's population professes in some way to be Christian. This is not to say that they have all truly been born again into the kingdom of God. Many, perhaps the majority, are Christian in name but not in heart, belief, commitment, or lifestyle, and they are proper objects of the evangelistic mandate. The remaining 70 percent of the world's population, or slightly over three billion individuals at the present time, does not even profess to be Christian. At least two billion of them have never heard of Jesus Christ and his kingdom in a way that has made sense in their particular culture. The Lausanne Covenant mentions these three billion (which were 2.7 billion when it was written in 1974), and goes on to say, "We are ashamed that so many have been neglected; it is a standing rebuke to us and to the whole church" (Art. 9). The missiological research done by the Church Growth Movement and others indicates that reaching the three billion is logistically possible for today's Christians if sufficient personnel and financial resources could be dedicated to completing the task. The main reason it has not been accomplished, I think, is that God's people have not fully grasped the urgency of the evangelistic mandate.

The Goals of the Evangelistic Mandate. The evangelistic mandate is implicit in virtually every book of the New Testament. Jesus' own mention of it is recorded at least five times, once each in Matthew, Mark, Luke, John, and Acts. Some scholars would add other statements of Jesus to the list as well. It is called by many the "Great Commission." While each appearance of the Great Commission adds to the richness of its total meaning, there is a substantial consensus among students of missiology that the best starting point for understanding it is Matthew 28:19–20.[1]

Go, then, to all peoples everywhere and make them my disciples: baptize them in the name of the Father, the Son and the Holy Spirit, and teach them to obey everything I have commanded you (GNB).

These words of Jesus are to the evangelistic mandate what his words in the synagogue of Nazareth, recorded in Luke 4:18–19, are to the cultural mandate. This text, more than any other, has provided the scriptural motivation of the Church Growth Movement throughout the quarter century of its history. For that reason, a considerable amount of attention has been paid to it by the movement's advocates and its critics alike. The discussion centers on two points, one minor, one major.

The minor point has to do with the phrase "to all peoples everywhere." The Greek phrase for this is *panta ta ethne. "Panta"* means "all" and this is not a point of debate. *"Ta"* simply means "the." But what does *"ethne"* mean? The translators of the Good News Bible (quoted above) say it means "peoples." It is the word from which our English "ethnic" is derived. Most of the other Bible translations use "nations."

The Church Growth Movement has understood *panta ta ethne* to mean the significant groups of people in the world who have not yet been reached by the gospel. McGavran refers to them as "the classes, tribes, lineages, and peoples of the earth."[2] The Strategy Working Group of the Lausanne Committee for World Evangelization agrees with the translation "peoples," and defines a people as "a significantly large sociological grouping of individuals who perceive themselves to have a common affinity for one another."[3]

During the past few years, some missiologists have raised their voices against this interpretation of *ethne.* For example, Johannes Verkuyl argues that it should not be translated "ethnic units", but is rather "a technical term referring to the whole humanity from which God is gathering his people."[4] David Hesselgrave is disturbed that church growth proponents "impose current anthropological and sociological understandings upon the Scripture," and he prefers the meaning "Gentiles."[5]

I think this is a minor point, because everyone concerned believes that The Great Commission refers, in some way or another, to those vast multitudes of people out there who have not yet been evangelized. *Ethne* does refer to Gentiles. But it also is used to refer to Jews in 14 places in the New Testament.[6] The version of the Great Commission given in Acts 1:8 actually lists geographical areas where *ethne* are to be found, including Jerusalem, Judea, Samaria, and the uttermost parts of the earth. The objects of the evangelistic mandate are all those yet outside the kingdom of God, whether church members or not. They are lost sheep that God wants found and brought safely into his fold.

Defining Evangelism

The second and major point of the contemporary discussion over the goals of the Great Commission, revolves around the phrase "make disciples." This underlies the church growth understanding of what evangelism is all about. A clear definition of evangelism will help clarify the goal of the evangelistic mandate.

Notice that the Great Commission in Matthew 28:19–20 contains four action verbs: go, make disciples, baptize, and teach. In the original Greek, three of them, go, baptize and teach, are participles or helping verbs. Only one, make disciples, is an imperative verb. It is clear exigetically that the goal of the Great Commission is to *make disciples.* Going, in itself, will not fulfill the Great Commission. Neither will baptizing or teaching. But at the same time, speaking practically now, no one can make disciples without going, baptizing or teaching. While these three activities cannot be understood as ultimate goals, they nevertheless do carry a sense of the imperative because they are necessary for the task.

We cannot measure the degree of success or failure in the evangelistic effort by quantifying the going, baptizing, or teaching, but we can measure it by the number of disciples made. To the degree the other activities help to make disciples, they are being successfully accomplished. For example, if I go around the world five times, preach one thousand evangelistic sermons and baptize thousands in water, as did the Spanish priests in sixteenth-century Latin America, but leave behind no ongoing disciples of Jesus Christ, I have not evangelized those people. I may have been engaged in evangelistic activities, but the people themselves are still unevangelized. They are not yet safely in the kingdom of God.

Including "making disciples" as an integral part of the evangelistic mandate leads us to what I call a "3-P" definition of evangelism. The three Ps are presence, proclamation, and persuasion.

Presence Evangelism. What might be called "1-P" evangelism stresses *presence* as sufficient evangelism. In the final analysis, it confuses the cultural mandate with the evangelistic mandate and argues that fulfilling the cultural mandate is, in effect, evangelism. This is the error I described in Chapter 2 as the failure to distinguish between sociopolitical liberation and evangelism. Advocates of presence evangelism argue that "it cannot be regarded as the goal of Christian mission to 'make' non-Christians Christian, to 'convert' them, to 'win' them,"[7] or that "contemporary evangelism is moving away from winning souls one by one to the evangelization of the structures of society,"[8] or that "to evangelize is not to convert, it is not to win souls to Christ, it is not to get members for the church . . . but rather to bring all the structures of this world toward their ultimate goal,"[9] or that evangelism means "to serve without thought of growth or proselytizing."[10]

Most evangelicals do not hesitate to criticize this view of presence evangelism. For example, Ronald Sider says, "There is no New Testament justification for talking about 'evangelizing' political structures.[11] David Bosch fears that it will throw wide open "the flood-gates of universalism."[12] In a more pragmatic vein, Princeton's George Sweazey warns, " 'Presence' is a code word for failure."[13]

Proclamation and Persuasion. While most evangelicals reject presence, or 1-P, as an insufficient definition of evangelism, they do agree that one cannot evangelize in an authentic way without being present and identifying with the people who are to hear the message. Presence is a prerequisite for evangelism, although being present does not in itself constitute evangelism, since the biblical goal goes considerably beyond that.

Evangelicals do not agree among themselves whether the goal of evangelism should be understood as simply to proclaim the Good News or to make disciples. Some hold to proclamation evangelism, or 2-P, which argues that to evangelize is "not to ask whether conversions are known to have resulted from your witness,"[14] but simply "to announce the good news."[15] Others, and the Church Growth Movement identifies with this view, feel that proclamation itself, while it is as necessary as presence to evangelize effectively, does not in itself constitute evangelism. Evangelism has only been accomplished when disciples are made. A focal point of the debate has been the famous definition of evangelism published by the Anglican Archbishops' Committee in 1918:

To evangelize is so to present Christ Jesus in the power of the Holy Spirit that men shall come to put their trust in God through Him, to accept Him as their Saviour, and serve Him as their King in the fellowship of His Church.

Proclamation (2-P) evangelism does not accept this definition because it includes the hoped for effect in the definition itself. Persuasion evangelism (3-P) applauds it because the definition includes the need to see signs of true discipleship through its mention of serving Jesus as king in the fellowship of his church. Church growth thinking has contended that Great Commission evangelism has not been completed unless and until men and women accept the gospel, believe in Jesus, are incorporated into the church as responsible members, and, as Luke said of those who were converted on the day of Pentecost, "continue steadfastly in the apostles' doctrine and fellowship and in breaking of bread and in prayers" (Acts 2:42).

After the better part of a decade of discussion over the difference between 2-P and 3-P evangelism,[16] John Stott and I, both engaged in the ongoing dynamic of the Lausanne Committee for World Evangelization, have agreed on a definition that, we feel, satisfies the concerns of both the 2-P people and the 3-P people. This definition has been accepted by both the Theology Working Group (of which Stott is chairperson) and the Strategy Working Group (of which I am chairperson). It goes somewhat beyond the Lausanne Covenant in stating that:

The *nature* of evangelism is the communication of the Good News.
The *purpose* of evangelism is to give individuals and groups valid opportunity
    to accept Jesus Christ.

The *goal* of evangelism is to persuade men and women to become disciples of
Jesus Christ and to serve him in the fellowship of his Church.

In my opinion, this, better than anything else to date, properly sets
forth the biblical ideal of the evangelistic mandate. There is more to be
said about exactly what constitutes a "disciple" and how that fits into
the contemporary use of the word "discipleship," but that discussion will
be postponed until Chapter 7.

Church Growth and the Evangelistic Mandate

If we accept that "the goal of evangelism is to persuade men and
women to become disciples of Jesus Christ and to serve him in the
fellowship of his church," as suggested above, it is clear that the growth
of the church is intimately related to the fulfillment of the evangelistic
mandate. Donald McGavran argues that "Evangelization intends the
redemption of individuals and the multiplication of Christ's
churches."[17] This is not acceptable to those who feel that the goal of
evangelism is to draw large crowds or count hands raised at the invitation
or distribute tracts or conduct a radio ministry. Those are 2-P approaches. A 3-P approach insists that the evangelistic process is not
concluded until the person has committed himself or herself to Jesus
Christ as Savior and Lord and also has committed himself or herself to
the body of Christ. Commitment to Christ is an essential first step, but
the Church Growth Movement questions the validity of that decision
unless the person becomes a responsible church member.

Some people continue to disagree, however. Bishop Lesslie Newbigin,
in a critique of the Church Growth Movement, argues that a study of
the Epistles discloses no interest in numerical growth. "We do not find
Paul concerning himself with the size of the churches, or with questions
about their growth," he says. In fact, in the whole New Testament
"there is no evidence that the numerical growth of the church is a
matter of primary concern."[18] Karl Barth asks, "What objection could
we really make if it should please God to carry his work onward and
reach his goal, not through a further numerical increase, but through a
drastic numerical decrease of so-called Christendom?"[19] Al Krass adds
his voice when he says, "I don't really want to silence the debate over
church growth. What I want to ask, quite seriously, is whether the Lord
intends for the church to grow."[20]

Two things need to be said about this point of view, which, of course, is not confined to Newbigin, Barth, and Krass. The first is that, in my opinion, it falls short of a biblical understanding of the evangelistic mandate and its goals. The theme of the Epistle to the Romans, for example, can be summed up by Paul's concluding paragraph. There he says that the "command of the eternal God" is made known to all nations *(panta ta ethne)* "so that all may believe and obey" (Rom. 16:26). This, Paul asserts, is the "Good News I preach about Jesus Christ" (Rom. 16:25). With three billion people in the world who have yet to hear the Gospel and "believe and obey," it is difficult for church growth leaders to understand how some theologians can sit back and calmly wonder whether or not it is God's will for his church to grow. Most of those in the world who presently believe and obey are to be found in Christian churches. When the evangelistic mandate is being implemented, men and women do, in fact, believe and obey, and they thereby add to the number of people who belong to existing churches and participate in the establishment of new churches. At the present time, approximately 1,600 new churches are being started every week around the world. My understanding of the evangelistic mandate is that such a phenomenon pleases the eternal God.

The second thing to be said about those who disagree with the church growth teaching is that there might be some lack of mutual understanding as to what is meant by "church." I notice that Newbigin mentions with some anguish the thousands baptized by the Spanish in Latin America, and obviously wonders if these are the "church." It would be well, then, to clarify what the Church Growth Movement means by "church," particularly in relationship to the kingdom of God.

Several theologians have objected to what Paul Fries calls the "axial postulate" of church growth theology, namely that "God wants his church to grow."[21] Fries argues that he finds this nowhere in the New Testament. But a major point of his article is that "it may be stated without the slightest equivocation that *God wants his kingdom to grow.*"[22] This is helpful. Orlando Costas asserts that the Church Growth Movement has a "questionable theological locus" and perceives that it is too ecclesiocentric. He argues that the locus of biblical theology should not be church-centered, but Christ-centered. And then, like Fries, he asks, "Isn't the gospel the good news of the *kingdom?* Who is the center of the kingdom—Christ or the church?"[23]

Undoubtedly, church growth writers in the past have been negligent in developing the relationship of the growth of the church to that of the kingdom of God. Perhaps they have not been Christocentric enough. These are, I think, acceptable criticisms. In Chapter 1, I asserted that all *church* growth is not *kingdom* growth. Anyone who reads Jesus' parables knows that Satan sows tares among the wheat. Church growth people are interested in the sowing, multiplication, and harvesting of wheat, not of tares. Some tares, of course, will creep in. I think the parable warns us not to be overly concerned about them. But church growth would agree with Fries and Costas that *kingdom growth* is the ultimate task, while *church growth* is a penultimate task within the evangelistic mandate.

The "Church" of Church Growth

The Church Growth Movement has consistently stressed that the outcome of fulfilling the evangelistic mandate is *responsible* church membership. The kind of "church" it aims for is the church which best glorifies God through faith, obedience, and a kingdom lifestyle. It is not content with mere names on a church roll, with inflated numbers of nonresident, nonactive, nongiving, nonworshipping nondisciples. It is critical, for example, of the growing number of persons in America who have committed themselves to Jesus Christ, but who do not commit themselves to a local congregation. Instead they use television as their "electronic church." (Shut-ins and invalids, of course, are an exception.) Church growth does not aspire to churches that are mere social clubs or ingrown churches that do not reach out to the community in obedience to both the cultural and the evangelistic mandate.

I detect, in much of the criticism of the Church Growth Movement, a concern that an overenthusiastic commitment to the evangelistic mandate will lead to neglect of the dimensions of what Costas calls "organic, conceptual and incarnational" growth. I agree that these must not be neglected by faithful Christians. But unbelievers who worship idols, beat wives and children, get high on drugs and rape teenage girls, underpay their employees, cheat on their income tax, and lie on expense accounts cannot be taught organic, conceptual, and incarnational growth. They must first become believers, and it is the evangelistic mandate that carries the gospel of the kingdom to them so that they, too, all have the opportunity to obey the king and enjoy his blessings. From this point of view it is hard to see how Christian people can get over-enthusiastic about the evangelistic mandate.

The "church" of the Church Growth Movement is the one that Jesus referred to in Matthew 16:18, where he said, "Upon this rock I will build my church." It is *his* church. Whether it is a Baptist or Lutheran or Episcopal or Pentecostal church is secondary. Whether it is large or small is secondary. Whether it is rural or urban, suburban or inner-city is secondary. The primary consideration is that it be the church of Jesus Christ and that by its lifestyle of obedience it bring glory to him.

Perhaps a paradigm of the kind of church that church growth people envision is found in Acts 2. It may be true that Acts 2 is largely a descriptive rather than normative portion of Scripture, yet few will deny that the quality of that Jerusalem church, while not identical with the kingdom, reflected to a substantial degree the lifestyle of the kingdom. It was a community of the king which began as a result of prayer and the filling of the Holy Spirit. The 3,000 people who founded it repented, placed their faith in Jesus, and were baptized. They improved their knowledge of Christian doctrine; they enjoyed each other's fellowship; they partook of the Lord's Supper; they prayed; they shared their belongings with each other; they preached the gospel; they saw miracles and wonders being done in their midst; they had humble hearts; they praised God; they met in the Temple; they established small groups in their homes. They obviously were doing God's will and bringing glory to him. But one thing more: they were active in obeying the evangelistic mandate. They reached out to the unbelievers around them, and *the Lord added daily to the church such as should be saved.*

Does God want his church to grow? He apparently wanted that church in Jerusalem to grow, and it did, because the believers were obedient in all things. And, although there might be some exceptions, God expects most churches today, those that are serious about the evangelistic mandate, to grow and multiply. As Chester Droog says, "Small, weak, struggling, stagnant churches do nothing to enhance the glory of Christ. Vibrant, alive, witnessing, throbbing congregations give Christ the glory and honor due him."[24]

Is It All Right to Count?

The use of numbers in fulfilling the evangelistic mandate has been so abused by otherwise well-meaning people that it has fallen under some harsh criticism. The phrase "evangelistically speaking" is not merely a jest. It has done a great deal, in some people's minds, to bring the use of numbers in the Lord's work into considerable disrepute. The Lausanne Covenant rightly warns that "we have become unduly preoccupied with statistics or even dishonest in our use of them" (Art. 12).

"The renewed interest in church growth and the stimulating studies of Donald McGavran are important," says Hans-Ruedi Weber of the Ecumenical Institute. But he goes on to caution that these studies "often use man's and not God's arithmetic as the measure of growth."[25] His concern is partly that churches need not only to grow in the number of members but also in grace. René Padilla feels that the "excessive emphasis on numbers" in church growth becomes "numerolatry." He objects to "the philosophy of statistical success."[26] Wes Michaelson also speaks of "the idolization of church growth."[27] Andrew Kirk warns against "the current evangelistic triumphalism of a concern for numbers."[28]

My view is that this kind of criticism emerges from Christian leaders who desire to uphold the banner of the cultural mandate. Many identify with the radical discipleship group and feel that the Church Growth Movement poses a serious threat to their vision of the lifestyle of the kingdom. A great deal of emotional heat must lie behind accusing fellow evangelicals of being idolatrous. This negative image may well have been fueled by church growth leaders themselves who have not in the past given enough emphasis to the cultural mandate alongside the evangelistic mandate. I hope that, as books like this one are published, it will help relieve some of that tension.

One reason I say this is that I know that many of these critics, as committed Christians, believe deeply in the evangelistic mandate. Padilla himself says, "The numerical expansion of the church is a legitimate concern for anyone who takes the Scriptures seriously."[29] He mainly wants to avoid promoting cheap grace or a commercialized gospel. Some who, like Padilla and Kirk, take a strong stand for the cultural mandate and the kingdom lifestyle, have perceived the triviality of attacking the use of numbers. John Howard Yoder, for example, calls them "quibbles" and "red herrings," matters of "style, not substance." He feels that "they are not fair to the intention and the creative contribution of 'Church Growth.'"[30] David Stowe considers Hans-Ruedi Weber's position "very mysterious." "I think there is only one arithmetic," Stowe says, "although there are many forms of higher mathematics. And surely every single person from number one to number three billion is distinctly and individually important to God."[31]

The Church Growth Movement is not about to forego the use of numbers and statistics. Donald McGavran says that "the numerical approach is essential to understanding church growth. The church is made up of countable people and there is nothing particularly spiritual in not counting them." He argues that there are both biblical and practical grounds for using numbers. In congregations and denominations, McGavran says, "It is as necessary as honest financial dealing." He admits that no one was ever saved by statistics, but then "no one was ever cured by the thermometer to which the physician pays such close attention."[32] Throughout the last couple of decades, church growth studies, based on as careful and objective quantitative reporting as possible, have greatly accelerated the fulfillment of the evangelistic mandate from the human point of view, and, I believe, brought glory to God.

Church growth people, however, will gladly accept the admonition that "the goal of added numbers must not be absolutized."[33] Not all growth, as human cancer research shows, is good. But every person who is taken by the power of the Holy Spirit from darkness to light, from the power of Satan to the power of God, and who becomes a member of the community of the king through whom the signs of the kingdom show through to the world, is a step in the right direction. Careful records evidently are being kept in heaven, for when this happens to even one person the angels of heaven rejoice (Luke 15:7). And we pray for God's will to be done on earth as it is in heaven. Not growth for denominational self-aggrandizement; not growth for a personal ego trip; not growth attributed to carnal or worldly desires; but growth that glorifies God is the objective of the Church Growth Movement.

Numbers and American Culture

There is one more thing to say about the use of numbers. When Samuel Escobar objects to "the strong tendency to measure the results of the missionary enterprise solely in quantitative terms," he ties this in with "our pragmatic, technological age, particularly in North America" where the "cult of success and efficiency" is prominent.[34] This is a very interesting comment because it unveils one of the underlying reasons why so many critics of church growth are either natives of other countries than the United States, or Americans who have rejected mainline American cultural values and are attempting to develop a countercultural lifestyle.

One of the most helpful books for understanding Americans is *American Cultural Patterns: A Cross-Cultural Perspective* by Edward C. Stewart.[35] Anthropologist Stewart compares American cultural values and behavior patterns to non-American cultures of other parts of the world. Studying this book not only helps Americans to understand themselves better and take themselves a little less seriously, but it also enlightens others as to why Americans often appear strange and even offensive to them. His perspective is certainly compatible with contemporary missiology and intercultural studies.

As an example, Robert Zuercher, in a recent article, warns fellow Britons to "reflect a bit more carefully on some of the basic presuppositions out of which Church Growth methodology and principles emerged," lest British churches (now losing 131,000 members per year) "get caught up with yet another American model for doing things."[36] What might be called "Americophobia" is a worldwide phenomenon.

One American cultural trait that others find offensive is the American tendency to quantify. Stewart observes that "to the American the essential quality is measurability. The world to him is seen as having dimensions that can be quantified." For Americans, "success and failure are measured by statistics," and it is difficult for them to understand the negative reaction of others to this mind set. Stewart points out, for example, how the Kpelle of Liberia never count chickens for fear some harm will come to them. And a typical American statement like "the average family contains two and one-half members" seems to some non-Americans to "impugn the dignity of the individual."[37]

I know of no good reason to deny that the Church Growth Movement has built into its methodology many reflections of American (more specifically Anglo-American) cultural values. In the Introduction I admitted to a degree of theological ethnocentrism, and I will admit here to a degree of methodological ethnocentrism. But very few anthropologists, missiologists, or people with in-depth cross-cultural experience would argue that American cultural values are either inferior or superior to those of any other given culture. Certainly there are demonic elements in American culture that need to be rejected by Christians—for example, killing 1.5 million babies per year by abortion (another statistic!). But this is true of any human culture. I myself do not think the American inclination to quantify is any better or worse than the Kpelle inclination not to.

Quantity and Quality

Lyle E. Schaller says that "the most widespread defensive response to the Church Growth Movement by the congregations on a plateau or declining in size is, 'We're not interested in the numbers game. We're concentrating on quality.' "[38]

The Church Growth Movement feels that it is not legitimate to set quantity against quality in church growth. No church growth advocates that I am aware of would deny the need for high-quality churches. I share the concern of those who strive to avoid "a new version of the old Constantinism," or churches that are little more than a "mass of baptized unbelievers."[39]

It is not easy to measure quality growth in a church, but some church growth researchers are attempting to develop helpful measuring scales. These scales will probably include such things as regularity of attendance at weekly worship services, percentage of individual giving, percentage of the church budget designated for the cultural and evangelistic mandates, proportion of church members volunteering time to serve the Lord, and other measurements of quality of Christian growth. The composite membership figure, already a standard component of church growth research methodology, combines qualities such as worship attendance and Sunday School attendance with communicant membership.[40] A major task is to discover scales which will be acceptable across the board and not confined to a particular denomination or philosophy of ministry.

Ralph Winter says it well when he argues that "highly important qualities do have quantitative, measurable dimensions, and quantitative statements cannot but refer to qualities of some kind, important or not. The challenge is to make sure the qualities we measure are important." He concludes that "the people who set the quantitative in opposition to the qualitative are really trying to say that we are not measuring the right things."[41] I think that he is partly right, but there are also some who object because they have cultural aversions to measuring anything, and they should feel free to abstain from measuring.

Notes

1. For example, Johannes Verkuyl states: "But there is no doubt about it: the concluding verses of Matthew's Gospel express it the most forthrightly. Not only is the conclusion of Matthew's Gospel extremely powerful compared to the others, but the final verses form a climax and present a summary of what was written before. They are the key to the understanding of the whole book." *Contemporary Missiology: An Introduction* (Grand Rapids: Eerdmans, 1978), p. 106. See also David J. Bosch, *Witness to the World: The Christian Mission in Theological Perspective* (Atlanta: John Knox, 1980), pp. 66–69.

2. Donald A. McGavran, *Understanding Church Growth*, rev. ed. (Grand Rapids: Eerdmans, 1980), p. 22.

3. Edward R. Dayton, *That Everyone May Hear* (Monrovia, CA: Missions Advanced Research and Communications, 1979), p. 22.

4. Verkuyl, *Contemporary Missiology*, p. 107.

5. David J. Hesselgrave, *Planting Churches Cross-Culturally: A Guide for Home and Foreign Missions* (Grand Rapids: Baker, 1980), pp. 47–48. See also Walter L. Liefield, "Theology of Church Growth," in *Theology and Mission: Papers Given at Trinity Consultation No. 1*, ed. David J. Hesselgrave (Grand Rapids, Baker, 1978), pp. 175–176; and David J. Hesselgrave, "Confusion Concerning the Great Commission," *Evangelical Missions Quarterly* 15, no. 4 (October 1979), p. 200; and the response to that by Tetsunao Yamamori, "A Sophisticated Misinterpretation?" *Global Church Growth Bulletin* 18, no. 1 (January/February 1980), p. 4.

6. Colin Brown, ed., *The New International Dictionary of New Testament Theology*, Vol. 2 (Grand Rapids: Zondervan, 1976), p. 793. See also G. Kittel, ed., *Theological Dictionary of the New Testament*, Vol. 2 (Grand Rapids: Eerdmans, 1964), pp. 364–372.

7. Quoted in Peter Beyerhaus, "Mission, Humanization and the Kingdom," in *Crucial Issues in Missions Tomorrow*, ed. Donald McGavran (Chicago; Moody Press, 1972), p. 70.

8. Quoted in Billy Graham, "Why the Berlin Congress?" in *One Race, One Gospel, One Task*, ed. Carl F. H. Henry and W. Stanley Mooneyham (Minneapolis: World Wide Publications, 1967), Vol. 1, p. 24.

9. Carlos Valle, "Presuposiciones teológicas de la evangelización," mimeographed paper, 1966, pp. 1–2 (translation mine).
10. Quoted in George E. Sweazey, *The Church as Evangelist* (San Francisco: Harper & Row, 1978), p. 27.
11. Ronald J. Sider, *Evangelism, Salvation and Social Justice* (Bramcote, Notts., U. K.: Grove Books, 1977), p. 14.
12. Bosch, *Witness to the World*, p. 215.
13. Sweazey, *The Church as Evangelist*, p. 27.
14. J. I. Packer, *Evangelism and the Sovereignty of God* (Downers Grove, IL: InterVarsity Press, 1961), p. 41.
15. John R. W. Stott, *Christian Mission in the Modern World* (Downers Grove, IL: InterVarsity Press, 1975), p. 40.
16. For some of the published exchanges in this discussion, see my *Frontiers in Missionary Strategy* (Chicago: Moody Press, 1971), pp. 125–134; James I. Packer, "What Is Evangelism?" *Theological Perspectives on Church Growth*, ed. Harvie M. Conn (Nutley, NJ: Presbyterian and Reformed, 1976), pp. 98–100; and Stott, *Christian Mission in the Modern World*, pp. 38–41; 54–57. For an independent opinion that responsible church membership should be included in the definition of evangelism, see Sweazey, *The Church as Evangelist*, pp. 53 ff.
17. McGavran, *Understanding Church Growth*, p. v.
18. Lesslie Newbigin, *The Open Secret* (Grand Rapids: Eerdmans, 1978), p. 140.
19. Karl Barth, "No Christian Marshall Plan," *Christian Century* 65, no. 49 (December 8, 1948), p. 1332. This was Barth's address to the inaugural assembly of the World Council of Churches in Amsterdam in 1948.
20. Alfred Krass, "Church Growth and the Methodology of the Kingdom: Reflections on My Personal Search for Direction," *The Other Side* 14, no. 12 (December 1978), p. 62.
21. Paul Fries, "Toward a Reformed Theology of Church Growth," *The Church Herald* 34, no. 17 (August 19, 1977), p. 13.
22. Ibid., p. 14.
23. Orlando Costas, *The Church and Its Mission: A Shattering Critique from the Third World* (Wheaton, IL: Tyndale, 1974), pp. 134–137.
24. Chester J. Droog, unpublished Letter to the Editor of *The Church Herald*, August 20, 1977, p. 1.

25. Hans-Reudi Weber, "God's Arithmetic," *Frontier* 6 (Winter 1963), p. 298.

26. C. René Padilla, "A Steep Climb Ahead for Theology in Latin America," *Evangelical Missions Quarterly* 7, no. 2 (Winter 1971), p. 102, 104.

27. Wes Michaelson, "Evangelicalism and Radical Discipleship," *Evangelicalism and Anabaptism*, ed. C. Norman Kraus (Scottdale, PA: Herald Press, 1979), p. 79.

28. J. Andrew Kirk, "The Kingdom of God and the Church in Contemporary Protestantism and Catholicism," in *Let the Earth Hear His Voice*, ed. J. D. Douglas (Minneapolis: World Wide Publications, 1975), p. 1080.

29. René Padilla, "Evangelism and the World," in *Let the Earth Hear His Voice*, ed. J. D. Douglas (Minneapolis: World Wide Publications, 1975), p. 138.

30. John H. Yoder, "Church Growth Issues in Theological Perspective," in *The Challenge of Church Growth: A Symposium*, ed. Wilbert R. Shenk (Elkhart, IN: Institute of Mennonite Studies, 1973), pp. 29–30.

31. David M. Stowe, *Ecumenicity and Evangelism* (Grand Rapids: Eerdmans, 1970), p. 25.

32. McGavran, *Understanding Church Growth*, pp. 93–94.

33. John M. L. Young, "The Place and Importance of Numerical Church Growth," in *Theological Perspectives on Church Growth*, ed. Harvie M. Conn (Nutley, NJ: Presbyterian and Reformed, 1976), p. 72.

34. Samuel Escobar, "The Return of Christ," in *The New Face of Evangelicalism*, ed. C. René Padilla (Downers Grove, IL: InterVarsity Press, 1976), p. 262.

35. Edward C. Stewart, *American Cultural Patterns: A Cross-Cultural Perspective* (LaGrange Park, IL: Intercultural Network, 1972).

36. Robert Zuercher, "Growing a Church," *Third Way* 4, no. 3 (March 1980), p. 31.

37. Stewart, *American Cultural Patterns*, p. 68.

38. Lyle E. Schaller, "Overlooked Characteristics of Growing Congregations," *Church Administration*, July 1979, p. 18.

39. Padilla, "A Steep Climb Ahead," pp. 102–103.

40. See Bob Waymire and C. Peter Wagner, *The Church Growth*

Survey Handbook (Santa Clara, CA: Global Church Growth Bulletin, 1980), p. 7.

41. Ralph D. Winter, "Quality or Quantity," *Crucial Issues in Missions Tomorrow,* ed. Donald McGavran (Chicago: Moody Press, 1972), p. 178.

CHAPTER 4

Consecrated Pragmatism

In the first three chapters I have attempted to establish the obligation of every faithful Christian, congregation, and grouping of churches to participate in fulfilling both the cultural mandate and the evangelistic mandate. I have said it before and I will say it again: neither the cultural nor the evangelistic mandate is optional for men and women who belong to the community of the king and for whom Jesus is Lord.

The Right and Duty to Specialize

While both mandates are obligatory, not every faithful Christian is expected to give equal emphasis to both, although some will. The Church Growth Movement, for example, feels called by God to special-ize in the evangelistic mandate. Donald McGavran says it all when he writes: "The long range goal of church growth is the discipling of *panta ta ethne,* to the end that rivers of water of eternal and abundant life flow fast and free, to every tongue and tribe and people in all the earth."[1] Church growth people do what they can to participate in the cultural mandate, and many of them do a great deal. But most of their time, energy, and money is dedicated to world evangelization.

Because the Church Growth Movement believes in all the obligations of the lifestyle of the kingdom of God, it does not consider this calling as selective obedience. The Bible teaches that all members of the body of Christ have been given "gifts differing according to the grace that is given to us" (Rom. 12:6). Church growth believes in "diversities of gifts but the same spirit" (1 Cor. 12:4). It believes that some members of the body are called to give themselves specifically to the fulfillment of the cultural mandate as part of God's total plan for the kingdom and for its outreach and testimony in the world. In my opinion, specific spiritual gifts such as service, prophecy, mercy, voluntary poverty, and others are given to those believers by God.[2] Groups of such Christians, banded together in organizations like the Sojourners of Washington D.C., the Jubilee Fellowship of Philadelphia, the Evangelicals for Social Action, and others, are leading the way in helping evangelical Christians fully to understand and participate in the cultural mandate. Similarly, groups of Christians with different sets of spiritual gifts, in organizations like the Billy Graham Evangelistic Association, the U. S. Center for World Mission, or the Lausanne Committee for World Evangelization, are leading the way toward fulfilling the evangelistic mandate.

Some local churches such as the Church of the Savior in Washington, D.C. or the Church of the Redeemer in Houston, or the La Salle Street Church in Chicago dedicate much of their ministry to the cultural mandate. Others such as the Coral Ridge Presbyterian Church of Fort Lauderdale, Florida, or Bellevue Baptist Church of Memphis, or the Full Gospel Tabernacle of Buffalo, specialize in the evangelistic mandate. None of the leaders of either group denies or neglects the other mandate, but each feels called by God to concentrate primarily on one.

It seems to me that, given the nature of the distribution of gifts by the Holy Spirit in the body of Christ, such specialization is pleasing to God. It is theologically sound. All the members of the body are important, but all do not have the same function. The eye cannot say to the ear, "I have no need of you." Cultural mandate specialists cannot say that they have no need of the evangelistic mandate specialists and vice versa. All are important in the body of Christ and all are making a substantial contribution to the kingdom of God.

I am aware that some Christian leaders will continue to object to this, feeling that every group of Christians should attempt to balance their activities rather than specialize. Some warn against the tendency to "balkanize" Christian activities. Some, for example, have objected to the Lausanne Committee's staunch determination to concentrate on the evangelistic mandate. But, in my opinion, rather than attempting to force more cultural mandate concerns on the LCWE they would do better to use their energies in establishing a parallel Committee for World Christian Social Concerns.

"Fierce Pragmatism"

The basis of the decision of the Church Growth Movement to concentrate on the evangelistic mandate is rooted in a principle of the
kingdom of God, namely, obedience to the king. When God calls, it is
the duty of believers to respond and obey. God has called some of his
people to specialize in worship, others in marriage and family counsel-
ing, others in relief and development, others in theological and biblical
scholarship, in Christian education, in music, social action, and so on.
If they are living a kingdom lifestyle, they will obey him and give primary
attention to their calling. Church growth people believe their duty is to
make whatever contribution they can toward sharing the Gospel and
persuading all men and women who have yet to believe in Christ to
accept him as their Savior and Lord and serve him in the fellowship of
his church. Such a decision is compatible with the kingdom of God.

The goal of the evangelistic mandate is clear. It is a goal established
not by human beings, but revealed by God in his Word. As shown in
the last chapter, it is nothing less than making disciples of all nations.
As long as there is one person in the world not yet reconciled to God
through Jesus Christ, the evangelistic mandate remains in effect. If 99
sheep are in the fold and one is missing, the faithful shepherd searches
for the missing one. In our world, however, for every sheep in the fold,
at least two are still outside. With three billion yet to believe, the task
is enormous.

Since God's goal is clear, church growth people approach the task of
accomplishing it in a fairly pragmatic way. The word "pragmatic,"
however, has drawn some criticism. Perhaps it is not the best word, but
since it is being used, it should be explained. My dictionary defines
pragmatic as "concerned with practical consequences or values." This
is the way church growth understands the term. It does not mean the
kind of pragmatism that treats people as objects and dehumanizes them.
It does not mean pragmatism that will compromise the doctrinal and
ethical principles of God, the Bible, and the kingdom. But it does mean
pragmatism as far as value-neutral methodologies are concerned.

In an address given at the Fuller School of World Mission in 1970,
Donald McGavran said, "We devise mission methods and policies in the
light of what God has blessed—and what he has obviously not blessed."
He expressed concern about methodologies that are supposed to bring

people to Christ and multiply churches, but don't. Or those that are designed to improve society, but don't. The best thing to do with such methods, he argued, was "throw them away," and get a method that works and brings glory to God. He then summed it up by saying, "As to methods, we are *fiercely pragmatic.*"[3]

Sources of Pragmatism in Church Growth

Because their pragmatism is used in obedience to God and for the ultimate purpose of glorifying God, church growth people feel it is "consecrated pragmatism." Where does this pragmatism come from? As I see it, it comes from at least three sources: cultural, historical, and theological.

Cultural Sources. There is undoubtedly some methodological ethnocentrism in the church growth approach to pragmatism. Stewart points out that Americans have an "incessant need to systematize the perception of the world into a form that enables the individual to act." In the academic world, the American intellectual "has been consistently pressed to show the utility of his ideas and theories," which is not the case, for example, with European intellectuals. In America the argument that "it may be all right in theory, but it's no good in practice" can often kill a new idea.

I have no inclination to argue whether this is a good or bad cultural trait. Most Americans simply participate in it as naturally as Germans arrive at appointments punctually or as Indian parents choose their children's spouses. Even those who stress the cultural mandate (and sometimes complain about the pragmatism of church growth) are pragmatic in their own way. If, for example, the most effective way to raise funds is through direct mail appeal letters, they will use well-designed Madison Avenue–type appeals, use computerized labels, offer credit, and advertise discount incentives on their magazines, which decry American consumerism and technology.

Historical Sources. One approach characteristic of church growth methodology is the attempt to observe, as McGavran mentions above, which evangelistic methods God has blessed and which he obviously has not blessed. If we can find cases in recent or more remote history where disciples have actually been made and where the evangelistic mandate has in fact been carried out, we can find valuable clues as to methodologies. This is the phenomenological approach which will be discussed in some detail in Chapter 8.

Here I will simply mention, as an illustration, the matter of motives for conversion. Many critics of church growth have questioned the use of certain evangelistic methodologies on the grounds that they might bring people to Christ for the wrong motives. They question strongly, for example, a church that will advertise a 100-foot-long banana split to get children to come to Sunday School, or churches that have a large bus ministry and serve bubble gum or Colonel Sanders chicken on the busses, or churches that hold square dances, or churches that build Crystal Cathedrals with water fountains up the center aisle. This all seems too pragmatic.

Research shows that the motives for becoming a Christian are very mixed indeed. In a well-publicized research project done by J. Waskom Pickett some years ago, it was found that Indians who had become responsible Christians did so from four basic sets of motives: spiritual, secular, social, and natal. While those who became Christians from spiritual motives showed higher levels of Christian attainment than the others, the difference was not a significant one.[4] Perhaps an understanding of this was one reason why the Apostle Paul, addressing the problem of motives, admitted that some were preaching from envy and strife while others were preaching from love. But in all cases, "Christ is preached; and therein I do rejoice" (Phil. 1:18).

Theological Sources. The Bible itself contains many references to a pragmatic approach that are impressive to church growth people. One could hardly read the story of Nehemiah, for example, without applauding his pragmatism. Without it he could hardly have accomplished the building of the wall of Jerusalem in 52 days, using volunteer help, while under attack of enemies. We see also, in the Book of Hebrews, that Jesus' going to the cross was a pragmatically determined action. It had been established by God that without the shedding of blood there would be no remission of sins. Jesus came in order to die for the sins of the whole world, once and for all. Although he had to break the news gradually to his disciples, the cross had been his goal from the beginning. With no cross he would have failed, but with it he accomplished his goal. Jesus, it seems to me, was an intensely task-oriented person.

No less task-oriented was the Apostle Paul. His goal was to save people —to fulfill the evangelistic mandate. Sometimes he obeyed the Jewish law, and sometimes he did not. One of the most pragmatic statements in the New Testament is Paul's willingness to be made all things to all men "that I might *by all means* save some" (1 Cor. 9:19–22). It is this same kind of single-minded obedience to the evangelistic mandate that is part of the lifestyle of the kingdom and a chief source of the "conse-crated pragmatism" of church growth people.

Planning Strategy for Results

The emphasis on planning strategy, found in church growth literature, flows from this pragmatic approach to doing the work of God. Setting goals and doing what is necessary to reach those goals is very much part of the lifestyle of church growth people. Behind the affirmation that it is God's will that his church grow is an assumption that churches that are not actively reaching out with practical methodologies to bring new people to Christ are to that degree less than God's ideal. This has drawn criticism from those who have developed a different concept of the church. Their assumption is that the church exists "to be the church." Richard Hutcheson calls this the "classical understanding" of the church. He reviews the historical confessions of the Reformed tradition, beginning with the Apostles' Creed, and finds that "not one of these classical statements so much as *mentions* the church's *goal,* its *mission,* or its *purpose.* "[5] Little wonder that the more recent goal-oriented per-spective on the nature of the church, which is being stressed by the Church Growth Movement, is distasteful to many. "Always the assump-tion has been," Hutcheson argues, "that the church exists, not to *do* something, but to *be* something—a people of God, a community of faith, the body of Christ."[6]

It seems to me that the church exists both to be and to do. Doing requires planning. It requires goal-setting and strategy development. I like Robert Schuller's slogan, "If you fail to plan you're planning to fail." If the cultural mandate and the evangelistic mandate are worthwhile, they're worth planning for.

Those who fear pragmatism are concerned lest the end be taken as justifying the means. However, a knee-jerk rejection of this concept may be too hasty. In Christian work it is axiomatic that *immoral* means are not to be used for any end. Both the means and the end must glorify God. For example, Christians who are obedient to Jesus as Lord cannot follow the Children of God sect in recommending the use of sexual relations as an evangelistic methodology. Fornication, lying, force, ma-nipulation, or any immoral activity cannot be used. But 100-foot banana splits? Bubble gum on the busses?

These questions concerning the evangelistic mandate run parallel to many questions that are asked about the cultural mandate, all on pragmatic grounds. Is civil disobedience, for example, a means that glorifies God? I am pragmatic enough to feel that it may at times be justified. I have seen, for example, a secret room in the basement of my ancestral home in New York's Mohawk Valley and learned that Fort Wagner was a station on the underground railway for the freeing of slaves. My family was disobeying the law, but I think God was pleased with that, and if I had been alive at the time, I too would have supported it. How about illegal strikes to gain rights for exploited factory workers? How about participating in a revolution to overthrow the government? How about the use of violence or war to bring about more just conditions in human society? Serving God, whether in evangelism or social ministry, inevitably has its ambiguities.

But while immoral means may not be used in God's work, on what basis does one choose between several equally moral or value-free methodological options for accomplishing a certain goal? The approach of consecrated pragmatism recommends the option which most effectively and efficiently accomplishes the goal. In that sense, but only in that sense, the end is the only thing that can possible justify the means. A means that fails to accomplish the goal is not, by anyone's measurement, a justifiable means.

Church Growth as a Science

Not only does church growth admit to using consecrated pragmatism in its methodology, it professes to be a science. Up to this point I have not defined church growth with any precision. Perhaps this is a good time to look at the most formalized definition of it to date, which appears in the Constitution of the Academy for American Church Growth:

Church growth is that science which investigates the planting, multiplication, function and health of Christian churches as they relate specifically to the effective implementation of God's commission to "make disciples of all nations" (Matt. 28:19–20, RSV).

Church growth strives to combine the eternal theological principles of God's Word concerning the expansion of the church with the best insights of contemporary social and behavioral sciences, employing as its initial frame of reference, the foundational work done by Donald McGavran.

In what way is church growth a "science?"

This question has been raised by others as well. In reviewing a book of mine where I mentioned this scientific aspect of the field, Howard Snyder says, "If Wagner wishes his conclusions to be taken as scientific, however, then it seems to me his evidence is rather thin." He speaks of examining a number of growing churches in similar social contexts and attempting to draw conclusions regarding growth principles they have in common. Snyder concludes, "This method may be valid as far as it goes, but it falls short of being 'scientific' unless it is part of a larger, more rigorous study."[7]

Snyder has a different perception of science from that of the Church Growth Movement. In my understanding, science is simply the attempt to explain certain phenomena in a reasonable and systematic way. Natural science, for example, attempts to explain the phenomena of nature in a reasonable and systematic way. It tries to answer questions such as: Why does the sun rise in the morning? Why do fish die when they are out of water? Why do volcanoes erupt? Social science attempts to do the same with phenomena of human behavior. Why do brothers not marry sisters? Why do Japanese take their shoes off in the house? Why don't Americans eat dog meat?

The methodology used by both these branches of science is similar. They (1) examine the facts, (2) construct a hypothesis that explains the facts, (3) test the hypothesis, and (4) revise the hypothesis in the light of feedback and new facts and start all over again. No scientist I am aware of thinks his or her findings are absolute. They are simply a useful way of explaining phenomena until a more useful way comes along. Up until 1905, for example, the hypothesis that matter and energy were separate was regarded as reasonable and scientific. Then came Einstein's $E = mc^2$, which hypothesized they were exchangeable, and that is now held as the most reasonable explanation. Few scientists, however, think that $E = mc^2$ will never be improved upon. Even if it is (and, for all I know, it already has been), it will not detract from the scientific quality of Einstein's theory of relativity.

In an age when science is practically idolized, it comes as a surprise to many just how tentative and subjective all science really is. Jim Neidhardt argues that failure to understand the nature of science contributes to the fact that many people either "worship science" or "hate it as lacking in true humanity." A balanced appreciation could be gained, he says, "if science could be more universally recognized for what it is—an activity that is just as dependent upon personal involvement as other parts of human experience." No scientist is free from personal judgments and commitments.[8]

With this in mind, we may get a clearer picture of the sense in which church growth can be considered a science. It is admittedly a "soft" science, because part of its data includes the surprising, unpredictable, spontaneous, sovereign work of the Holy Spirit, a factor most natural and social sciences exclude. Because of this, no church growth principles are to be considered absolute. Every one I know of has exceptions. Some, in fact, have so many exceptions that the exceptions congeal and form a new church growth principle. Every such development is welcome.

Computerizing Resistance and Receptivity

One of the major scientific contributions the Church Growth Movement has made toward the practice of evangelism is the resistance-receptivity theory. George Hunter calls it "The Church Growth Movement's greatest contribution to this generation's world evangelization."[9] This is a direct outcome of a pragmatic outlook on the task.

Resistance-receptivity theory postulates that at a given point in time certain people groups, families, and individuals will be more receptive to the message of the Gospel than others. The empirical and biblical aspects of this have been developed in detail elsewhere and will not be rehearsed here.[10] Much research is being carried on to identify the world's distinct peoples and to gauge their present degree of receptivity to the gospel. Under supervision of the Strategy Working Group of the Lausanne Committee for World Evangelization and the MARC division of World Vision International, data are being gathered worldwide, entered into the computers at World Vision, and published in a series of annual volumes called *Unreached Peoples.*[11] By means of the computer, lists are now available which classify people groups as "very receptive," "receptive," "indifferent," "reluctant," and "very reluctant."

The value of resistance-receptivity theory for planning evangelistic strategy is self-evident. Since resources of time, personnel, talent, money, and energy are all limited, decisions have to be made as to where they can best be used. This necessarily involves setting priorities. Although God can and does intervene and indicate otherwise, it only makes good sense to direct the bulk of the available resources to the areas where the greatest numbers are likely to become disciples of Jesus Christ. The resistant are not to be neglected or bypassed, but they are to be held lightly. This makes good sense to those who take the approach of consecrated pragmatism.

There are those for whom this is offensive, however. René Padilla, for example, objects to the use of the computer, for he fears it will turn the gospel into a syncretistic "culture-Christianity" and make the gospel "a product it also has to distribute among the greatest number of consumers of religion." He says that through the use of technology, evangelistic strategy "becomes a question of mathematical calculation."[12] He does not say whether he objects to the use of computers to speed up and improve the quality of Bible translation. Padilla's colleague, Samuel Escobar, labels resistance-receptivity theory "classist missiology."[13] Because this relates directly to a point of convergence between church growth theory and social issues, it is worthwhile examining it in some detail.

Escobar commends Donald McGavran for demonstrating that the Bible shows a preference of God for the poor. But then he goes on to point out that, for McGavran, the principal meaning of this is that the gospel should be shared on a priority basis with the poor, since they are the ones most receptive to the gospel message. He objects that "poverty is taken as a datum only in order to define a strategy that has nothing to do with either the impact of the Christian message on the fact of poverty or social change directed to the elimination of poverty."[14]

While it can be shown that McGavran and other church growth writers are concerned for the poor and oppressed whether or not they become Christian, I think this is a minor point. More important is Escobar's implicit objection to professional specialization on the part of Christians. Church growth leaders like McGavran feel called to concentrate on the evangelistic mandate. From McGavran's perspective, then, the biblical goals of this mandate can best be accomplished by "winning the winnable," and the church's plan for outreach should be directed by the observed fact that "the masses are growing increasingly responsive and will continue to listen to the Good News."[15]

To scorn this as "classist missiology" is, from the church growth point of view, to question the primary importance of poor people being reconciled to God through Jesus Christ. Although I am reasonably sure Escobar would not do this, it does point to an area where those flying the banners of, respectively, the cultural mandate and evangelistic mandate need to meet in love on kingdom soil. There should be no contradiction or mutual recrimination. Howard Snyder brings the two concerns together when he says, "I am convinced that Jesus commands us to preach the gospel to the poor not only because their need is most acute but also precisely because they are most ready to accept."[16]

Is Church Growth the Point?

The term "remnant theology" has been a catchword with church growth people for many years. It describes the point of view of those who, for many reasons, feel uncomfortable with growing churches. They often mention Gideon's 300 as God's ideal for the church. McGavran says, "Remnant theology proves attractive. A glorification of littleness prevails, in which to be small is to be holy. *Slow* growth is adjudged good growth."[17]

One very enlightening theological treatise justifying nongrowth is *Church Growth Is Not the Point* by Robert K. Hudnut. Despite the title, the book does not address the Church Growth Movement directly. Still, Hudnut argues that decreasing numbers in America's mainline denominations mean "increasing power." "People are leaving the church," says Hudnut. "It could not be a better sign." His principal thesis is: "Church growth is not the point. Faithfulness to our Lord Jesus Christ is."[18]

Contrasting church growth on one hand against faithfulness to God on the other has been a predominant theme of remnant theologians over the past few years. Because of the task-oriented nature of the Church Growth Movement and the stress on consecrated pragmatism, many observers associate it with "success." For example, Martin Marty argues that " 'success,' in the way the world defines it, is not and never has been the goal of the Christian life. The church is called to be obedient and faithful."[19] Another articulate theologian, Robert Evans, argues that "God's demand of faithfulness carries no guarantee for growth, health, prosperity, or even temporal survival."[20]

What is behind the church-growth-is-not-the-point position?

I believe I discern in these authors a desire to protect the integrity of the sovereignty of God. Evans, for example, says "I do not suggest that God never desires the church to grow," but "the point is the Holy Spirit alone knows if, when and how the increase will be given."[21] Hudnut, who was Evans' pastor for some years, adds, "We do not choose to become church members. We are chosen."[22] Certainly these statements are biblical. God is sovereign.

A second concern is that the gospel not be cheapened. Christian commitment is more than verbal assent to a creed or the repetition of a prayer or a decision for Christ. Too many who use the name "Christian" are Christian only in name, not in living a lifestyle characteristic of the kingdom of God.

A third concern is for the cultural mandate. Faithfulness to God is lived out in love for God and for the neighbor. Evans stresses that "it is to the culture that the church addresses its gospel in word and deed."[23]

The desire to uphold the sovereignty of God, the integrity of the gospel, and the cultural mandate is a noble desire that church growth people understand and agree with. What is much more difficult for me to understand is how these things can be set *against* growth. Part of the same faithfulness to God is to be fishers of men, to preach the gospel to every creature, to make disciples of all nations, to baptize believers in the name of the Father and the Son and the Holy Spirit. It is a theological truism that salvation, redemption, justification, or regeneration are exclusively sovereign works of the Holy Spirit which do not admit any synergism. Paul plants, Apollos waters, but it is God and God alone who gives the increase (1 Cor. 3:6). Nevertheless, in evangelism as in agriculture, while God gives the increase he does not harvest the crop. Jesus tells us to pray the Lord of the harvest to send forth laborers into the harvest field (Matt. 9:38). He was referring not to angels, but to human beings: faithful men and women who, in Jesus' name, would recognize where God had whitened the harvest fields and who would come back "bringing in the sheaves." The natural, spiritual result of faithful harvesting is "the Lord add[ing] to the church daily such as should be saved" (Acts 2:47).

Faithfulness and Success

A verse of Scripture frequently cited by remnant theologians to justify nongrowth is 1 Corinthians 4:2: "It is required in stewards that a man be found faithful." I once heard a theologian pray, with a note of relief in his voice, "Lord, we thank you that you have not called us to be *successful*, only *faithful.*" The inherent contradiction in what he said struck me so deeply that I had a hard time following the rest of his prayer. Setting faithfulness against success reflects a superficial view of

New Testament stewardship as I understand it. One of the key passages describing the responsibilities of a steward or a servant[24] is Matthew 25:14-30, commonly known as the Parable of the Talents. Three servants were entrusted by their master with sums of money, $1,000, $2,000, and $5,000, as the Living Bible translates it. The purpose of the money is not mentioned because in the commercial world the task is to use capital to make more money. This was the master's desire, and the servants had an "investment mandate." The one who had $2,000 brought back $4,000, and the one who had $5,000 brought back $10,-000. They were called by the master "good and *faithful*" servants." Why were they faithful? Very simply, because they were successful. They successfully used the resources that the master had given them for the purposes that the master had predetermined and brought glory to the master through fulfilling the "investment mandate." The servant who got $1,000 had buried it and brought it back intact. He was not faithful, but "wicked and slothful," because he had not carried out the master's desires and fulfilled the "investment mandate." The consistent view of stewardship in the New Testament maintains a close relationship between faithfulness and success, both being understood in terms of the will of the master.

Notice that, in the parable, the quantity was not a principal concern to the master. The one who gained $2,000 received the same verbal reward as the one who gained $5,000. One simply had a different quantity of resources, and of him to whom much is given much is required. In church growth, bigger is not necessarily better. God is pleased with small churches and he is pleased with large churches, provided they all are churches where people are living the lifestyle of the community of the king. Jim Jones' Peoples' Temple of Guyana, for example, was a big "church," but obviously not pleasing to God. On the other hand, Paul (Yonggi) Cho's Full Gospel Central Church of Korea, now the largest church in the world with 200,000 members and gaining 5,000 new ones each month, seems to be a church that is pleasing to God. Even Methodist Bishop James Armstrong, who has not been very friendly to the Church Growth Movement, uses the Korean churches as examples of responsible growth, because they are involved in the cultural as well as the evangelistic mandate.[25]

I see a problem when people with an aversion to large churches claim that "small is beautiful," presumably because smaller churches better implement the cultural mandate. This appears to be the assumption of

Jean Caffey Lyles in questioning whether United Methodists should "buy the Church Growth package." Lyles opposes the church growth "apostles of cheap growth" and the "numbers game," and suggests that Methodists should aim for "a few committed people impacting the structures of society to make the world a more humane place."[26] How about considering *many* committed people impacting the structures of society? Wouldn't many be better than few? It might well turn out that larger, growing churches are, as a matter of empirical fact, impacting society more than smaller nongrowing ones. The impact that churches have on society should not be measured exclusively by the cultural mandate, but by both the cultural and the evangelistic mandates.

I like the way Orlando Costas puts it. He advocates "holistic growth." He argues that only when church growth "affects *in depth* both the personal life of men and women and their structured life situations" can it be understood "as the legitimate expression of God's mission."[27]

Pouring Church Growth into Theological Molds

Does the Church Growth Movement carry with it a set of theological assumptions that can be characterized by any of the traditional theological labels? This matter has not been discussed to any extent in the literature and demands more than I am able to give it here. The question was raised recently by Ralph P. Martin of the Fuller Seminary School of Theology. Martin feels that Hudnut's *Church Growth Is Not the Point* is "a tract for the times" and that God's mandate is "to be faithful in witness, not necessarily successful in growing." Martin considers that a title such as McGavran and Arn's *How to Grow a Church* "reduces the concept of the church to a vegetable plot."[28] Although he does not make the accusation, he does raise the question whether church growth could be interpreted in a "Pelagian, synergistic fashion."[29] I think it is basically the cordial acceptance of "consecrated pragmatism" that Martin feels is dangerous.

Pelagianism, the theological contention that salvation is a cooperative (or synergistic) relationship between God and humans, is far from the thoughts of any church growth leaders I know of. Salvation, the new birth, conversion, redemption, justification, and all that is involved in making a person a "new creature in Christ Jesus" is a unique work of the sovereign God, which he performs without any human help whatsoever.

Donald McGavran, though his theological roots are in the Restoration Movement (Christian Churches, Disciples of Christ), has assiduously attempted not to allow church growth teaching to identify itself with any particular paradigm of systematic theology. Church growth principles have intentionally been kept as atheological as possible, on the assumption that they can be adapted to fit into virtually any systematic theological tradition. McGavran's first colleague in the Fuller School of World Mission, for example, was Alan R. Tippett, who, as a Methodist, came out of a Wesleyan theological tradition. He found church growth principles compatible, and had a great deal to say about how they fit in with prevenient grace.[30] McGavran's successor as Dean of the School was Arthur F. Glasser, a Reformed Presbyterian, who sees church growth theology from the point of view of a "somewhat modified Reformed hermeneutic."[31] Through the years the Arminian-Calvinism issues latent here have never seemed to pose a problem.

Increasingly, books developing the principles of church growth are being written and published by denominationally oriented leaders for specific denominational and theological audiences.[32] They differ from one another in theological terminology, authors cited, illustrations presented, writing style, and emphasis. But these authors all have felt to date that nothing in their particular theological tradition has been incompatible with the general principles of church growth.

My impression is that church growth cannot reasonably be labeled as Reformed or Wesleyan or Lutheran or Calvinistic or Pietistic or Pelagian or Arminian. It can, however, be labeled as evangelical. But, I repeat, this is a subject for future research and awaits much enlightenment.

Notes

1. Donald McGavran, *Understanding Church Growth*, rev. ed. (Grand Rapids: Eerdmans, 1980), p. viii.
2. For more details, see my *Your Spiritual Gifts Can Help Your Church Grow* (Glendale: Regal Books, 1979).
3. Donald McGavran, "For Such a Time as This," unpublished address given at the Fuller Seminary School of World Mission, 1970.
4. This originally appeared in J. Waskom Pickett, *Christian Mass Movements in India* (Lucknow, India: Lucknow Publishing House,

1933), and is reported in McGavran, *Understanding Church Growth*, pp. 173–175.

5. Richard G. Hutcheson, Jr., *Wheel Within the Wheel: Confronting the Management Crisis of the Pluralistic Church* (Atlanta: John Knox Press, 1979), p. 69.

6. Ibid., p. 71.

7. Howard A. Snyder, "How Some Churches Grow—Sometimes," *Eternity* 27, no. 11 (November 1976), p. 63.

8. W. Jim Neidhardt, "Schematic Portrayals of the Personal Component in Scientific Discovery," *Journal of the American Scientific Affiliation*, March, 1980, p. 63.

9. George G. Hunter III, *The Contagious Congregation: Frontiers in Evangelism and Church Growth* (Nashville: Abingdon, 1979), p. 104.

10. For extended discussions of resistance-receptivity theory, see McGavran, *Understanding Church Growth*, pp. 245–265; my *Frontiers in Missionary Strategy* (Chicago: Moody, 1971), pp. 106–121; Hunter, *The Contagious Congregation*, pp. 104–129; and Edward R. Dayton and David A. Fraser, *Planning Strategies for World Evangelization* (Grand Rapids: Eerdmans, 1980), pp. 178–181.

11. Three volumes have appeared thus far: *Unreached Peoples '79, Unreached Peoples '80,* and *Unreached Peoples '81,* ed. C. Peter Wagner and Edward R. Dayton (Elgin, IL: David C. Cook).

12. René Padilla, "Evangelism and the World," in *Let the Earth Hear His Voice,* ed. J. D. Douglas (Minneapolis: World Wide Publications, 1975), p. 126.

13. Samuel Escobar and John Driver, *Christian Mission and Social Justice* (Scottdale, PA: Herald Press, 1978), p. 45.

14. Ibid., p. 47.

15. McGavran, *Understanding Church Growth*, p. 290.

16. Howard A. Snyder, *The Problem of Wineskins: Church Structure in a Technological Age* (Downers Grove, IL: InterVarsity Press, 1975), p. 46.

17. McGavran, *Understanding Church Growth*, p. 168.

18. Robert K. Hudnut, *Church Growth Is Not the Point* (New York: Harper & Row, 1975), pp. x–xi.

19. Martin Marty, "Congregations Alive," *A.D. Magazine* 7, no. 4 (April 1978), p. 29.

20. Robert A. Evans, "Recovering the Church's Transforming Middle:

Theological Reflections on the Balance Between Faithfulness and Effectiveness," in *Understanding Church Growth and Decline: 1950–1978,* ed. Dean R. Hoge and David A. Roozen (New York: Pilgrim, 1979), p. 292.

21. Ibid., p. 296.
22. Hudnut, *Church Growth Is Not the Point,* p. x.
23. Evans, "Recovering the Church's Transforming Middle," p. 293.
24. The word *oikonomos* (steward) is used in 1 Cor. 4:1–2, and the word *doulos* (servant or slave) is used in Matt. 25:14–30, but these terms are interchanged in Luke (the only gospel that uses *oikonomos*) and in Paul's writings. See *The New International Dictionary of New Testament Theology*, Vol. 2, ed. Colin Brown (Grand Rapids: Zondervan, 1976), pp. 254–255.
25. Chesnutt, Clyde, "Emphasis on Statistics Claimed to be 'Faithless,'" *United Methodist Reporter,* February 8, 1980, p. 4.
26. Jean Caffey Lyles, "Should Methodists Buy the 'Church Growth' Package?" *Christian Century* 94, no. 43 (December 28, 1977), p. 1215. A weakness of Carl S. Dudley's excellent book *Making the Small Church Effective* (Nashville: Abingdon, 1978), is his failure to show how small churches can do their part to fulfill the evangelistic mandate.
27. Orlando E. Costas, *The Church and Its Mission: A Shattering Critique from the Third World* (Wheaton, IL: Tyndale, 1974), p. 310.
28. Ralph P. Martin, "Church Growth Is Not the Point," *Life of Faith* (England), January 10, 1976.
29. Ralph P. Martin, "End of Term Report," *Life of Faith* (England), June 11, 1977.
30. Alan R. Tippett, "Conversion as a Dynamic Process in Christian Mission," *Missiology* 5, no. 2 (April, 1977), pp. 219–220.
31. Arthur F. Glasser, "Church Growth Theology," in *Church Growth Movement: Proceedings of the Eleventh Biennial Meeting of Association of Professors of Missions*, June, 1972, p. 18.
32. Some of these denominationally-oriented works include: Charles Chaney and Ron Lewis, *Design for Church Growth* (Southern Baptist) (Nashville: Broadman, 1977); Paul R. Orjala, *Get Ready to Grow* (Church of the Nazarene) (Kansas City: Beacon Hill Press, 1978); Hunter, *The Contagious Congregation* (United Methodist); Floyd G. Bartel, *A New Look At Church Growth* (Mennonite)

(Scottdale, PA: Herald Press, 1979); and Wayne Williamson, *Growth and Decline in the Episcopal Church* (Pasadena: William Carey Library, 1979). Unpublished manuscripts have been completed by Lutheran, Presbyterian, and Advent Christian authors as of this writing.

CHAPTER 5

Holistic Mission Versus Holistic Evangelism

This chapter takes up the most crucial points at which church growth and social issues intersect. My desire is to see the greatest improvement in society, especially liberation and justice for the poor and oppressed, while at the same time seeing the greatest number of people, especially the poor and oppressed, reconciled to God through Jesus Christ. In this chapter I deal with priorities, and I do not want to be misunderstood. When I argue that the evangelistic mandate has priority over the cultural mandate, this does not mean that I have any intention of neglecting the cultural mandate. But recognizing the priority of the evangelistic mandate is, in my opinion, the best starting point for the maximum fulfillment of *both* the cultural and the evangelistic mandates. Some may judge that I do not succeed well in my argument. So be it. But I have at least made my motives and intentions clear.

Is Mission Evangelism?

Precise definitions are always an aid to clear thinking. If two of us use a word that carries different meanings for each, intelligent discussion is impossible unless or until we agree on our definitions. This chapter deals with a very important theoretical discussion of "mission" and "evangelism." It is necessary, therefore, to define these two terms as precisely as possible from the beginning. I do not expect everyone to agree with the ways I define these words—the vast literature on the subject contains many differing opinions. But my use of the terms will be clear and consistent, and this will enlighten the subsequent discussion of their relationship and the role of the cultural mandate.

Rodger Bassham argues that "church growth theology has some serious weaknesses," one of them being "the narrow conception of mission as evangelism." He feels that church growth runs the risk of being "distorted and imbalanced" if it does not seriously take into account "the whole task of mission." The Church Growth Movement at this point, Bassham says, "appears to have neglected a substantial discussion which has taken place over the past twenty-five years, in which the meaning of mission, evangelism, witness, service, and salvation have been explored and developed."[1] This is a challenge which needs to be acted upon.

One of the problems we must face at the outset is that the word "mission" is not a biblical word. Our English word is derived from the Latin *missio*, a sending. The concept of sending is, of course, found in the New Testament, but there is no literal equivalent to "mission." Therefore we cannot argue exigetically that "mission" *ought* to mean so and so. Our starting point needs, rather, to be a more phenomenological understanding of how the term is being used in real life by those to whom it is important.

Until fairly recently the word "mission" meant, roughly, evangelism. The mission was to send missionaries to propagate the faith. The unquestioned task of a missionary was to make converts. Harvey Hoekstra correctly labels as "classical mission" that "complex of activities whose chief purpose is to make Jesus Christ known as Lord and Savior and to persuade men to become his disciples and responsible members of his church."[2] One implication of this view was that social service, or the cultural mandate, was not considered an essential part of missions. Some, like Rufus Anderson, Secretary of the American Board of Commissioners for Foreign Missions, argued that once the gospel was preached and converts were won, then "social renovation will be sure to follow." Anderson rejected as a direct objective of missions the "reorganizing, by various direct means, of the structure of that social system of which the converts form a part."[3]

During that period of time, what might be called the *classical period,* another key distinction was made in the minds of most church and mission leaders. While missions were evangelism, not all evangelism was missions. Missions had a clear geographical connotation, usually *"foreign missions."* Evangelism was an activity done at home, but missions were out there in heathen darkness. Missionaries were those recruited and sent out by Western nations to parts of the world that were being colonized. The danger of confusing the motives of missionaries with those of the colonial powers was one reason why such mission leaders as Rufus Anderson tended to exclude the cultural mandate. Most missiologists did not agree that civilization must precede Christianization, as some others were advocating. As we see now in retrospect, many missionaries confused sharing the gospel with sharing their own Western culture, and Anderson, rightly, wished to avoid that to the degree possible.

Changing the Classical Definition of Mission

During our century, a change in this classical understanding of mission has been taking place. Sydney E. Mead traces the roots of this change to the last quarter of the nineteenth century and the opening years of the twentieth, when "real belief in the all-sufficiency of this kind of missions declined." He associates it with the impact the social gospel movement was having on churches at that time. The result was that "missions were metamorphosed from the simple task of winning converts . . . to the complex task of participating actively in social betterment and reconstruction."[4] The strongest expression of this new view of missions came in 1932 with the publication of Hocking's *Re-Thinking Missions*, the result of the "layman's inquiry." It began a process which later, as we will see, drastically eroded the place of the evangelistic mandate in the mission of the church.

In the classical period, the word *missions* was sufficient to describe the task of spreading the faith in foreign countries. But with the broadening of the concept, a change from *missions* (plural) to *mission* (singular) also took place. For example, the ecumenically oriented journal *International Review of Missions* changed its name in April 1969, to *International Review of Mission*. In technical usage today, *mission* means the task of the church, while *missions* means the agencies and activities implementing the task, although they are interchanged somewhat in popular usage.

Notice that the period of time in which the concept of mission was undergoing a change was the same period in which evangelicals were building defenses against the social gospel, as I described in Chapter 1. Evangelicals were in the "Great Reversal." They had eclipsed the concept of the kingdom of God, among other things. For evangelicals throughout this period, mission continued to mean evangelism. To allow the cultural mandate to creep into the technical definition of mission would have been interpreted as a capitulation to the enemy. Evangelicals maintained the classical definition of mission long after the ecumenical camp had abandoned it.

A change in evangelical thinking began in the 1960s. Two events significant to evangelicals took place in 1966, the Congress on the Church's Worldwide Mission held in Wheaton, Illinois, and the World Congress on Evangelism held in Berlin. In the Wheaton Congress a plenary address was given by Horace L. Fenton on "Mission—and Social Concern." In it, Fenton suggested that it was unbiblical to separate evangelism and social concern in the mission of the church.[5] The Wheaton Declaration was still somewhat tentative on this, but it pledged to "demonstrate anew God's concern for social justice and human welfare," and to "urge all evangelicals to stand openly and firmly for racial equality, human freedom, and all forms of social justice throughout the world."[6]

The Berlin Congress, by and large, held to the classical definition of mission. Arthur Johnston of Trinity Evangelical Divinity School, in *The Battle for World Evangelism,* the most comprehensive treatment of these concepts to date, observes that "Berlin gave little more than token theological consideration to the social pressures of the 1960s." Berlin did not develop a view of mission that would embrace the cultural mandate. "It stood firm on proclamation evangelism as *the* mission of the Church."[7]

Lausanne and Holistic Mission

The period between the Berlin Congress of 1966 and its successor, The International Congress on World Evangelization, held in Lausanne, Switzerland, in 1974, was a time of transition in evangelical thinking on the definition of mission. Arthur Johnston says, "The crisis of Christianity during the period between Berlin 1966 and Lausanne 1974 may be summarized theologically as the definition of the mission of the church."[8] The "Great Reversal" was coming to an end. The "young evangelicals" were on the rise with civil rights demonstrations and draft card burning. Radical discipleship movements began with their communes and magazines. The cultural mandate was being stressed. A collective social conscience was beginning to develop among evangelicals in general. By the time of the Lausanne Congress, a significant number of evangelical leaders were ready to go public with a revised definition of mission.

Key to this was a person whom God had raised up to assume a strong, influential position in the shaping of evangelical thought, John R. W. Stott, Rector of All Souls Church, Langham Place, London. In Berlin, Stott had presented three plenary session Bible studies on the Great Commission. There he held to the classical definition of mission. He argued that "the commission of the church is not to reform society, but to preach the Gospel."[9] Stott himself affirms that this was his thinking in 1966.[10]

"Today, however," Stott says, "I would express myself differently."[11] Stott was one of the chief authors of the Lausanne Covenent, which states: "We affirm that evangelism and sociopolitical involvement are both part of our Christian duty" (Art. 5). While the word "duty" appears here instead of "mission," most post-Lausanne interpreters have considered them synonymous. Stott himself says, "The word 'mission' . . . includes evangelism and social responsibility, since both are authentic expressions of love which longs to serve man in his need."[12] By the time of Lausanne, then, a significant group of missiologically oriented evangelicals had accepted the position that ecumenicals had embraced decades earlier, namely that the mission of the church includes *both* the cultural and the evangelistic mandates. They have not, however, allowed this to carry them to the unbiblical conclusions of the ecumenical group.

My own thinking on the issue also changed during this time of transition. Previous to Lausanne, I had published my book *Frontiers in Missionary Strategy.* In my mind mission and evangelism were synonymous, and I was using them interchangeably. The "composite definition of mission" that I formulated there was, as I see it now, not so much a definition of mission as of evangelism. In fact, I argued there that the definition was "3-P *evangelism.*"[13] This was before I went to Lausanne and heard such speakers as René Padilla, Samuel Escobar, and Orlando Costas. I was influenced by the Lausanne Covenant, the writings of John Stott, and the ongoing dynamic of the Lausanne Committee, of which I have been a part since its founding. I now believe that the mission of the church embraces both the cultural and the evangelistic mandates. *I believe in what is now being called "holistic mission."*

Potential Dangers of Holistic Mission

I am fully aware that not all evangelicals agree with me and with the Lausanne Covenant at this point. They continue to hold high the banner of classical mission. Peter Beyerhaus, for example, argues that "the semantic distinction between 'evangelism' and 'mission' as allegedly comprising both evangelism and sociopolitical involvement is irrelevant," and that to allow it, as did Lausanne, may have us awaken one day to the realization that we are "importing ecumenical ideology in the belly of the Trojan horse!"[14] Beyerhaus, it might be mentioned, is also a member of the Lausanne Committee (LCWE), maintaining an insider's dissenting voice. Arthur Johnston is himself an articulate evangelical spokesperson for the classical view of mission. While he is in general sympathy and agreement with the Lausanne Covenant, he detects in Lausanne a "theological blurring of the evangelism focus that has characterized evangelicalism in the nineteenth and twentieth centuries." He feels that, although the Lausanne Covenant may not have been so intended, some who want to "equate sociopolitical involvement with evangelism" can use that document to do so.[15]

Johnston's colleague, David Hesselgrave, also insists on continuing to use missions and evangelism in the classic sense as "having essentially the same meaning."[16] Hesselgrave argues that missionary experience has shown that even when social activities are used simply as evangelistic methods, they often end up as distractions from the central task of soul-winning and church-planting. "How much more difficult," he says, "will they find it if social ministry and political action come to be considered more or less equal partners of evangelism and church development!" Hesselgrave fears that holistic mission "may well result in a frustrated generation of missionaries who will neither change the world nor disciple the nations."[17]

I share with Johnston and Hesselgrave the concern that the cultural mandate not be equated with the evangelistic mandate. But at the same time I do not think the rejection of the concept of holistic mission is needed to prevent it from happening. More about this later.

Beyerhaus, Johnston, and Hesselgrave, are well aware of the current debates on the meaning of the words mission and evangelism and have decided to stay with the classical definition. Others, particularly writers in the ecumenical camp, tend to use them interchangeably because of confused thinking. I will refrain from citing specific cases here, but

Philip Potter, General Secretary of the World Council of Churches, informs us "that 'mission,' 'evangelism,' and 'witness' are, as a rule, interchangeable concepts in ecumenical literature."[18]

It is a caricature of holistic mission to pretend that it stands for "everything God wants to do in the world." If everything is mission, nothing is mission. God, for example, brings rain upon the just and the unjust—this is hardly mission. God makes the earth orbit the sun, gives the gift of life to new babies, punishes injustice, sets up and takes down world rulers. Those activities are not what most people mean by mission. Many things God does through his own people are not properly mission. Worship, prayer, giving, Christian education, fellowship, the sacraments, and numbers of other things that Christians do in obedience to God are not contemplated in holistic mission. The central concept of holistic mission embraces what God sends his redeemed people out from their own congregations to do: principally implement the cultural mandate and the evangelistic mandate.

The Scope of Holistic Mission

Once the concept of holistic mission is accepted as embracing both the cultural and the evangelistic mandates, it is necessary to understand that the execution of mission will vary according to those to whom the efforts are directed. Missiologists in the Church Growth Movement, and many others as well, have agreed that the cultural perspective is useful in looking at the spheres in which mission is accomplished. Some mission is accomplished within one culture and some crosses cultural boundaries.

Church growth specialists have found it helpful to assign value-neutral letters and numbers to different kinds of mission activity as follows:

M-1 (Mission One): Mission directed to those who share the same culture as the missionary.

M-2 (Mission Two): Cross-cultural mission directed to those of different culture, but a culture which has a significant similarity to that of the missionary. For example, an Anglo-American missionary to the French would be an M-2 distance.

M-3 (Mission Three): Cross-cultural mission directed to those of a quite distinct culture having very little in common with the culture of the missionary. For example, the same Anglo-American missionary ministering to Thai fishing people would be at an M-3 distance.

Culture, not geography, is the decisive factor. Mission seen in this perspective does not distinguish between home and foreign missions. Within one metropolitan area, for example, all three cultural distances will frequently be found, sometimes even in one neighborhood. I mention this because many who have attempted to master and use this terminology have inadvertently brought geographical considerations into the picture and confused the issues.[19] Our Anglo-American missionary, if sent to minister to Anglo-American oil workers in Saudi Arabia, would be an M-1 missionary even after traveling half way around the globe. He or she does not have to learn a new language or adapt to new customs to minister to the people who meet the airplane.

While "M" for mission is the all-embracing term, three subcategories have been found helpful for analysis: evangelism (E), Christian nurture (N), and service (S). For those who accept the holistic definition of mission, all three are part of the whole, but, while naturally there is overlap, they describe different tasks.

Evangelism (whether E-1, E-2, or E-3) is, as we defined it in Chapter 3, making disciples of Jesus Christ. It is presenting Jesus Christ in the power of the Holy Spirit in such a way that men and women will believe in him as their savior and serve him as their Lord in the fellowship of his church. The message of evangelism is directed to the unbeliever, not to believers. Its goal is to win souls, to see sinners saved by the grace of God, and enter into the kingdom of God as responsible disciples.

Christian nurture (whether N-1, N-2, or N-3) is a ministry directed toward Christians, not unbelievers. Its objective is helping them develop in their faith. It enables spiritual "children" who may be "carried about with every wind of doctrine" to grow into perfect people "unto the measure of the stature of the fullness of Christ" (Eph. 4:13–14). Helping a Christian pray more fervently, read the Bible more intelligently, sing more melodiously, witness more aggressively, or give more generously is not evangelism. It is nurture.

Service (whether S-1, S-2, or S-3) is neither evangelism nor nurture. Its focus is the implementation of the cultural mandate. It helps meet the physical, social, or material needs of people. It can be directed toward believers or unbelievers or both. It includes social action and social service. God may use service to open the hearts and minds of men and women to the message of the gospel, or he may not. But service doesn't save sinners—evangelism does.

Evangelism and service are clearly part of mission as the word is commonly understood. Nurture can be part of mission when it is used to help get new converts established in their faith. We could call this Phase I nurture. But I do not believe it is helpful to include Phase II nurture, the ongoing lifetime care and feeding of Christians, as mission, technically speaking. While it is proper to say that an average Sunday School teacher who meets week after week with the same group of believers is serving God, carrying out a ministry, or fulfilling a Christian duty, it is not proper to say that the teacher is engaged in *mission.*

Holistic Evangelism?

Clearly not everyone agrees that evangelism and service should be separated as two distinct parts of mission. Many evangelicals disagree with the Lausanne Covenant's affirmation that social action is not evangelism (Art. 5). Their position has been called "holistic evangelism." In this section I will attempt to explain the position of the advocates of holistic evangelism and also why I disagree with them. I find the concept of holistic mission helpful, but not that of holistic evangelism.

Holistic evangelism people agree among themselves that to make a distinction between evangelism and social ministry is illegitimate. They see it as dangerous "dichotomizing." Alfred Krass, for example, argues that evangelicals frequently avoid social issues because they have "learned to read scripture in such a way as to dichotomize between the personal and the social, between the private and the historical," and he quotes Article 5 of the Lausanne Covenant to illustrate his point.[20] René Padilla calls it "driving a wedge,"[21] an expression used in the "Response to Lausanne" drawn up by a group of dissenters at the Lausanne Congress: "We must repudiate as demonic the attempt to drive a wedge between evangelism and social action."[22]

The use of the term "demonic" seems rather harsh, but it reveals the depth of feeling of the holistic evangelism group against the Lausanne position. Orlando Costas continues just as fervently, five years later. He calls the distinction between "teaching and preaching the gospel" and "engaging in the socio-political liberation of the weak and oppressed" a "diabolic polarization," a "useless debate" and a "senseless and satanic waste of time, energies and resources."[23] Costas' self-identity is, of course, that of an evangelical. But, Richard J. Coleman, in analyzing the theological issues that separate evangelicals from liberals, sees the holistic evangelism view not as evangelical, but as liberal. He says that "the liberal begins with the supposition that the spiritual and the physical are so interdependent that it is misleading to exalt one over the other."[24] I point this out, not to show that Costas is a liberal, but to help explain why the position of the Lausanne dissenters on holistic evangelism has not been embraced to any significant degree by the contemporary evangelical community. It runs counter to the way most evangelicals understand their faith.

Partnership in Mission, an organization that existed for a number of years in the 1970s, sought to popularize the concept of holistic evangelism among evangelicals and others. The history of the term, the Lausanne debate, and its current usage is traced in their newsletter, *Partnership*. Holistic evangelism, it argues, "is not simply a matter of improving the balance between two separate elements, evangelism and social action." It goes beyond this concept and contends that "to be biblically faithful, the church must arrive at a gospel that fuses both elements inseparably into *one* conceptual framework and *one* incarnational ministry." *Partnership* will not accept a "separate but equal" theory. It insists on "authentic integration." Anything short of this is likely to produce "an incomplete, defective Gospel."[25]

The holistic evangelism point of view has some weighty supporters. For example, Carl F. H. Henry, now being called the dean of evangelical theologians, agrees with them. Henry argues that the Lausanne Covenant leaves "in doubt whether social concern . . . is a legitimate aspect of—and not simply compatible with and supplementary to—evangelism."[26] Henry later contributed to a symposium volume edited by René Padilla, *The New Face of Evangelicalism*. In it Padilla contends that the Lausanne Covenant "eliminates the dichotomy between evangelism and social involvement."[27] If by this Padilla means that, from Lausanne on, evangelicals recognized that both the cultural and the evangelistic mandates are part of holistic mission, he is right. But if he goes beyond this and means that Lausanne makes no distinction between evangelism and social concerns, he is mistaken. The Lausanne Covenant clearly does not advocate holistic evangelism. *Partnership* correctly says that "holistic evangelism takes issue with the prioritizing that surfaces in the Lausanne Covenant."[28]

Pattaya and Holistic Evangelism

Advocates of holistic evangelism attempted to make their point during the six years between the Lausanne Congress and the Consultation on World Evangelization held in Pattaya, Thailand, in 1980. During that same period, the issue was raised in the Lausanne Committee itself. A minor flaw in Arthur Johnston's excellent book, *The Battle for World Evangelism*, is his perception that holistic evangelism "quite accurately represents the concept of evangelism developed implicitly by the [Lausanne] Continuation Committee."[29] He is wrong. An extremely lively debate occurred at the very first meeting of the Lausanne Committee, in Mexico City in 1975, and it was decided there that the Committee would recognize as legitimate the Covenant's distinction between evangelization and social concerns and concentrate its particular efforts on world evangelization. The Lausanne Committee has been faithful to its intent. When Johnston says that it "has adopted 'holistic' evangelism and is implementing its understanding and acceptance around the world,"[30] he is describing, not the Lausanne Committee, but the Partnership in Mission group and some of the contributors to *The New Face of Evangelicalism*.

In Pattaya, the holistic evangelism bloc tried once again to promote their position, but failed. The Thailand Statement says, "Although evangelism and social action *are not identical*, we gladly reaffirm our commitment to both, and we endorse the Lausanne Covenant in its entirety." While the Thailand Statement says "yes" to holistic mission, it says "no" to holistic evangelism. About 200 participants saw fit both to vote for the Thailand Statement and to sign a "Statement of Concerns" drafted by the holistic evangelism advocates, wherein they criticized the Lausanne Committee for not giving sufficient attention to social concerns. But the initial decision to emphasize evangelism taken in Mexico City in 1975 was maintained.

Giving Priority to Evangelism

Establishing a legitimate distinction between the cultural mandate and the evangelistic mandate is indispensable to recognizing the priority of the evangelistic mandate. If the two cannot be separated, as proponents of holistic evangelism contend, no granting of priority would be possible. But if they can, then priority is an open question. Therefore those who oppose this granting of priority find themselves obliged to argue strongly against what they call "satanic dichotomization."

The Lausanne Covenant is clear on this point: "In the church's mission of sacrificial service evangelism is primary" (Art. 6). To maintain clarity, the Thailand Statement of 1980 not only reaffirmed the Lausanne Covenant in general, but went on specifically to state that evangelism is still considered primary. "This is not to deny that evangelism and social action are integrally related, but rather to acknowledge that of all the tragic needs of human beings none is greater than their alienation from their Creator and the reality of eternal death for those who refuse to repent and believe."

It must be stated clearly that neither *distinction* nor *dichotomization* nor *granting priority* is equivalent to *polarization.* Paul Hiebert warns against polarization as being "to set these concerns in *opposition* to one another."[31] I know of no one who subscribes to the Lausanne Covenant who would want to do this. The Lausanne Movement is making every effort to bring concern for the cultural mandate back into the mainstream of evangelical mission. At the same time it recognizes that the most powerful and effective way to promote the fulfillment of the cultural mandate is to keep it in proper relationship to the evangelistic mandate.

Orlando Costas calls the position of the Lausanne Covenant "the syndrome of evangelistic prioritization." He feels that the Lausanne Congress which produced the Covenant suffered from "Western domination," "closed organizational structure," and "limited democratic process." He agrees that Lausanne was "a sign of hope," but he would have preferred that it declare for holistic evangelism rather than giving first priority to the evangelistic mandate.[32] The opposition of Costas and other evangelicals to granting priority comes neither from rejection nor neglect of the evangelistic mandate. That view appears mostly in ecumenical circles. It comes rather from a fear that, with the granting of priority to evangelism, the cultural mandate may soon slip out of sight. Alfred Krass argues that if the Lausanne position is accepted, "One will not be surprised if a certain hesitancy enters into our Christian social action."[33] As I read the evangelical scene today, their fears do not seem well grounded. I share their desire to uphold the cultural mandate, but my view is that granting priority to evangelism will help, rather than retard, the implementation of the cultural mandate.

The general idea of priority is common to human experience and was used by biblical personalities, including Jesus and Paul. Any battlefield surgeon, for example, knows that persons wounded in conflict must be separated into three categories: those with minor wounds, those with severe wounds who will die without immediate attention, and those who are so badly wounded they are likely to die whether or not they get attention. First priority is given to the middle group—those who need emergency surgery, but who have a relatively good chance of recovering. This is a difficult decision. A great deal of subjectivity enters into choosing which person to operate on first. While the middle group is being cared for, some in the critical group are bleeding, moaning, and dying. But the battlefield surgeon is trained and conditioned to handle the distasteful job and, when it is over, is considered an "angel of mercy."

Limited resources necessitate assigning priorities. With three surgeons for three wounded, priorities are not necessary. With unlimited resources, a family would not have to make difficult decisions concerning how to spend their money—on a trip to the city to get medical attention rather than on new clothes for the family, for example. Or on schooling expenses for the children rather than adding a bathroom to the house. These kinds of decisions would not be necessary if they had enough money to do it all.

Another factor that determines priority is a sense of values. An affluent businessman, for example, may decide that it is a higher value to him to stay home with his wife and children than to go on a business trip. I believe that in America today, too many people, both men and women, have this priority wrong, resulting in a breakdown of the family unit. In my opinion, the family should be given priority over occupational involvement, even when that involvement is full-time Christian service.

Biblical Priorities

The argument in Chapter 2 that there is a biblical bias toward the poor as against the rich dichotomizes and prioritizes. Curiously, holistic evangelism advocates do not scold themselves for doing this. God loves *both* the poor and the rich, but the poor have priority. Jesus did not hesitate to say, "Blessed are the poor," and "It is difficult for the rich to enter into the kingdom of God." Paul does not hesitate to assign priority when he says that the gospel is to be preached *first* to the Jew, and also to the Greek.

Jesus not only gives priority to the poor over the rich, but also to the soul over the body. "Fear not them which kill the body," he says, "but are not able to kill the soul: but rather fear him which is able to destroy both soul and body in hell" (Matt. 10:28). Since the evangelistic mandate relates to saving the soul and the cultural mandate to feeding the body, it seems that Jesus is giving priority to the evangelistic mandate here. To me, it seems unfair that holistic evangelism advocates commend giving priority to the poor, but condemn giving priority to the soul over the body. Jesus did them both, and both should be accepted by Jesus' disciples.

Suppose the cultural mandate is highly successful and a poor family or a poor community "gains the whole world." This is good, but "what shall it profit a man, if he shall gain the whole world, and lose his own soul?" (Mark 8:36). Saving the soul is held above gaining the social or the physical or the material world. Jesus ministered to both body and soul, but he died on the cross primarily for the forgiveness of sins. His death was different from Martin Luther King's or Polycarp's or David Livingstone's or Ché Guevara's or Patrick Henry's. They all died for one cause or another, but none of them died for his own sins, much less the sins of the world.

Jesus, as far as we know, would never have left heaven and been incarnated except that human beings were alienated from God by sin. God so loved the world that he gave his only begotten son. Why? So that "whoever believes in him should not perish but have eternal life" (John 3:16, RSV). The evangelistic mandate makes the difference between unbelief and belief, between eternal death and eternal life. Sociopolitical liberation, relief, development, justice, sharing the wealth, saving the whales, or any other part of the cultural mandate are temporal, not eternal. It is doubtful that God would have become human and suffered on the cross if all that was wrong were social problems.

The Apostle Paul's understanding of the gospel was the preaching of the death and resurrection of Jesus Christ, who "died for our sins according to the scriptures" (1 Cor. 15:1–4). He preached it knowing that "it is the power of God unto salvation" (Rom. 1:16). As he traveled throughout the Mediterranean world, he left behind disciples of Jesus Christ. A study of Paul's ministry shows that the evangelistic mandate was his overriding and overwhelming motivation. John Stott points out that one of the most severe cries of anguish we have from Paul is his concern for his fellow Jews: "I am speaking the truth in Christ, I am not lying; my conscience bears me witness in the Holy Spirit, that I have great sorrow and unceasing anguish in my heart. For I could wish that I myself were accursed and cut off from Christ for the sake of my brethren, my kinsmen by race" (Rom. 9:1–3, RSV). Stott then raises the question as to the cause of Paul's anguish. Was it that the Jews "had lost their national Jewish independence and were under the colonial heel of Rome?" Or that "they were often despised and hated by Gentiles, socially boycotted and deprived of equal opportunities?" Of course not. It was Paul's heart's desire and prayer "that they may be saved" (Rom. 10:1, RSV).[34] Being saved, in the biblical sense, is not a slave being freed or a beggar getting a meal or a despot being overthrown by revolutionaries or a law being passed opening up job opportunities for minorities. The cultural mandate doesn't save. That is why, in the total sweep of Christian mission and the kingdom of God, the evangelistic mandate is primary.

The kingdom of God, with all its manifold blessings and signs, is manifested in the world primarily by those who have already been touched by the evangelistic mandate. Jesus said "You are the light of the world. You are the salt of the earth." The "you" does not refer to unbelievers, still unsaved, still in their sins, still serving the powers of darkness. It refers to those who, by someone sharing the evangelistic message with them, have been born again, baptized into fellowship with other Christians, and are living a lifestyle of obedience and discipleship in the community of the king. No evangelistic mandate—no light. No evangelistic mandate—no salt. In other words, without the *prior* operation of the evangelistic mandate, there would be no one to work on fulfilling the other part of holistic mission—the cultural mandate.

I repeat that fulfilling the cultural mandate is not *optional* for Christians. It is God's command and a part of Christian mission. But it is true that, when a choice must be made on the basis of availability of resources or of value judgments, the biblical indication is that the evangelistic mandate must take priority. Nothing is or can be as important as saving souls from eternal damnation.

The Issues and the Advocates

The question of the relative place of the cultural and the evangelistic mandates in the total mission of the church is one of the most important missiological issues being discussed today. I find it helpful, as a way of understanding the options, to use a diagram, as follows:

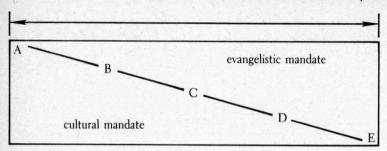

Conceptions of God's Mission in the World

Notice that as one moves from left to right along the spectrum, the cultural mandate decreases and the evangelistic mandate increases proportionately. There are probably an infinite number of positions that Christians could choose to take, but I have located five as being typical of the options open to those who feel involved in God's mission in the world.

Position A holds that God's mission includes only the cultural mandate, and not the evangelistic.

Position B holds that mission includes both the cultural and evangelistic mandates, but that the cultural mandate has the priority.

Position C holds that the cultural mandate and the evangelistic mandate have equal part in mission.

Position D holds that the evangelistic mandate has priority over the cultural mandate.

Position E holds that mission includes only the evangelistic mandate, and not the cultural.

It will be obvious to those who study the spectrum that the position I have been arguing in this chapter is Position D. But it may also be helpful to see where some contemporary Christian leaders fit into the picture.

Position A probably doesn't exist except in the mind of a secular humanist. Few Christians would agree that there is no place for winning people to Christ. Most Christians who find themselves toward the extreme left would probably be at A.1 or A.2. The Section II statement that emerged from the World Conference on Salvation Today, held by the World Council of Churches in Bangkok in 1973, furnishes an example at this end of the spectrum. On careful examination, fleeting references can be found to "salvation of the soul" and "reconciliation with God," but it is hardly more than a tip of the hat. If the position is not A, it is scarcely more than A.1. It sees the "comprehensive notion of salvation" in four social dimensions:

1. Salvation works in the struggle for economic justice against the exploitation of people by people.
2. Salvation works in the struggle for human dignity against political oppression by their fellow men.
3. Salvation works in the struggle for solidarity against the alienation of person from person.
4. Salvation works in the struggle of hope against despair in personal life.[35]

Position B is probably the most common position of ecumenical missiologists and church leaders. Some would lean toward A, some toward C. Emilio Castro's pleading for the proclamation of the gospel in the meeting of the CWME in Melbourne in 1980, for example, would lean from B toward C. Evangelical consultants at the Uppsala Assembly of the World Council of Churches, held in 1968, described the WCC view in Position B terms. While Philip Potter, then Director of the CWME and now General Secretary of the WCC, did acknowledge "the hundreds of millions who have not heard the gospel of forgiveness of God in Christ,"[36] concern for their souls never became a central topic of the Assembly. David Hubbard, for example, was baffled by the reluctance of the Assembly to "see both evangelism and social concern as essential, unchanging, binding obligations."[37] John Stott was worried that, while the cultural mandate came through clearly, he "found no comparable compassion or concern for the spiritual hunger of the unevangelized missions."[38] Clearly, Uppsala is located on the left of our spectrum, probably Position B leaning toward A.

Position C was previously described as "holistic evangelism." There is no need repeating statements made by Orlando Costas, René Padilla, Partnership in Mission, Alfred Krass, Carl Henry, and others. Joining them at this position would be Harvie Conn of Westminster Theological Seminary. Conn feels that the Lausanne Covenant errs in attempting to resolve dualisms by dualisms. He does not feel it legitimate to separate proclamation and service. "There can be no ordered priority or duality even of a temporal sort," Conn says.[39]

Ronald Sider agrees, although he differs with other Position C advocates in admitting that it is legitimate to recognize evangelism and social action as "quite distinct aspects of the total mission of the church." He goes on to add, however, that this "does not mean that evangelism is more important than social action," and says he finds no indication in the Gospels "that Jesus considered preaching the Good News more important than healing sick people."[40]

Position D is my own position and that of the Lausanne Covenant. It recognizes at the same time holistic mission and the priority of evangelism. Arthur Glasser concurs when he says: "Although not a few evangelicals are rightly concerned to participate in the worldwide struggle for social justice and reconciliation within human society, they refuse to retreat from affirming that the primary task of the church's mission of sacrificial service to the world is evangelism."[41]

Although I am not an expert in Roman Catholic thought, it does seem to me that Pope Paul's Apostolic Exhortation, *"Evangelii Nuntiandi,"* of 1975 is a Position D statement. In Article 34, the Pope affirms that, while the Church is "preaching liberation and associating herself with those who are working and suffering for it," nevertheless, "she reaffirms the primacy of her spiritual vocation and refuses to replace the proclamation of the kingdom by the proclamation of forms of human liberation." As a result of this, some visible changes have come about in the evangelistic efforts of Roman Catholics, at least in America.

Position E is identified as the classical definition of mission. It is maintained by many who are generally in sympathy with the Lausanne Covenant but disagree on Lausanne's acceptance of holistic mission. I used to hold to classical mission myself, but I have changed over the years to holistic mission. Arthur Johnston defends Position E. Johnston says, clearly, "The mission of the Church is evangelism."[42] He agrees that the cultural mandate must be fulfilled, but refuses to see it as a legitimate component of biblical mission.

Where Does McGavran Fit?

The Church Growth Movement as a whole falls between Position D and Position E on the spectrum. Most church growth people hold to either classical mission or holistic mission. Very few, if any, would move farther left. I have intentionally avoided mentioning Donald McGavran, the founder of the Church Growth Movement, in this discussion because I feel his position needs separate treatment.

I know of no one who has written more on the role of evangelism in missions than Donald McGavran. Indeed, he first coined the phrase "church growth," after 30 years of ministry as a missionary to India, when he became irritated at the erosion of the biblical content of the words *mission* and *evangelism.* I have before me ten of his statements on the relationship of evangelism to mission, arranged in chronological order from 1958 to 1980. His views have not changed. Despite some small confusion, I think that if McGavran is not squarely at Position E., he would not be farther back than, say D.9.

The problem in exegeting McGavran arises out of the fact that through the years he has made two kinds of statements, and he still does. In *Understanding Church Growth* he adopts what he calls the "narrow" definition of mission: "an enterprise devoted to proclaiming the Good News of Jesus Christ, and to persuading men to become His disciples and dependable members of His Church."[43] This is Position E. In 1972 he discussed his definitions with the Association of Professors of Missions. There he said that, while he was conscious of attempts to redefine mission to mean "everything God wants done," he nevertheless "declines to use the terms that way." He reserves the term "mission" for "propagating the Gospel and reconciling men to God in the Church of Jesus Christ." He prefers to call the cultural mandate "our Christian duty," but not *mission.*[44] Again, this is Position E.

But in the same paper, McGavran also says that evangelism is "a chief and irreplaceable purpose of Christian mission. It is not the *only* purpose. It is not even *the* chief purpose. It is, however, a chief and irreplaceable purpose."[45] If evangelism is a chief and irreplaceable purpose of mission, one might conclude that there would be other chief purposes of mission, among them, presumably, the cultural mandate. McGavran believes in the cultural mandate. In his most careful statements, however, he insists that classical *mission* is winning souls and that social action is a legitimate *program* of the church, but not mission itself.[46] In other words, despite occasional hints that lend themselves to other interpretations, it is accurate to describe McGavran's view of mission as Position E, or classical mission.

It should be noted here briefly that, while the Church Growth Movement clearly gives priority to evangelism, whether from the classical or the holistic mission perspective, allowance is made under certain circumstances for changing these priorities. This will be discussed in some detail in the next chapter.

Notes

1. Rodger C. Bassham, *Mission Theology: 1948–1975, Years of Worldwide Creative Tension: Ecumenical, Evangelical and Roman Catholic* (Pasadena: William Carey Library, 1979), pp. 194–195.

2. Harvey T. Hoekstra, *The World Council of Churches and the Demise of Evangelism* (Wheaton, IL: Tyndale, 1979), p. 12.

3. Quoted in Sydney E. Mead, "Denominationalism: The Shape of Protestantism in America," in *Denominationalism*, ed. Russell E. Richey (Nashville: Abingdon, 1977), pp. 85–86.

4. Ibid., pp. 86–87.

5. Horace L. Fenton, Jr., "Mission—and Social Concern," in *The Church's Worldwide Mission*, ed. Harold Lindsell (Waco: Word Books, 1966), pp. 193–203.

6. "Wheaton Declaration," in Lindsell, *The Church's Worldwide Mission*, p. 235.

7. Arthur Johnston, *The Battle for World Evangelization* (Wheaton, IL: Tyndale, 1978), p. 221.

8. Ibid., p. 227.

9. John R. W. Stott, "The Great Commission," in *One Race, One Gospel, One Task*, ed. Carl F. H. Henry and W. Stanley Mooneyham (Minneapolis: World Wide Publications, 1967), Vol. 1, p. 50.

10. John R. W. Stott, *Christian Mission in the Modern World* (Downers Grove, IL: InterVarsity Press, 1975), p. 23.

11. Ibid.

12. Ibid, p. 35.

13. See my *Frontiers in Missionary Strategy* (Chicago: Moody Press, 1971), p. 134.

14. Peter Beyerhaus, "Foreword," in Johnston, *The Battle for World Evangelism*, p. 11.

15. Johnston, *The Battle for World Evangelism*, p. 327.

16. David J. Hesselgrave, *Planting Churches Cross-Culturally: A Guide for Home and Foreign Missions* (Grand Rapids: Baker Book House, 1980), p. 34.

17. David H. Hesselgrave, "Tomorrow's Missionaries: To Whose Drumbeat Will They March?" *Christianity Today*, 24, no. 13 (July 18, 1980), p. 27.

18. Cited in David J. Bosch, *Witness to the World: The Christian Mission in Theological Perspective* (Atlanta: John Knox Press, 1980), p. 14.

19. This type of confusion of geographical with cultural considerations contributed to the insertion of cross-cultural evangelistic situations (E-2) into the monocultural category (E-1) by George G. Hunter, III. For example, he calls upper class Americans reaching blue-collar workers in Appalachia a type of E-1 (he uses E-1-C). Whereas Ralph Winter, the originator of the scheme, and I would argue that there is enough cultural difference between the two (though located in the same nation) to classify it as an E-2 distance. Hunter's typology was originally published in *Global Church Growth Bulletin* 17, no. 2 (March/April, 1980), pp. 24–25, and later used by Donald A. McGavran in *Understanding Church Growth*, rev.ed.(Grand Rapids: Eerdmans, 1980), pp. 69–72.

20. Alfred C. Krass, *Five Lanterns at Sundown: Evangelism in a Chastened Mood* (Grand Rapids: Eerdmans, 1978), pp. 78–79.

21. René Padilla, "Evangelism and the World," in *Let the Earth Hear His Voice*, ed. J. D. Douglas (Minneapolis: World Wide Publications, 1975), p. 144.

22. "Theology and Implications of Radical Discipleship," in *Let the Earth Hear His Voice*, ed. Douglas, p. 1294.

23. Orlando E. Costas, *The Integrity of Mission: The Inner Life and Outreach of the Church* (San Francisco: Harper & Row, 1979), p. 75.

24. Richard J. Coleman, *Issues of Theological Warfare: Evangelicals and Liberals* (Grand Rapids: Eerdmans, 1972), p. 178.

25. *Partnership*, September 21, 1976, pp. 2–3.

26. Carl F. H. Henry, "The Gospel and Society," *Christianity Today* 18, no. 24 (September 13, 1974), p. 67.

27. C. René Padilla, "Introduction," in *The New Face of Evangelicalism: An International Symposium on the Lausanne Covenant* (Downers Grove, IL: InterVarsity Press, 1976), p. 11.

28. *Partnership*, p. 3.

29. Arthur Johnston, *The Battle for World Evangelism* (Wheaton, IL: Tyndale, 1978), p. 347.

30. Ibid., p. 350.

31. Paul G. Hiebert, "Holism and the Integrated Christian Life," in *Crucial Dimensions in World Evangelization*, ed. Arthur F. Glasser, et. al. (Pasadena: William Carey Library, 1976), p. 83.

32. See Orlando Costas, "A Sign of Hope: A Latin American Appraisal of Lausanne '74," *Latin America Evangelist*, November/December, 1974, pp. 2, 10.

33. Krass, *Five Lanterns*, p. 79.

34. See Stott, *Christian Mission in the Modern World*, p. 36.

35. "Salvation and Social Justice: Report of Section II of the Bangkok Conference," *International Review of Mission* 62, no. 246 (April 1973), p. 200.

36. Philip Potter, "Renewal in Mission," in *The Conciliar-Evangelical Debate: The Crucial Documents 1964–1976*, ed. Donald McGavran (Pasadena: William Carey Library, 1977), p. 263. It is highly likely that Potter's statement was in part a defensive reaction to the widely circulated pre-Uppsala article by McGavran, "Will Uppsala Betray the Two Billion?" published in the May, 1968, *Church Growth Bulletin*.

37. David Allan Hubbard, "The Theology of Section Two," in *The Conciliar-Ecumenical Debate*, ed. McGavran, p. 270.

38. John R. W. Stott, "Does Section Two Provide Sufficient Emphasis on World Evangelism?" in *The Conciliar-Ecumenical Debate*, ed. McGavran, p. 268.

39. Harvie M. Conn, "The Mission of the Church," in *Evangelicals and Liberation*, ed. Carl E. Armerding (Nutley, NJ: Presbyterian and Reformed, 1977), p. 68.

40. Ronald J. Sider, *Evangelism, Salvation and Social Justice* (Bramcote, Notts, U.K.: Grove Books, 1977), p. 17.

41. Arthur F. Glasser, "China Today and the Christian Movement," unpublished paper presented at the China Consultation, Overseas Ministries Study Center, Ventnor, N.J., April 15–17, 1980, p. 5.

42. Johnston, *The Battle for World Evangelism*, p. 303.

43. McGavran, *Understanding Church Growth*, p. 26.

44. Donald McGavran, "What Is the Church Growth School of Thought?" in *The Church Growth Movement*, Proceedings of the Eleventh Biennial Meeting of the Association of Professors of Missions, June 12–14, 1972, p. 8.

45. Ibid., p. 9

46. See Donald McGavran, "Salvation Today?" *Church Growth Bulletin*, September 1972, p. 16; and Donald McGavran, "Introduction," in *Crucial Issues in Missions Tomorrow*, ed. Donald McGavran (Chicago: Moody Press, 1972), pp. 9–10.

CHAPTER 6

Priorities and Their
Practical Consequences

The Church Growth Movement holds that it is theologically and biblically defensible to make a distinction between the evangelistic mandate
and the cultural mandate. It also argues that the evangelistic mandate
maintains priority over the cultural mandate if the revealed will of God
is properly understood. Those concepts were developed in a theoretical
way in the last chapter. This chapter is intended to be more practical.
It will discuss what difference this priority makes in the actual field
application of both mandates.

The Social Disaster Area: Reversing Priorities

As mentioned previously, the evangelistic and cultural mandates can
be differentiated one from another, but they must not be polarized. One
must not be set against the other, since both are part of the working out
of the kingdom of God in our day. While in theory the evangelistic
mandate has the long range priority, in some concrete situations faithfulness to God and his kingdom may demand that the cultural mandate
take priority. This concept apparently has not been understood by some
critics of the Church Growth Movement, although it is not new to
church growth teaching. I suspect that it may not have been emphasized
enough in the literature.

Edward Dayton and David Fraser argue that when one leaves the
realm of the theoretical and gets into concrete situations, the issue of
social action or evangelism becomes a "non-question." It can be a

meaningful question, but only when understood in a specific context. The question must be qualified: "Social action or evangelism where? When?"[1] Church growth leader Tetsunao Yamamori suggests that the relationship be seen as "contextual symbiosis." He argues that the particular aspect of the ministry of God's kingdom which must be underscored at any given moment is best determined by "the nature of needs, problems, opportunities, and available resources within a given context."[2] The context, then, determines the precise relationship of the evangelistic to the cultural mandate.

The term I prefer in describing a concrete situation where the cultural mandate may take priority is "social disaster area." The Road to Jericho is an example. There was no question as to the priority of action when the fellow who had been beaten by thieves was lying in the dust, and the Samaritan took appropriate action. Donald McGavran makes allowances for the social disaster area when he says, "under some circumstances, to be sure, and for a limited time, Christianizing some aspect of the social order may legitimately be assigned a higher priority and receive greater attention than evangelism."[3] This is taught in church growth classes.

As I see it, there are two significant types of social disaster areas: (1) *social service* disaster areas and (2) *social action* disaster areas (to continue with the terms defined in Chapter 2). The decisions that need to be made in social service areas are relatively easy. Those for social action areas are much more difficult.

A good example of the social service disaster area is famine. When people are actually dying from starvation it is a Jericho Road situation. The cultural mandate takes priority: people must be fed; lives must be saved. Dead people can't hear the gospel anyway, so what good is prioritizing the evangelistic mandate? Compassion for bodies, not only souls, shows forth the values of the kingdom of God. If a building is burning, holding an open-air evangelistic meeting is inappropriate. It is more important to put out the fire and help the victims to escape. I agree with John Stott, who says that an "evangelist could not with integrity proclaim the good news to the victims of flood or famine while ignoring their physical plight."[4]

Social action disaster areas are somewhat more complex. Do we wait for matters of injustice, oppression, racism, unemployment, exploitation, war, consumerism, and human rights to be resolved in a way congruous with the kingdom of God before we vigorously implement the evangelistic mandate? McGavran feels that it was appropriate for "some Christian leaders, under the circumstances prevailing in the sixties, and for a limited time, to turn from winning men to Christ to winning the civil rights battle."[5] At times I have raised the question of the practice of *apartheid* in South Africa today. Could South Africa be regarded as a legitimate social action disaster area? Would it not be appropriate for some white churches there to take in black members and thus visibly display the acceptance of all races in Jesus Christ, knowing ahead of time that such action would in all probability reduce their evangelistic effectiveness? I only raise the question because I do not feel that those of us outside the South African context have a right to superimpose our answers on them. But my outsider's inclination is to answer it in the affirmative.

The Church Growth Movement affirms the need to change priorities in certain situations, but it also holds tenaciously to the D-E positions on the mission issues spectrum, as described in Chapter 5. Notice how McGavran qualifies his statements with "some circumstances" and "for a limited time." He adds, "But as a rule, the multiplying of cells of reborn Christians continues to have a higher priority."[6] Church growth people intuitively question the kind of statements that came out of the World Council Geneva Conference on Church and Society (1966), stating that "in certain situations political and economic liberation must precede the preaching of personal conversion and reconciliation with God."[7] It usually takes more than a "limited time" to bring about socio-political liberation, and, furthermore, not all Christians are agreed as to what the ideal society should look like before we can begin evangelizing. Should evangelism be postponed in the Soviet Union until totalitarianism is crushed? Should it be postponed in the Philippines until the Marcos regime is ousted? Should tribal peoples be "civilized" before they are evangelized? Should abolishing India's caste system be a prerequisite to evangelism?

The answers to such questions can only be given, as Dayton, Fraser, and Yamamori remind us, in the context of the concrete situation. But it is equally true that individuals and groups that finally make the decision will be governed by previous assumptions. This is why, in complex situations such as social action disaster areas, the matter of the relative priorities of the two mandates is really not a "non-question." It may be a non-question on the Road to Jericho, but it is more likely a burning question on the road to Havana or to Taipei. Previous assumptions derived from Positions A or B on the mission issues spectrum will argue one kind of decision in a given context, while assumptions from Positions D or E demand quite another in the identical context.

Evangelicals on Social Change

Evangelicals and church growth advocates who hold to the priority of the evangelistic mandate, as a matter of historical record, have not neglected their social responsibilities under the cultural mandate, particularly in social service but also in areas of social action.

Evangelical Christians who would argue the priority of evangelistic mandate have made significant and even outstanding contributions to the fulfillment of the cultural mandate. Samuel Escobar asserts that throughout the history of modern missions, the "intention of these evangelicals was basically evangelistic." But, despite the priority given to this spiritual aspect of ministry, "the evils of society were such that out of their Christian vocation they could not but become involved in the fight for social change." Their missionary work, says Escobar, "has always been accompanied by results that affected social and political structures."[8] Orlando Costas adds that "the modern missionary movement, whatever its theology, has served men's and women's social needs."[9]

Historical scholarship continues to uncover ways in which evangelistically minded people have contributed to social improvement. One outstanding breakthrough in this field was Timothy L. Smith's *Revivalism and Social Reform*, written in 1957.[10] Previous to Smith the common scholarly assumption was that liberal intellectual and socio-economic forces were the major determining factors in the social development of America, with the influence of more evangelistically minded Christians peripheral at best.[11] Timothy Smith, in his prize-winning book, proposed a new thesis. Martin Marty, for example, remarks that Smith "claimed to discover that [American revivalists] were more oriented toward social reform than their critics saw them to be," and that Smith's book "represented one of those rare moments in the study of American church history: the development of an original thesis," one that, in fact, has survived.[12]

Timothy Smith finds that, "Far from disdaining earthly affairs, the evangelists played a key role in the widespread attack upon slavery, poverty, and greed. They thus helped prepare the way both in theory and in practice for what later became known as the social gospel."[13] Smith, a minister in the Church of the Nazarene, argues that the doctrines of holiness and perfectionism in the Wesleyan tradition were powerful social forces. He quotes, for example, Methodist William Arthur as saying, "Nothing short of the general renewal of society ought to satisfy any soldier of Christ."[14] Social Christianity in America originated, says Smith, "long before the slavery conflict erupted into war." Whatever may have been the role of other factors, "the quest for perfection joined with compassion for poor and needy sinners and a rebirth of millennial expectation to make popular Protestantism a mighty social force."[15]

Professor J. Edwin Orr, of Fuller Seminary's School of World Mission, is the recognized authority on the history of awakenings. In several works, Orr links significant social reform to the effects of evangelistically oriented awakenings. Ever since the First Great Awakening of the 1720s, the kind of ministry which gives top priority to the spiritual dimension of human beings has resulted in great benefits to the physical and social dimensions as well. Orr's works describe advances in education, prison reform, health care, treatment of mental illness, trade unionism, public libraries, slum housing, courts of justice, and many other social improvements. He shows how revivals led to the reduction of such practices as gambling, child labor abuse, rape, arson, drunkenness, swearing, slavery, robbery, assault, and the exhibition of insane people in cages for general ridicule. Orr says, "The outpouring of the Holy Spirit, reviving the Church and awakening the masses, not only promotes evangelism and teaching the Word, but accelerates social action."[16]

Missions and Social Improvement

Any cursory reading of missionary history will turn up many examples of how people who went out to evangelize the world also promoted the cultural mandate with considerable success. In his excellent book *The Social Conscience of the Evangelical,* Sherwood Wirt says of "all the pioneers of the modern evangelical missionary movement" that they "possessed two things in common: evangelistic fervor and an active social conscience." This is to be expected of those who are living lives worthy of the kingdom of God. He points out how they, through the power of God, were able to reform such practices as black magic, child-stealing, slavery, cannibalism, and head hunting.[17] One could look further to such practices as infanticide, widow burning, warfare, geno-cide, drunkenness, and other dehumanizing abuses that were radically changed by the introduction of the gospel through missionary evangel-ists.

One of the most significant changes affecting the balance of power worldwide in our century has been the demise of Western colonialism and the emergence of independent nation-states since World War II. Donald McGavran points out that few people are aware that this inde-pendence movement "through which at least one billion people became self-governing is itself a triumph of the Christian faith."[18] Samuel Escobar concurs. "It is recognized today," Escobar says, "that many of those who fought for independence in the anti-colonial movements . . . were people that had been educated, and probably motivated in their love for freedom, by the missionary schools. . . ."[19]

It would be inaccurate to leave the impression that all missionary work has been exemplary in the fulfillment of the cultural mandate. Alas, many mistakes have been made. The imposition of Western cultural values on other peoples, under the guise of the gospel, has been a common mistake, now widely recognized. Billy Graham admitted this publicly in Lausanne when he said, "When I go to preach the Gospel, I go as an ambassador for the kingdom of God—not America."[20] While praising the good that has been done by missionaries, Orlando Costas also points out that their negative impact "has been far greater than what many of us would like to admit."[21] But, despite some possible effects of the "Great Reversal" on evangelical missionaries, the balance seems favorable. Most evangelicals continue to believe and practice the cultural mandate. In preparation for the Lausanne Congress, for exam-ple, W. Stanley Mooneyham surveyed 150 evangelical leaders around the world. He reported that "from every part of the world came reports that evangelicals are ministering to human needs, as well as spiritual needs, in the name of Christ."[22]

The Magnetic Field of the Evangelistic Mandate

It is my opinion, as I argue in Chapter 4, that the Scriptures have a bias toward the evangelistic mandate. While the cultural mandate is also an important part of the kingdom lifestyle and is not optional for Christians, it nevertheless is not as important as the evangelistic man-date.

I visualize the evangelistic mandate as a magnet. Depending on its position, it will tend to pull the cultural mandate one way or another. If evangelism is kept in its biblical position of number one priority, the cultural mandate will also have the potential of maximum fulfillment. If, however, it is dropped to a priority below the cultural mandate, it will in turn drag down the social ministry of the church. The best starting point for the vigorous and effective implementation of Christian social concerns is to win multitudes of people to Christ and multiply Christian churches.

I do not mean that evangelism will automatically bring about social change. Like evangelism, Christian social ministry takes doing. It takes prayer, financial resources, human time and energy, the prophetic word, exhortation, determination, commitment, planning, and goal setting. Above all, it takes the sovereign blessing of God. God usually most abundantly blesses those who are obedient to him. Part of obedience is listening carefully to the Word of God and subscribing to biblical priorities. While I respect those who disagree, I nevertheless do operate under the strong *conviction* that the most important message of the kingdom of God is "be ye reconciled to Christ," the evangelistic mandate. In this I can safely say that I represent evangelicals in general and the Church Growth Movement in particular.[23]

It is frequently said that peace on earth and goodwill toward men are works of almighty God who, however, sees fit to work his works through the instrumentality of human beings. Most of the time he chooses those of his own family, those who have been born again into the kingdom of God, as his instruments of good in the world. That is why Jesus told believers that *they* were salt of the earth and lights of the world. God, of course, is not limited to using his own people. He can and does occasionally use a Cyrus or a Herod or a Mao to accomplish his own purposes, but this is not the usual way. Justice today can best flow like a mighty stream in Cambodia or Libya or Taiwan if the people there bend their knee to their Creator and obey him. I like the way Montgomery and McGavran put it: "As the gospel spreads, men and women are converted, soundly Christian congregations multiply and the Holy Spirit causes both individual and corporate changes. Through his redeemed, he causes justice to roll down in families, neighborhoods, cities and states."[24] Nothing can better assist the cultural mandate than the previous application of the evangelistic mandate.

The Three Priorities

Several years ago I attempted to identify what I called the "seven vital signs" of healthy, Anglo-American churches. In the book *Your Church Can Grow,* I used as the title of a chapter, "Are Your Priorities in Order?" Then I listed the priorities of ministry as I perceived they were arranged in the most healthy, growing churches. As more evidence has come in, I continue to feel that they are sound. The first priority is commitment to Christ, the second is commitment to the body of Christ, and the third is commitment to the work of Christ in the world. All three are essential for a well-rounded Christian life of discipleship and obedience, but all three are best implemented if kept in proper order.

Priority three—the work of Christ in the world—is also divided into sub-priorities. The first is the evangelistic mandate and the second is the cultural mandate. The cultural mandate has its own two sub-priorities: social service and social action. Our discussion in this chapter obviously relates to priority three and, in particular, the need to maintain the evangelistic over the cultural mandate if both are to have their maximum impact.

Priorities and the Collapse of Christian Movements

Christian movements that have switched the priorities have frequently become frustrated. A clear example from fairly recent history is the Student Volunteer Movement. It was founded in the latter part of the last century by John R. Mott and Robert Wilder, around the watchword: "The evangelization of the world in this generation." Its chief priority was the evangelistic mandate. God blessed, and the SVM flourished. At one time it counted 40,000 members from the colleges and universities of America. Over 20,000 men and women actually reached the mission fields of the world as a direct result of the Student Volunteer Movement. It was probably the single strongest force for missions in America in the early part of this century.

But there is no Student Volunteer Movement today, primarily because it allowed its priorities to shift. The SVM hit its peak in 1920, enrolling 2,783 new volunteers; in 1938 they enrolled twenty-five new volunteers. By 1940 the SVM "had almost ceased to be a decisive factor either in student religious life or in the promotion of the missionary program of the churches."[25] One account of the demise of the SVM reflects the fatal shift of priorities:

Their emphasis shifted away from Bible study, evangelism, lifework decision and foreign mission obligation on which the SVM had originally been built. Instead they now emphasized the new issues such as race relations, economic injustice and imperialism.[26]

The priorities did not shift all of a sudden. The process began in 1924 when J. C. Robbins succeeded John R. Mott as chairperson. In his first address Robbins redefined the evangelistic mandate, saying that the kind of evangelism he was interested in means "to permeate with the spirit of the Gospel." He went on to say, "Our purpose is to permeate with the spirit of the Gospel not only individuals, but also society and international relationships."[27] This sounds something like proponents of "holistic evangelism" in our day. With remorse, Timothy Wallstrom points out that "The well-outlined sense of purpose the watchword had originally served to focus so vividly now was projected as fuzzy and diffuse."[28] Giving priority to the cultural mandate in the SVM ultimately resulted in not fulfilling the cultural mandate at all.

The Student Volunteer Movement is not the only case study scrutinized by historians. Arthur Johnston, for example, describes how a similar thing happened to the World Student Christian Federation when it began to switch priorities to the cultural mandate in 1902.[29] Sidney Mead sees the YMCA as passing through a similar process. The YMCA, Mead says, "had as its original objective the evangelization of uprooted men in traditional fashion." It added libraries, recreational facilities, inexpensive hotel rooms, and other facilities in order better to win men and women to Jesus Christ. But, sadly, "as belief in simple evangelism declined, the facilities themselves tended to take the leading role."[30] A similar priority shift almost caught InterVarsity Christian Fellowship in the 1960s. The climax was the Urbana Student Missionary Convention in 1970, when rousing cheers and applause greeted speakers stressing the cultural mandate, while icy indifference, barely short of audible booing, was aimed at those stressing the evangelistic mandate.[31] But the leaders of IVCF had read the history of the Student Volunteer Movement well, and they immediately took steps to keep the evangelistic mandate as a high priority. They succeeded, and the Urbana Conventions have enjoyed an uninterrupted growth under the blessing of God.

Unprecedented American Church Decline

"An unprecedented period in the life of the North American church began in the mid-1960s. For the first time since records allow us to recall, many major denominations actually stopped growing in membership and began to decline, and the growth rate of most others slowed considerably."[32] So reads the opening sentence of the report of a two-year consortium of theologians, sociologists of religion, denominational statisticians, historians, and church consultants who met at Hartford Seminary between 1976 and 1978.

Between 1965 and 1975 the United Methodist Church lost a net of 1,110,000 members (10 percent); the United Presbyterians lost 375,000 (12 percent); the United Church of Christ lost 250,000 (12 percent); and the Episcopal Church lost 575,000 (17 percent). At the beginning of the great decline, most mainline denominations were indifferent to the losses and interpreted the figures rather casually. Some said, "We're just getting rid of the dead wood," or "We're not in the numbers game," or as Robert K. Hudnut said, "People are leaving the church. It could not be a better sign."[33] Many expected that the trend would be just a slight dip and then pick up again. But when it stretched to five, then ten, and now fifteen years, the indifference turned to concern. The Hartford Consortium, of which I was privileged to be a member, was one manifestation of the concern.

Those of us who participated in the Hartford study agreed on a typology of sets of conditions which enter into the complex causes of church growth or decline. This typology itself was worth the consortium, since it has provided a standardized vocabulary that researchers can now use to talk to each other. Here are the four sets of conditions:

National Contextual Factors. These are forces operating at the national level external to the church. Population shifts, wars, economic changes, human rights, religious freedom—these and other similar considerations, usually beyond the control of the church, make up this category.

National Institutional Factors. These are factors controlled by the church at the level of the denominational, or in some cases, judicatorial level. In mission situations these would include decisions made by the mission but affecting the national church.

Local Contextual Factors. Sociological forces operating at the level of the community in which the local church or congregation is located.

Changing neighborhoods, opening or closing of factories, new housing starts, and the like—these factors are also outside the control of the church but influence growth to one degree or another.

Local Institutional Factors.   These factors have to do with the particular congregation or parish. They might include pastoral and lay leadership, small group structure, outreach programs, worship format, giving patterns, etc.[34]

While there was agreement as to the usefulness and nomenclature of this typology, the Hartford group did not agree on the relative weight the sets of factors had in influencing church growth in America. The conclusion of Hoge and Roozen themselves, representing the majority of the consortium, is that contextual factors are more important than institutional factors. They also suggest that in studying *denominational* trends the local factors, whether contextual or institutional, are relatively unimportant. In their opinion, mainline denominations declined primarily because of national contextual factors.[35]

At least two people there, Dean M. Kelley and myself, disagreed both orally and in our contributions to the symposium volume, *Understanding Church Growth and Decline.* We both feel that institutional factors are prior to contextual factors in explaining the decline of mainline churches. It is my opinion that in the total picture of American church growth (including the evangelical denominations that the consortium did not study) local institutional factors are the most important. But, in terms of the mainline denominations only, I agree with Dean Kelley that the national institutional factors are the most determinative.

My hypothesis is that the most important single cause of the startling membership decline in American mainline denominations, beginning in 1965, was a subtle priority shift on the part of the denominational bureaucracies, clearly a national institutional factor. The switch from the evangelistic to the cultural mandate proved in real life to be devastating.

One fact that made me suspicious of the contextual advocates was that during the time the *mainline* churches were declining, most *evangelical* denominations were growing. While United Methodists were losing 1,110,000 members, Southern Baptists were picking up 1,460,-000. During the 1965–1975 period the Church of God (Cleveland) grew 67 percent; the Assemblies of God grew 33 percent; and the Church of the Nazarene grew 29 percent, to name a few. Presumably the national contextual factors were constant for all American denominations concerned. The Hartford consortium came to their conclusions from study-ing mostly *declining* churches, while Kelley and I studied both growing and declining churches.

On the other hand, my inclination toward national contextual factors was stimulated by the publication of Dean Kelley's landmark book, *Why Conservative Churches Are Growing.*[36] He convinced me that the basic function of churches in society is to provide their members answers to the deepest questions about the meaning of life. My interpretation of the meaning of life is sharing the message of the gospel that through Jesus Christ men and women can be born again and be reconciled to God, at which point they begin to understand for what purpose they have been placed on this planet. In other words, the thing that churches do first and best is to implement the evangelistic mandate.

Dean Kelley makes an extremely significant observation on how the contextual advocates handled the empirical data upon which they based their conclusions. They found that the national contextual factors (fam-ily income, percent of people living in the West, and the number of children in the family) accounted for "over half the total variance in denominational growth rates," *if they are taken first.* But, Kelley points out, if four institutional factors are taken first (theological conservatism, emphasis on evangelism, distinctive lifestyle and morality, and unitary set of beliefs) "they explain virtually *all* the total variance, and little is left for contextual factors to explain!"[37] Notice the presence of "empha-sis on evangelism" in the list. The growing churches are the ones which hold the evangelistic mandate high.

The Great Priority Shift

The decade of the 1950s in America was a time of burgeoning church growth in virtually every denomination. Attendance was up. New churches were being planted regularly. In 1950, for example, 57 percent of Americans were church members; by 1958 the number had increased to 67 percent. Needless to say, the evangelistic mandate was in operation and effectively so.

Then came the 1960s, a decade of turmoil and change. The civil rights movement, the Vietnam war, the hippie counterculture, the death-of-God viewpoint, situation ethics, new morality, and other social and psychological factors convulsed the religious world. Consciences of

Christian leaders were aroused to social injustices. The cultural mandate became prominent. Enter what Richard Hutcheson calls "prophets in the bureaucracy." Certain religiously motivated social activists "were naturally attracted to church bureaucracies as seats of power for social change."[38] They had the big budgets. It did not matter that the people in the pews who contributed to the budgets may not have approved their social agenda, as Jeffrey Hadden's studies show.[39] The climate was ripe for a takeover, and the social activists moved into the denominational executive suites with zeal.

It wasn't long before priorities were changed. The cultural mandate was supreme. As William Willimon and Robert Wilson observe, "The really significant activity for church leaders was not in carrying out the traditional ministries that had always occupied congregations, but being a part of the protest marches and helping correct the evils in society."[40] The national bureaucracies embarked on programs which were "grandiose and costly," launched with "considerable publicity and heavy rhetoric," to use the terms of Mickey and Wilson.[41] The Great Priority Shift had begun in earnest.

If my hypothesis that the evangelistic mandate should have top priority in carrying out God's work in the world is valid, it would be expected that the Great Priority Shift would lessen the effects of both the evangelistic and cultural mandates in the mainline churches. This, in fact, has happened.

The decline of the evangelistic mandate has been seen in membership losses. Major studies done on the losses in both the United Methodist and United Presbyterian denominations have shown that the evangelistic mandate is weak. As church growth leader George Hunter points out, the losses in the United Methodist church are not due to "losing more prople out the *back* door than we used to," but rather that "fewer people are coming in through the *front* door." No wonder he accuses his fellow Methodists of being "keepers of the aquarium" rather than "fishers of men."[42] The official United Methodist report, compiled by Warren Hartman, recognizes the "reordering of priorities" and "notable shifts in program emphases" particularly in the reduction of evangelism and Christian education.[43] The shift has been toward a relatively small group in the church "strongly supportive of all ministries of the church which are designed to bring about social and political changes in society."[44]

The United Presbyterian report is somewhat more complex because it raises a further question. It says, for example, "We conclude that the frequently argued theory that church involvement in social action has caused membership loss has at best a very limited validity."[45] This theme is picked up again in the Hartford Consortium study. However, their conclusion should not be taken at face value. It fails to make the important distinction between social *service* and social *action,* explained in Chapter 2. Lumping them together produces a distorted picture of reality. I will take this up again in Chapter 10, and I mention it here only to keep the record as complete as possible. In my opinion the Great Priority Shift was as much at the root of United Presbyterian losses as it was at the root of United Methodist losses.

Effectiveness in Social Ministries

At this point, some may think I am letting the cultural mandate slip. I want to clarify this with another important finding of the empirical studies of growth trends in the mainline denominations. The studies I have cited show fairly conclusively that a strong emphasis on the cultural mandate is not *in itself* a significant cause of membership decline. Churches can be very active socially and still enjoy vigorous membership growth *if they do not give the cultural mandate a higher priority than the evangelistic mandate.* However, if biblical priorities are reversed, not only will membership suffer, but so will social ministry. There is a spiritual magnetic force in the evangelistic mandate. I agree with Arthur Johnston, who says that "history seems to indicate that when the church has departed from its biblical ministry and functions, it has inevitably declined—both in spiritual power and in its influence upon the society it sought to uplift."[46]

Donald McGavran has frequently pointed out that Christian social causes "will not triumph unless we have great numbers of Christians."[47] This is the mathematical rationale for the priority of the evangelistic mandate. An experienced observer of the world ecumenical scene and one of the foremost historians of mission, Anglican Bishop Stephen Neill, observes that after more than a century it is possible on purely empirical grounds to pronounce a judgment on the relative position of the evangelistic and the cultural mandates. He is convinced from experience that "the order of priority must always be first conversion and then social change." Once the inner spiritual transformation has been cared for, "the problem of social change and uplift can be tackled with far greater prospects of success."[48]

A similar lesson has been learned by some leaders in those American mainline denominations that executed the Great Priority Shift in the 1960s. Mickey and Wilson report that the new bureaucrats expended vast sums of money on social programs "with little or no evidence concerning what was in fact actually accomplished." This would not have been so bad except for the subsequent sad spectacle of a "sense of impotence by the bureaucrat as he sees his elaborate programs quietly fold."[49] Perhaps they experienced a type of ecclesiastical Peter Principle when they faced the fact of their own incompetence at doing some things the church as such was never intended to do, at least as a first priority.

The trend had gone so far, according to Willimon and Wilson that "the pastor whose main interest was winning adherents to the church and nurturing them in the faith was perceived as not being devoted to the real mission of the church."[50] Not only is that giving priority to the cultural mandate (Position B on the mission issues spectrum), it approaches an eclipse of the evangelistic mandate (Position A). It is somewhat akin to the admitted position of some contemporary radical Christians in America who, as John Alexander says, "don't evangelize," even though they recognize the fact that they "can't do much because not enough people care about justice," and that "to have much effect, we have to add thousands and thousands of new recruits."[51] But the attitude that correcting social evils is the only, or even the primary task of the church (Positions A and B), Willimon and Wilson argue, "had a negative impact on the congregations, particularly the small churches. The effect was to communicate to such congregations that what they did, and often did very well, was not what the church was all about."[52]

The Evangelical Track Record

On the other side of the spectrum, evangelicals who typically adopt Positions D or E on the mission issues spectrum and unhesitatingly give priority to the evangelistic mandate do reasonably well at applying the cultural mandate. There certainly is a great deal of room for improvement. Nevertheless, David Bosch says that the judgment that evangelicals are "devoid of compassion and humanitarian concern," is incorrect. Rather, Bosch argues, "They often reveal greater sacrificial involvement with the existential needs of the victims of society—drug addicts, refugees, the exploited poor, the sick, and so forth—than many ecumenicals who malign them for their lack of social concern."[53]

Although we have insufficient research on this as yet, I am reasonably sure that the evangelical churches which give first priority to the evangelistic mandate, are in the long run actually doing more for the poor, the dispossessed, the exploited, and the marginal citizens of America's cities than the more liberal ones. Study a major metropolitan area and see where the physically and mentally handicapped are attending church in considerable numbers. Locate the churches that have active and growing programs for the deaf. Find the churches of the very poor and see if their theology is of the gospel-preaching, soul-saving variety or if it is oriented to the cultural mandate and concerned with saving the whales or boycotting grapes or outlawing nuclear energy. Most likely such a church will be of an evangelical nature.

The Gallup Organization recently took a national survey of the involvement evangelicals actually had in social work. They asked, "Do you, yourself, happen to be involved in any charity or social service activities, such as helping the poor, the sick or the elderly?" Evangelical Christians registered a 42 percent positive answer as against nonevangelical Christians with only 26 percent. Gallup concluded that this seems to "contradict one of the major criticisms of evangelicals—that they are socially apathetic and concerned only with the winning of souls."[54]

Soon after that the Gallup Organization, together with *Christianity Today,* took another poll. In it evangelicals scored significantly higher than the general public (almost twice as high) on the questions that reflected concern for the cultural mandate. Kenneth Wilson sums it up by saying:

Evangelicals, this survey indicates, have been underestimating their own regard for, support of, and participation in "social action." Indeed, the more frequently they read the Bible, attend church, tithe, witness, watch religious television, and listen to religious radio, the more committed they are to social involvement.[55]

George Hunter, speaking to his colleagues in the United Methodist Church, sums it up when he argues that it is "intrinsically worthwhile" to invite people to receive Christ. No external justification is needed for the evangelistic mandate. But, Hunter goes on to say, "it is also because I want *Christ's social cause to prevail* that I implore our once great

Church to once again make evangelical outreach an indispensable and ongoing priority in every congregation"[56] (italics added).

Notes

1. Edward R. Dayton and David A. Fraser, *Planning Strategies for World Evangelization* (Grand Rapids: Eerdmans, 1980), p. 66.
2. Tetsunao Yamamori, "Toward the Symbiotic Ministry," *Missiology: An International Review* 5, no. 3 (July 1977), p. 272.
3. Donald A. McGavran, *Understanding Church Growth*, rev. ed. (Grand Rapids: Eerdmans, 1980), p. 25.
4. John R. W. Stott, "The Battle for World Evangelism: An Open Response to Arthur Johnston," *Christianity Today* 23, no. 7 (January 5, 1979), p. 34.
5. McGavran, *Understanding Church Growth*, p. 25.
6. Ibid.
7. See Klaus Bockmuehl, *Evangelicals and Social Ethics: A Commentary on Article 5 of the Lausanne Covenant* (Downers Grove, IL: InterVarsity Press, 1979), p. 9.
8. Samuel Escobar, "Evangelism and Man's Search for Freedom, Justice and Fulfillment," in *Let the Earth Hear His Voice*, ed. J. D. Douglas (Minneapolis: World Wide Publications, 1975), pp. 307–308.
9. Orlando E. Costas, *The Integrity of Mission: The Inner Life and Outreach of the Church* (San Francisco: Harper & Row, 1979), p. 63.
10. Timothy L. Smith, *Revivalism and Social Reform in Mid-Nineteenth-Century America* (New York: Abingdon, 1957).
11. Compare, for example, Henry F. May, *Protestant Churches and Industrial America* (New York: Harper, 1949); and Charles Howard Hopkins, *The Rise of the Social Gospel in American Protestantism; 1865–1915* (New Haven: Yale University Press, 1940). A more balanced view is presented by John D. Woodbridge, Mark A. Noll, and Nathan O. Hatch, *The Gospel in America: Themes in the Story of America's Evangelicals* (Grand Rapids: Zondervan, 1979).
12. Martin E. Marty, jacket notes on paperback edition of Timothy L Smith, *Revivalism and Social Reform* (New York: Harper & Row, Harper Torchbook series, 1965).
13. Smith, *Revivalism and Social Reform* (1957), p. 8.

14. Ibid., p. 154.
15. Ibid., p. 149.
16. J. Edwin Orr, "Revival and Social Change," *Fides et Historia* 6, no. 2 (Spring 1974), pp. 1–12. See also "Evangelical Dynamic and Social Action," in *God, Man and Church Growth*, ed. Alan R. Tippett (Grand Rapids: Eerdmans, 1973), pp. 273–280.
17. Sherwood Wirt, *The Social Conscience of the Evangelical* (New York: Harper & Row, 1968), p. 33.
18. Donald McGavran, "Introduction to the 1972 Edition," in *The Conciliar-Evangelical Debate: The Crucial Documents 1964–1976*, ed. Donald McGavran (Pasadena: William Carey Library, 1977), p. 24.
19. Escobar, "Evangelism and Man's Search . . . ," p. 307.
20. Billy Graham, "Why Lausanne," in *Let The Earth Hear His Voice*, ed. J. D. Douglas (Minneapolis: World Wide Publications, 1975), p. 30.
21. Costas, *The Integrity of Mission*, p. 64.
22. W. Stanley Mooneyham, "Acts of the Holy Spirit '74," in *Let the Earth Hear His Voice*, ed. J. D. Douglas (Minneapolis: World Wide Publications, 1975), p. 445.
23. I can state the evangelical position with some empirical backing due to the 1979 *Christianity Today*-Gallup Organization poll, which indicated that "evangelicals maintain a high profile in giving world evangelism top priority, compared to other options," *Christianity Today*, July 18, 1980, p. 28.
24. James J. Montgomery and Donald A. McGavran, *The Discipling of a Nation*, (Santa Clara, CA: Global Church Growth Bulletin, 1980), p. 22.
25. A quotation from William H. Beahm, "Factors in the Development of the Student Volunteer Movement for Foreign Missions," unpublished Ph.D. dissertation, University of Chicago, 1941, p. 4, appearing in David M. Howard, *Student Power in World Missions* (Downers Grove, IL: InterVarsity Press, 1979), p. 99.
26. Ibid., p. 100.
27. Quoted in Timothy C. Wallstrom, *The Creation of a Student Movement to Evangelize the World: A History and Analysis of the Early Stages of the Student Volunteer Movement for Foreign Missions* (Pasadena: William Carey International University Press, 1980), p. 86.

28. Ibid., pp. 86–87.

29. See Arthur Johnston, *The Battle for World Evangelism* (Wheaton, IL: Tyndale, 1978), pp. 39–42.

30. Sidney E. Mead, "Denominationalism: The Shape of Protestantism in America," in *Denominationalism,* ed. Russel E. Richey (Nashville: Abingdon, 1977), pp. 70–105.

31. I know this because I happened to be one of those stressing the evangelistic mandate at Urbana '70. See John R. W. Stott, et. al., eds., *Christ the Liberator* (Downers Grove, IL: InterVarsity Press, 1971), pp. 93–102.

32. Dean R. Hoge and David A. Roozen, "Introduction," in *Understanding Church Growth and Decline: 1950–1978,* ed. Hoge and Roozen, (New York: Pilgrim, 1979), p. 17.

33. Robert K. Hudnut, *Church Growth Is Not the Point* (New York, Harper & Row, 1975), p. xi.

34. These categories are used extensively throughout Hoge and Roozen, *Understanding Church Growth and Decline.* They are introduced on pp. 38–41.

35. See Ibid., pp. 317–319, also Chapters 4, 8 and 10 in the same book.

36. Dean M. Kelley, *Why Conservative Churches Are Growing* (New York: Harper & Row, 1972), 1977.

37. Dean M. Kelley, "Commentary: Is Religion a Dependent Variable?" in *Understanding Church Growth and Decline*, ed. Hoge and Roozen, p. 338.

38. Richard G. Hutcheson, Jr., *Wheel Within the Wheel: Confronting the Management of Crisis of the Pluralistic Church* (Atlanta: John Knox, 1979), p. 132.

39. Jeffrey K. Hadden, *The Gathering Storm in the Churches* (New York: Anchor Books, 1969), p. 111.

40. William H. Willimon and Robert L. Wilson, *Preaching and Worship in the Small Church* (Nashville: Abingdon, 1980), p. 31.

41. Paul A. Mickey and Robert L. Wilson, *What New Creation?* (Nashville: Abingdon, 1977).

42. George Hunter, "Can United Methodists Recover Evangelism?" *Church Growth Bulletin* 13, no. 4 (March 1977), p. 111, 112.

43. Warren J. Hartman, *Membership Trends: A Study of Decline and Growth in the United Methodist Church 1949–1975* (Nashville: Discipleship Resources, 1976), p. 5.

44. Ibid., p. 47.

45. C. Edward Brubaker, Dean Hoge, Margaret Thomas, and John Dyble, *A Summary Report of the Committee on Membership Trends* (New York: United Presbyterian Church, 1976), p. 16.

46. Johnston, *The Battle for World Evangelism,* p. 246.

47. McGavran, *Understanding Church Growth,* p. 26.

48. Stephen Neill, *Call to Mission* (Philadelphia: Fortress Press, 1970), p. 56.

49. Mickey and Wilson, *What New Creation?* p. 23.

50. Willimon and Wilson, *Preaching and Worship*, p. 32.

51. John F. Alexander, "Evangelism?" *The Other Side* 16, no. 12 (December 1980), pp. 10–11.

52. Willimon and Wilson, *Preaching and Worship,* p. 32.

53. David J. Bosch, *Witness to the World: The Christian Mission in Theological Perspective* (Atlanta: John Knox Press, 1980), p. 33.

54. *Emerging Trends* (Princeton Religious Research Center) 1, no. 1 (January 1979), pp. 1–2.

55. Kenneth L. Wilson, "Concern for Society," *Christianity Today* 24, no. 17 (October 10, 1980), p. 41.

56. Hunter, "Can United Methodism Recover Evangelism?" p. 118.

CHAPTER 7

The Gospel, Conversion, and Ethical Awareness

A fairly widespread consensus among critics of the Church Growth Movement is that church growth promulgates "cheap grace." This arises from the critics' concern with the distinction made by church growth advocates between "discipling" and "perfecting." Robert Zuercher, for example, says, "Evangelicals and church growth advocates share an inadequate understanding of what it means to be saved."[1] For those who give priority to the evangelistic mandate and whose lives are dedicated to seeing the maximum number of people saved, such a statement is a significant challenge. Just what *does* it mean to be saved? How should the gospel message be addressed to a particular audience? What does it mean to repent and be converted? What are the ethical demands of the gospel as it is presented according to the Bible?

To set these answers in the proper context, it will be well first to understand the position of the Church Growth Movement.

McGavran on Discipling and Perfecting

In the book that sparked the Church Growth Movement twenty-five years ago, *The Bridges of God*, Donald McGavran proposed that a useful way of understanding the process of spreading the gospel around the world is to distinguish between discipling and perfecting. The two are never to be set in opposition to each other, but are, rather, two stages in the total process of Christianization. Those who see McGavran as an advocate of discipling, but not perfecting, are misinformed. He advocates both. He argues that these two stages in the growth of a church are "as distinct as stages in the growth of a child."[2] But if they are confused, the confusion is likely to stunt the growth of the church.

The concept of discipling was originally focused on the evangelization of a new people group. How can one tell when a given group is discipled? Negatively, McGavran says, "a people is discipled when the claim of polytheism, idolatry, fetishism or any other man-made religion on its corporate loyalty is eliminated." Positively, a people can be considered discipled when "its individuals feel united around Jesus Christ as Lord and Savior, believe themselves to be members of His Church, and realize that 'our folk are Christians, our book is the Bible, and our house of worship is the church.' "[3] When a people is discipled, the decision that an individual member of that group makes to become a Christian is a religious one, encumbered with a minimum of socio-cultural baggage.

If discipling is the first stage, the second is perfecting. Once a people recognizes that Jesus is Lord, members of the group begin to obey him. They learn more and more of his will and do it. The Holy Spirit is now present in their lives, and he makes their hearts tender for the good life of the kingdom of God. Perfecting is "bringing about an ethical change in the discipled group, an increasing achievement of a thoroughly Christian way of life for the community as a whole," the kind of holy living which includes "social, racial and political justice."[4] In his first published remarks on discipling and perfecting, McGavran affirms the cultural mandate.

While McGavran never minimizes the biblical emphasis that "the constant improvement of the existing Church is mandatory on all Christians" and that the church must strive to "rectify injustices in her neighborhoods and nations," he insists on a sequential order. "Undiscipled multitudes," he argues, "must be 'added to the Lord' before they can be perfected."[5] Reversing the order will retard the fulfillment of the evangelistic mandate. McGavran warns: "Discipling precedes perfecting. The second stage overlaps the first, but it cannot precede it without destroying it."[6]

Three Kinds of Discipling

The use of the verb "to disciple" and the noun "discipleship" has increased dramatically in Christian circles over the past two decades.[7] Bonhoeffer's *The Cost of Discipleship* gave the terms prominence as did the emphasis on a "ministry of discipleship" by the Navigators and other Christian organizations. In the Church Growth Movement the word has also expanded past McGavran's original meaning. The recent tendency toward confusion in use of the term provoked McGavran to refine the definition of discipling, breaking it down into three separate categories that he calls D_1, D_2, and D_3.[8]

D_1 is the original meaning of discipling. It refers to the "turning of a non-Christian society for the first time to Christ."[9] It is a collective concept closely related to the prominent church growth principle of the efficacy of people movements. A people group is said to be discipled in the D_1 sense of the word when "a large percentage of the citizens of a given people renounce all other gods, confess Christ as God and Savior, are baptized and organized into on-going congregations."[10] It is evident that some individuals in that discipled group may not yet be born again into the kingdom of God. If, for example, middle-class white Anglo-Americans of Los Angeles County can be considered a people group, they would currently be a discipled group—D_1, although there are many non-Christians among them.

D_2 signifies a meaning of discipling that has appeared in the Church Growth Movement more recently. It means "the turning of any *individual* from non-faith to faith in Christ and his incorporation in a church."[11] In fact, the D_2 discipling is the most prominent use of the term at this time. Most advocates and critics alike, when referring to the church growth use of discipling, mean D_2. Some of the more perceptive, such as John Howard Yoder, recognize that discipling refers either to "a person or a population."[12] But even when the distinction is understood, the criticisms are still directed against D_1 and D_2 alike.

The D_3 meaning of discipling has grown up mostly outside the Church Growth Movement. It means "teaching an existing Christian as much of the truths of the Bible as possible."[13] It is what church growth people call Christian nurture. It fits more into the stage of "perfecting" than "discipling." The Church Growth Movement is not inclined to oppose the use of "discipling" as D_3 so long as it is not confused with D_1 or D_2. The raw materials, so to speak, for D_1 and D_2 are unbelievers; the raw materials for D_3 are Christians.

It should be noted that the most common biblical use of disciple, or to make disciples, is the D_1 and/or D_2 sense, not the D_3. Disciple is a common biblical word, but it is used exclusively in the Gospels and

Acts, not once in the epistles. The Gospels and Acts are the books of the origin and growth of the Christian movement, while the Epistles are chiefly nurture books. A disciple in the New Testament is almost always a disciple of *Jesus,* although some disciples of John the Baptist and of the Pharisees are also mentioned. Timothy, for example, is not called a disciple of Paul in the Bible. When Paul first joined Timothy in Lystra, the account says that Timothy was already a disciple. Paul helped nurture Timothy, and today that ministry is called by many a "discipling ministry" (D3). But it must be understood that the Bible does not use discipling as Christian nurture, but rather as winning non-Christians to the faith (D1 or D2).

Why Critics Call It "Cheap Grace"

While the Church Growth Movement has found it useful to distinguish between discipling (D1 and D2) and perfecting (D3), some others are concerned that such a distinction may lead Christians to neglect their social and ethical responsibilities. David Bosch questions the kind of gospel preaching that does not inform unbelievers as to "their relationship to their fellow men, on racism, exploitation and blatant injustice." To leave these things out is "not to proclaim the gospel." It is "the quintessence of what Bonhoeffer has called 'cheap grace,'" according to Bosch.[14]

Lesslie Newbigin argues that "there cannot be a separation between conversion and obedience." He questions a form of evangelism which produces "baptized, communicant, Bible-reading and zealous Christians," people "committed to church growth" who, at the same time, are not equally committed to "radical obedience to the plain teaching of the Bible on the issues of human dignity and social justice." If evangelism does not bring forth people who enter the struggles against the "big ethical issues" such as "racism" and "militant sectarianism" and "blind support of oppressive economic and political systems," Newbigin doubts its integrity. When the evangelist announces to an unbeliever what it requires to be saved, the "original announcement of the gospel" must include spelling out Jesus' teaching on social concerns. "Can there be any real 'discipling,'" asks Newbigin, "which does not include as an essential element the ethical commitments which McGavran puts into the category of 'perfecting?'"[15]

These critics focus the problem on the social implications of the gospel and how much its initial presentation needs to include issues of social ethics. Samuel Escobar argues that "A spirituality without discipleship in the daily social, economic and political aspects of life is religiosity and not Christianity." He feels that the Church Growth Movement may exhibit an "eagerness for quantitative growth of the church" that would "render us silent about the whole counsel of God." Escobar wants to make sure that a person who "is exploiting others and swindling them" repents of this and changes his ways if he becomes a Christian.[16]

Making a distinction between discipling and perfecting appears to some, particularly to strong advocates of Christian social responsibility, as "lack of integrity"[17] at best and as "heresy" or "grace without discipleship"[18] at worst. Orlando Costas argues that the biblical understanding of conversion is limited when church growth theology "pushes the issue of ethical change to a post-conversion stage."[19] Robert Evans agrees: "The distinction and prioritizing of discipling over perfecting violates the biblical understanding of conversion and straitjackets the perception of religious experience." It contradicts the New Testament teaching on conversion, Evans argues, when we "attempt to make the gospel as attractive and palatable as possible."[20]

"Obey Everything I Have Commanded You"

Obviously the issues raised by those who advocate holistic evangelism or who give priority to the cultural mandate touch crucial questions of New Testament theology. They are raising questions of salvation and conversion and repentance. They have taken up the expression "cheap grace," which is useful rhetoric, but not a biblical term. I suspect that while rejecting "cheap grace" they might at the same time be advocating "exorbitant grace," and end up with a spiritual exploitation of gospel preaching. Socio-economic exploitation certainly needs to be avoided by Christians, but spiritual exploitation may be equally dangerous. When suggesting that the adoption of certain socio-political views is a condition of receiving God's grace, overpricing the gospel becomes a distinct threat. Evangelism can be manipulated as a useful means of promulgating certain socio-political views. The gospel is then in danger of being treated as an ideology. Here it is well to look at one of the key biblical passages that deals with the issue: The Great Commission (Matt. 28: 19–20, GNB):

Go, then, to all peoples everywhere and make them my disciples: baptize them in the name of the Father, the Son, and the Holy Spirit, and teach them to obey everything I have commanded you.

Critics of the church growth principle of discipling and perfecting frequently refer to this text, particularly the last line, "teach them to obey everything I have commanded you." Orlando Costas argues it is improper to separate the first part, "make disciples," as discipling, from the second part "teach them," as perfecting. "It forces on that passage an interpretation contrary to the structure of the sentence that begins in verse 19."[21]

In his exposition of Matthew 28:19–20, Jim Wallis argues that modern evangelism "takes the liberty to conceal the cost of discipleship" and that it all but obliterates "the radical demands of Christ" that are included in the "teaching them to observe all things." In his effort to raise the price of discipleship, Wallis would include the kind of fundamental change which would "disrupt the social order" and "threaten the power of the state" and "challenge the needs and character of the economic system."[22] Robert Evans warns against the "selective interpretation" of the Great Commission, which "puts stress on 'making disciples' rather than 'sharing the fullness of the Gospel.'" Evans feels that we need to present, with the gospel, all of Christ's teaching, "including his demands of humility, loving our enemies, forgiving seven times seventy, and selling what we have to give to the poor."[23]

I both agree and disagree with the critics. I agree that the Great Commission is a unitary whole. The imperative sense in the passage is "make disciples," while the rest describes activities without which disciples will not be made. I agree that if an unbeliever is not taught "to obey everything Jesus has commanded you" that person cannot become a disciple (D2). Now what exactly does this mean?

Obedience Is the Key

The answer can be found in an exhaustive exegetical and missiological study of the Matthew 28 passage done by Dennis Oliver, then professor of New Testament at Canadian Theological College. Oliver argues that the Greek text allows, as the object of the verb "teaching" *(didaskontes)*, either the "all things" or the "to obey." In his judgment, the "to obey" should be understood as the object of "teaching them." He says that it "mistakes the fundamental nature of what it means to become a disciple" if the "all things," rather than "to obey," is taken as the object of "teaching them." Oliver contends that "great commission teaching" is the teaching "designed to produce disciples," but that is not "to follow up Christians in their ongoing discipleship."[24] Oliver regards the basis of one's first becoming a disciple as being the relationship to a person, namely Jesus Christ, more than the acceptance of a detailed ethical code. The essence of this part of the Great Commission "is first and foremost calling them *to obey,* that is, instructing them in the necessity of an obedient will."[25]

Oliver's exegesis avoids the two extremes of "cheap grace" and "exorbitant grace." It denies, for example, the rather common evangelical teaching that you can accept Jesus as your Savior and be saved today, but later you should also accept him as your Lord and obey him. Accepting Jesus as Lord, in my view, is not part of perfecting, but of discipling itself. No one can become a disciple of Jesus Christ without first agreeing to obey him. If you doubt that Jesus is your Lord, I doubt that you are Jesus' disciple. This is not "cheap grace"; far from it. It is turning from idols to serve the living and true God. It is a lifelong relationship with a new person, Jesus Christ. It is becoming a "new creature in Christ."

But neither is it "exorbitant grace." It does not argue that in order to be saved one must agree to an ethical code. Deciding on a position that will "disrupt the social order" and "threaten the power of the state" is not a condition of salvation in any teaching of Jesus and the apostles. Relationship and obedience to a person certainly is. This is not to deny that as new disciples mature in their obedience to their Lord they might honestly conclude that full obedience to Jesus demands taking a public stand against their government, developing a Christian counterculture in the urban slums, joining the guerrillas, or picketing against nuclear energy. But none of this is a precondition of salvation or a price tag on God's grace.

The Postponement of Ethical Awareness

I am quite aware that there are other ways of interpreting the process of salvation. Those who suggest that the price of grace needs to be raised are disturbed at the tendency of church growth people toward the "postponement of ethical awareness." They want much more ethical content in the initial preaching of the gospel than evangelicals and especially church growth advocates, think needs to be included.

The argument is not *whether* the preaching of the gospel ought to have ethical content. As we will see in analyzing repentance and conversion, no one is arguing against ethical content in preaching. The question concerns the *amount*. How much ethical teaching is necessary for a person to be saved?

John Howard Yoder sharpens the issue by suggesting that converts should not get ethical surprises after they become Christians. He asks, "Assuming that nurture is separate from evangelism and must come second, how long can it wait?" If it waits too long, Yoder argues, you undercut the validity of the evangelism task. To illustrate, he chooses a hypothetical case in "racist Mississippi." He says that the church growth position is that "you can only win people if you accept racism. You can only win whites if you accept their racism, and you can only win blacks if you are just as black." Once you have them in the church you can tell them that racism is wrong. But he says that if he were the convert "I would think the missionary was cheating if he told me after I was baptized that I had to love the blacks when he had not wanted to tell me before."[26] In other words, Yoder objects to the postponement of ethical awareness from the discipling to the perfecting stage. He wants ethical awareness at the point of discipling.

What Is Repentance?

Some misunderstanding has crept into the discussion of the church growth position on repentance. For example, Robert Zuercher says, "In church growth thinking, conversion can be separated from repentance."[27] This is inaccurate. I know of no church growth advocate who would separate repentance and conversion. "Repent," as J. Edwin Orr says, is "the first word of the gospel."[28] The message, "Repent for the kingdom of heaven is at hand" was preached by John the Baptist, Jesus, and the apostles. At Pentecost, when the unbelievers asked Peter what to do, he said, "Repent" (Acts 2:38).

But repentance is not the only word which must not be separated from conversion. In fact, three words, to be converted *(epistrepho)*, to repent *(metanoeo)*, and to believe *(pisteuo)* are closely associated with each other and with salvation. *Epistrepho* and *metanoeo* both mean to turn oneself around, and either of them could be translated "be converted." The King James Version translates Peter's words as "repent [*metanoeo*] and be converted [*epistrepho*]" (Acts 3:19). Jesus said, "Repent ye, [*metaneo*] and believe [*pisteuo*] the gospel" (Mark 1:15). *Epistrepho* always includes faith *(pisteuo),* so it is the broadest concept.[29]

To put it in clear English, conversion always involves repentance and faith, as in John Stott's "biblical equation": repentance + faith = conversion.[30]

Repentance, then, means turning, and so does conversion. This turning is both turning *from* and turning *to.* True conversion involves turning from the old way of life to a new way of life, from the power of darkness to the power of light, from self to God, from Satan to Jesus. It is turning from what enslaves to what liberates. It involves turning from unbelief to believing that Jesus is Lord and making a lifetime, unconditional commitment to whatever that might imply in the future. This is how the Church Growth Movement now understands, and so far as I know, has always understood salvation.

Why, then, is there a debate? It is because of differing views of what the specific *content* of that turning involves. The tendency, among those deeply committed to a Christian cause other than getting people saved, is to load their favorite cause on repentance and say that this is what repentance means. Much criticism has come to Campus Crusade for Christ, because of their *Four Spiritual Laws* booklet, which is used for leading people to Christ. It has been maligned as "easy believism," and "simple formulas" and "gospel without repentance." However, not only has God wonderfully used this booklet in the salvation of countless thousands of people, but Law Four clearly teaches repentance as we have defined it: "Receiving Christ involves turning to God from self (repentance) and trusting Christ to come into our lives. . . ." What irritates the critics, as I understand it, is not that repentance is absent, but that it is so general. Padilla, for example, says that true repentance must be "more than generalizations—it has to do with specific acts of self-sacrifice in concrete situations."[31]

In looking at specifics we begin to see the favorite causes promoted by some evangelists. A member of the Woman's Christian Temperance Union, for example, might say that repentance means turning away from alcoholic beverages to total abstinence. A supporter of the Equal Rights Amendment might say that repentance is to turn away from the exploitation of women to women's liberation. Husbands whose wives now do the cooking and change the diapers, they might argue, should not consider themselves truly converted until they agree to share those labors. Western missionaries might preach that an African man married to four wives needs to turn away from three of them before God will accept him. Whenever the specific ethical cause of the evangelist is promoted in the preaching of the gospel there is a risk of overpricing the gospel and ending up with "exorbitant grace."

Conversion and Ethics in Biblical Times

The tendency to load the gospel with excessive ethical content is not new in church history. Michael Green traces the change which took place in the early church. He argues that in the early days "baptism was administered straight away on profession of faith and repentance." He cites the Philippian jailer who was baptized "without delay or catechesis," as were Paul, the Corinthians, and the Ethiopian eunuch. The book of Acts contains many conversion experiences that record no ethical content at all in connection with the gospel, although we of course do not have a verbatim transcript of what was said. Behavioral conditions as qualifications for baptism began to be prescribed, and by the end of the second century there were in some places "detailed ethical regulations and a three year period of instruction" as prerequisites to baptism. At that point, Green says, "We have certainly traveled a long way from the New Testament."[32] Many church leaders today have traveled a similar distance.

In the New Testament the evangelistic mandate was held high. Paul writes to Timothy, "This is good and it pleases God our Savior, who wants everyone to be *saved* and to come to know the truth" (1 Tim. 2:3–4, GNB). This word "save" is important. Paul says of the gospel: "It is God's power to *save* all who believe" (Rom. 1:16, GNB). A faithful church, such as the one in Jerusalem recorded in Acts 2 had this experience: "And every day the Lord added to their group those who were being *saved*" (Acts 2:47, GNB).

Peter was sent to the house of Cornelius to "speak words to you by which you and all your house will be *saved.*" What were Peter's words? Did he tell Cornelius that since he was a centurion in the army of Rome which had oppressed the Jewish people, one of the ethical demands of repenting and being saved was to stop representing Roman oppression? John Howard Yoder might have asked, "In oppressive Caesarea, named after the oppressor himself, can you accept their oppression?" Peter did not bring up the issue as far as we know. He said that everyone who believes in Jesus "will have his sins forgiven through the power of his name" (Acts 10:43, GNB). These sins were not specifically enumerated. No ethical code was drawn up that Cornelius had to affirm before he could be converted. He was simply to turn from his lord, who was Caesar, and assert that Jesus was Lord.

Many true disciples of Jesus Christ, mentioned as such in the New Testament, were far from being perfect. The Colossians, for example, were presumably true disciples; Paul called them, "God's people in Colossae, who are our faithful brothers in union with Christ" (Col. 1:2, GNB). Yet Paul has to tell them to "put to death" such things as "sexual immorality, indecency, lust, evil passions, and greed" (Col. 3:5, GNB). I can hear some people shouting "cheap grace" now. "How can you be a faithful brother in union with Christ" and have lust and greed? Even the eleven who were with Jesus through his earthly ministry and who were witnesses to his resurrection and to whom Jesus gave the Great Commission were not perfect. They went so far as to doubt Jesus (Matt. 28:17), yet they were considered bona fide disciples. They were brought to him not by "cheap grace" but through the grace that is ready to pardon, to forgive sins, and that costs nothing at all. God brought them into his family not by *cheap grace* but by *free grace*.

In the early stages of growth it is sometimes difficult to tell true disciples from counterfeits. But that judgment is not usually the responsibility of the evangelist, who is concerned more with discipling than perfecting. Jesus said that the kingdom of heaven is like a man who sowed good seed in his field. Later the enemy sowed some tares. The master told the servants not to bother the tares, that they would all be taken care of in the harvest (Matt. 13:24–30). There is some risk in keeping the ethical content of discipling to a minimum, in preaching free grace. But to me there seems a greater risk in prematurely trying to uproot the tares and destroying some of the wheat in the process.

I know of many evangelists who do not insist, as a prerequisite to salvation, that unbelievers agree to tithe their income. But after they become Christians they learn that their new Lord expects them to tithe their income. This is not bothersome to the average Christian. Initial repentance and conversion means turning to Christ as the Lord of Life, and when, over a lifetime of discipleship, the Lord speaks and brings new requirements to their attention, they are cordially accepted. Taking the step of tithing is an advance in Christian obedience, more a part of perfecting than of discipling.

The Point of Guilt

If some specific, concrete content must be present in preaching the gospel, at what is it to be directed? This is largely a question of the ethical agenda. In other words, in presenting the gospel, is it more proper to work from the ethical agenda of the evangelist or the ethical agenda of the hearer? Many of those who use the rhetoric "cheap grace" tend to bring their own agendas—open or hidden—to the presentation of the gospel. They tend to superimpose their own ethical agendas on their hearers. I object to this as a kind of unintentional oppression. It tends spiritually to dehumanize people. Repentance is necessary for conversion, but what, specifically, an unbeliever must turn from as he or she turns to God should be determined by what the Holy Spirit has been doing in the life of the hearer, not in the life of the preacher.

For one thing, not all unbelievers whom the Holy Spirit has prepared to hear the gospel are under the burden of sin, as such. This comes as a surprise to many, but, as several missiologists have pointed out in recent years, not all human beings happen to be members of a guilt-oriented culture, as most of us Westerners are. Being guilty of sin is so common to us that we leave little room for other worldviews. For example, Hans Kasdorf argues that conversion experiences in guilt cultures are quite different from those in "animistic fear cultures" or "tribal shame cultures." "In the one," Kasdorf says, "conversion frees man from existential guilt, in the other from haunting fear, and in still another from defeating shame."[33] The way that authentic discipling takes place in each context depends largely on the dynamics from the *inside,* not the *outside.*

To be specific, Joseph Cooke, says that the Thai person "is very unlikely to find himself burdened with conviction of sin in the theological sense." The Thai feel "little or no anguish over the guilt of sin" or "religious hunger for forgiveness." For that reason the Pauline doctrines of sin, guilt and atonement "have singularly little effect upon the Thai." In order to reach the Thai, Cooke argues, the first thing we need to do is to "temper our contempt for a morality governed largely by shame."[34] The preaching of "an agenda for biblical people," for example, would predictably do little to fulfill either the evangelistic or the cultural mandate among the Thai. Wallis' agenda may be an agenda appropriate for *some* biblical people, but it is a mistake (common among monocultural persons) to universalize it.

For others, such as Africans in Burundi, using the story of Elijah's confrontation with the prophets of Baal may be a better biblical starting point than the Sermon on the Mount for the purpose of making disciples. The Bugongo people, as Donald Hohensee tells it, lived in fear of evil spirits. The preacher did not come with his own agenda of the virtues of monogamy, or to inform them they had been crushed under the heel of Western colonialism. The Bugongo agenda was quite different. They wanted to be liberated, not so much from colonialism as from evil spirits. So the missionary got a sledge hammer and broke to pieces one of their sacred rocks to prove that his God was more powerful than their gods. Once that was done, the demand of repentance was to turn from their charms and fetishes and burn them up. Those who did were delivered by the power of God. They believed that Jesus was more powerful than the spirits, and they were thereby discipled. But they were not perfected. Once they burned their fetishes, they began a long process of learning what the ethical implications of their new faith were.[35] They did not feel that the missionary had cheated them.

Receptor-Oriented Ethics

Even in a more familiar Western guilt culture, the point of guilt is better determined by the ethical agenda of the hearer than that of the preacher. Missiologists are calling it "receptor-oriented ethics."[36] Lesslie Newbigin raises the right question when he asks, "Who has the right to decide the ethical content of conversion at any time or place—the evangelist or the convert?" Newbigin's answer is that a "virus of legalism" can enter the picture if the evangelist presumes he or she has the right and "can tell the potential convert what the ethical content of conversion will be."[37]

The alternative is to trust the Holy Spirit so to work in the life of the unbeliever that a specific point of guilt can be established. There are two things to keep in mind here. The first is that the point of guilt, so called, may not involve guilt at all. We have already mentioned that it might be a point of shame in some cultures or a point of fear in others. Perhaps a more general term would be "point of need." An evangelist can assume that every person whom the Holy Spirit has brought under conviction and prepared to receive the message of salvation has some point of need which should be addressed by the preacher.

The second thing to keep in mind is that this point of need may be active and conscious or latent and subconscious. It was conscious, for example, in the case of the woman caught in adultery in John 8. Adultery was probably not her only sin. But it clearly was her point of guilt, and at that point Jesus dealt with her and forgave her. When it is more latent, the Holy Spirit may often use the word of the evangelist to bring the specific guilt or other need to the surface.

I see this as what happened on the day of Pentecost. It is unlikely that the Jews in Jerusalem were going around wringing their hands and having bad dreams about Jesus' death. Their guilt was latent. But in Peter's sermon he perceived that killing the Messiah was their point of guilt, and he preached to it. "You killed him," he said (Acts 2:23, GNB). "This Jesus, whom you have crucified, is the one that God has made Lord and Messiah" (Acts 2:36, GNB). As a result "they were deeply troubled" (Acts 2:37, GNB) and three thousand of them were saved. Peter did not tell them to sell their goods to feed the poor; this they learned and practiced *after* they had become disciples of Jesus and were in the perfecting stage (Acts 4:32). Peter was not guilty of ethical overload or "exorbitant grace."

On this issue, John Howard Yoder asks if there is "some concept of what might be called a moral 'curriculum,' which distinguishes between what you learn first and what you learn later?" Or again, "Is there some scale of moral priority issues, some of which are indispensable and others dispensable?"[38] I think that, yes, such priority issues exist, but no generalized list of them can ever be compiled. In each specific evangelistic event the precise "moral curriculum" must be discerned by the evangelist on the terms of the receptors, not from a predetermined list of sins. I think Carl Henry overstates his case by insisting that "social concern is an indispensable ingredient of the evangelistic message."[39] Social concern is certainly indispensable in the perfecting stage of Christian nurture, but it is irrelevant to receptor-oriented evangelism in a large number (perhaps the majority) of cases.

My own point of guilt concerned drunkenness, which to me at that moment was a highly personal affair. When I repented I specifically turned from drunkenness. But I was also a gambler, and no one told me then that I had to give up gambling in order to be a Christian. I found that out later and gave it up, but I did not feel cheated because no one had given me that information before. Later I found out I couldn't cheat on exams. Jesus was my new Lord and I wanted to obey him. Day by

day and week by week, *after I had become a disciple,* I discovered new
areas of obedience. I even gave up dancing. Social concern came much
later, but it was far from an "indispensable ingredient" in my salvation
experience.

Lists of ethical agendas predetermined by the evangelist are difficult
enough to draw up in one's own culture, to say nothing about the
infinitely more complex cross-cultural situations in the world. Missiologists have shown that great sensitivity is needed even to determine what
is concrete sin in a different culture. Wayne Dye argues that "in another
culture the differences between their convictions and mine will be much
greater" than between individuals in my own culture. "I should speak
out about principles, or better yet, encourage them to read what the
Bible says about a topic."[40]

Some read the story of the rich young ruler and do not realize that
Jesus was speaking to a point of guilt. They generalize and make selling
one's goods to feed the poor a condition of everyone's salvation regard-
less of their personal point of need. It is a common mistake of those who
fail to understand the biblical distinction between the two stages of
Christianization, discipling and perfecting. It is "exorbitant grace."

Prophets and Evangelists

Many of those who criticize the distinction between discipling and
perfecting are themselves prophets. As such they don't always recognize
another important distinction, that between prophets and evangelists.
In 1972, when the protests against the Viet Nam war were at a peak,
Billy Graham was publicly scolded because in his evangelistic preaching
he did not condemn America's bombing of Hanoi. His response was that
God had not called him to be an Old Testament prophet but rather a
New Testament evangelist. This was not an acceptable answer to the
Christian social activists of the day, and it was used widely against
Graham and his ministry. They believed that he should have introduced
more prophetic content into his evangelistic preaching.

The accusation was both unfair and unbiblical. There is a significant
biblical distinction between prophets and evangelists. They are listed
separately in Ephesians 4:11. They are given different spiritual gifts.
They make contributions to the body of Christ as distinct as the diges-
tive and reproductive systems in the human body. A prophet is not an
evangelist. A prophet's audience is believers—the people of God. There

are some exceptions in the Old Testament, but very few. An evangelist's audience is unbelievers. Prophets are part of the perfecting stage. Evangelists deal with discipling. Prophets tell God's people what their ethical agendas *ought* to be. Evangelists ask unbelievers what their ethical agendas *are.* As Howard Snyder says, "evangelism is good news and prophecy is bad news."[41] Bombing Hanoi did not happen to be a prominent issue of guilt on the ethical agendas of many who were in Billy Graham's crusade audiences. For Billy Graham to include it as a part of the price tag of grace would have been to preach a gospel of "exorbitant grace." He is right to invite the people to come "Just as I am without one plea."

The Church Growth Movement believes there is a middle road between "cheap grace" and "exorbitant grace." The Church Growth Movement refuses to endorse a gospel of legalism or salvation by works. As Montgomery and McGavran say, "The Lord and His apostles did not build around the Church a six-foot wall and admit only those spiritual athletes who could jump over it."[42] But, disciples must acknowledge both in word and in deed that Jesus is their Lord. Faith without works is dead. By their fruits you shall know Jesus' disciples. Many who say "Lord, Lord" will not enter the kingdom of heaven. Once an unbeliever becomes a disciple, the fruits worthy of repentance will be produced. Such fruits, however, are not in unbelievers and will not be seen until they are discipled. As disciples grow from babes in Christ to the fullness of the stature of Christ, they will obey their Lord, become responsible members of the community of the king and do their part to fulfill both the evangelistic and the cultural mandates in their world.

Notes

1. Robert Zuercher, "Growing a Church," *Third Way* 4, no. 3 (England, March 1980), p. 31.
2. Donald A. McGavran, *Understanding Church Growth*, rev. ed. (Grand Rapids: Eerdmans, 1980), p. 170.
3. Donald McGavran, *The Bridges of God* (New York: Friendship Press, 1955), p. 14.
4. Ibid., p. 15.
5. McGavran, *Understanding Church Growth*, p. 170.
6. Donald A. McGavran, "Discipling Precedes Perfecting," *Church Growth Bulletin* 2, no. 6 (July 1966), p. 168.

7. Actually, "to disciple" was not altogether a new verb in 1955. It is listed as archaic in the *Oxford Universal Dictionary* of 1955 and, in the Random House *American College Dictionary* of 1956, as "to convert into a disciple."

8. McGavran's original essay on the subject appeared in the May, 1979, *Church Growth Bulletin:* "How About that New Verb To Disciple," See also James H. Montgomery and Donald A. McGavran, *The Discipling of a Nation* (Santa Clara, CA: Global Church Growth Bulletin, 1980), p. 18; and *Understanding Church Growth*, pp. 170–171.

9. McGavran, *Understanding Church Growth*, p. 170.

10. Montgomery and McGavran, *The Discipling of a Nation*, p. 18.

11. McGavran, *Understanding Church Growth*, p. 170.

12. John H. Yoder, "Church Growth Issues in Theological Perspective," in *The Challenge of Church Growth: A Symposium*, ed. Wilbert R. Shenk (Elkhart, IN: Institute of Mennonite Studies, 1973), p. 32.

13. McGavran, *Understanding Church Growth*, p. 170.

14. David J. Bosch, *Witness to the World: The Christian Mission in Theological Perspective* (Atlanta: John Knox Press, 1980), p. 206.

15. Lesslie Newbigin, *The Open Secret* (Grand Rapids: Eerdmans, 1978), pp. 150–151.

16. Samuel Escobar, "Evangelism and Man's Search for Freedom, Justice and Fulfillment," in *Let the Earth Hear His Voice*, ed. J. D. Douglas, (Minneapolis: World Wide Publications, 1975), p. 310.

17. Zuercher, "Growing a Church," p. 32.

18. Jim Wallis, *Agenda for Biblical People* (San Francisco: Harper & Row, 1976), p. 47.

19. Orlando E. Costas, *The Church and Its Mission: A Shattering Critique from the Third World* (Wheaton, IL: Tyndale, 1974), p. 143.

20. Robert A. Evans, "Recovering the Church's Transforming Middle: Theological Reflections on the Balance Between Faithfulness and Effectiveness," in *Understanding Church Growth and Decline: 1950–1978*, ed. Dean R. Hoge and David A. Roozen (New York: Pilgrim, 1979), pp. 302–303.

21. Costas, *The Church and Its Mission*, p. 142. At times, Donald McGavran has suggested a distinction between the "first half of the Great Commission" and the "second half." See *Understanding*

Church Growth, p. 439; *The Bridges of God*, p. 15. My view is that Costas' exegesis is sound, although his conclusions are not, and that the distinction between discipling and perfecting can be defended biblically in a more convincing way without postulating a separation of the passage into two halves.

22. Wallis, *Agenda for Biblical People*, pp. 23–24.
23. Evans, "Recovering the Church's Transforming Middle," p. 294.
24. Dennis Oliver, "Make Disciples," Doctor of Missiology dissertation, Pasadena: Fuller Seminary School of World Mission, 1973, p. 20.
25. Ibid.
26. Yoder, "Church Growth Issues," pp. 37–38.
27. Zuercher, "Growing a Church," p. 31.
28. J. Edwin Orr, "The First Word of the Gospel," unpublished.
29. See *The New International Dictionary of New Testament Theology*, Vol. 1, ed. Colin Brown (Grand Rapids: Zondervan, 1975), pp. 353–359.
30. John R. W. Stott, *Christian Mission in the Modern World* (Downers Grove, IL: InterVarsity Press, 1975), p. 114.
31. René Padilla, "Evangelism and the World," in *Let the Earth Hear His Voice*, ed. J. D. Douglas (Minneapolis: World Wide Publications, 1975), p. 128.
32. Michael Green, *Evangelism in the Early Church* (Grand Rapids: Eerdmans, 1970), pp. 154–155.
33. Hans Kasdorf, *Christian Conversion in Context* (Scottdale: PA: Herald Press, 1980), p. 113.
34. Joseph R. Cooke, "The Gospel for Thai Ears," unpublished paper presented to a group at the Consultation on World Evangelization, Pattaya, Thailand, 1980, p. 2.
35. Donald Hohensee, " 'Power Encounter' Paves the Way for Church Growth in Africa," *Evangelical Missions Quarterly* 15, no. 2 (April 1979), pp. 85–87.
36. For a technical discussion of receptor-oriented communication see Charles H. Kraft, *Christianity in Culture, A Study in Dynamic Biblical Theologizing in Cross-Cultural Perspective* (Maryknoll, NY: Orbis, 1979), pp. 147–166, 214, 299, 394.
37. Newbigin, *The Open Secret*, p. 152.
38. Yoder, "Church Growth Issues," p. 36.
39. Carl F. H. Henry, "The Purpose of God," in *The New Face of*

Evangelicalism 1. C. René Padilla (Downers Grove, IL: InterVarsity Press, 1976), p. 29.

40. T. Wayne Dye, "Toward a Cross-Cultural Definition of Sin," *Missiology: An International Review* 4, no. 1 (January 1976), p. 34.

41. Howard A. Snyder, *The Community of the King* (Downers Grove, IL: InterVarsity Press, 1977), p. 99.

42. Montgomery and McGavran, *The Discipling of a Nation*, p. 165.

CHAPTER 8

How Methodology Influences Social Perspectives

The Church Growth Movement has not yet paid enough attention to a critical self-assessment of its methodological presuppositions. Critics of the movement have raised important questions that need to be addressed. This chapter is directed to some of the pertinent issues, but acknowledges that much more reflection is necessary for the Church Growth Movement to develop sufficiently solid methodological and theological foundations.

Waking Up to Methodology

Samuel Escobar has prompted reflection with his concern that in the Church Growth Movement "the totality of the biblical message is reduced and partialized at the service of an ideology." He feels that church growth has "postulated a key to read the missionary situation and Christian history" (that is, a paradigm) and has called in "American functionalist social sciences" to buttress its case. Worse yet, he argues that "McGavran's followers do not appear to be aware of their method- ology."[1] Escobar, for reasons I have pointed out in the Introduction, has made a special cause of uncovering weaknesses in the teaching of church growth and thereby has forced church growth advocates to reexamine some of their positions. This has been very helpful, on the whole.

The formal definition of church growth, given in Chapter 4, affirms that church growth "strives to combine the eternal theological princi- ples of God's Word" with "the best insights of contemporary social and behavioral sciences." Some observers feel that church growth has too much social science and too little theology. David Hesselgrave says that "it is all too easy to fall into the trap of allowing our contemporary culture and experience to determine our understanding of the biblical text."[2] Roger Greenway's opinion is that the theological bases of church growth "have been worked out *after* the methodological insights and mission principles were arrived at through field observation and experience."[3]

It is true that the one social science providing the greatest input not only to the church growth field, but to missiology itself, is cultural anthropology. Orlando Costas may be right in suggesting that it has "overly depended on anthropology" and done too little with contemporary sociology and social psychology. He is dated, however, when he suggests (in 1974) that church growth "has hardly related to communication theory."[4] Since then Charles Kraft's epochal *Christianity in Culture* has been published, examining communication theory in detail within the context of missiology and, in particular, providing a reference point for the Church Growth Movement.[5] It remains true that cultural anthropology is the key social science in the church growth paradigm. Kraft's work, along with that of Paul G. Hiebert, has greatly helped church growth advocates become more conscious of their methodology.

Keeping the Balance: The "Ought" and the "Is"

A central concern of the Church Growth Movement is to be faithful to the Scriptures. I agree when Arthur Johnston suggests that the continuing development of the Church Growth Movement "will not depend as much upon its research into the social and behavioral sciences as in its deeper and deepening theological insights." Such insights must be based on (1) "the solid bedrock of a 'verbally inerrant' Scripture" and (2) a subordination of the social sciences to "the rigorous evaluations of the Scripture."[6] The authority of the Bible must be upheld. That is why the definition of church growth does not fail to mention as a starting point "the eternal theological principles of God's word." It would be a mistake, as Harvie Conn warns, to fall into the trap of continuing to develop theory "on a purely functional level, without the operative judgment of biblical theology."[7]

The crucial issue is not to choose sides between the Bible on the one hand and social science on the other, but to strike a satisfactory balance between the two. The pendulum may well swing too far in one direction, but eventually it can come to a center position of neither overemphasis nor neglect. It may be helpful to think of the biblical side as theological (the "ought") and the social science as phenomenological (the "is"). A diagram with three positions (X, Y, and Z) will help conceptualize the issues:

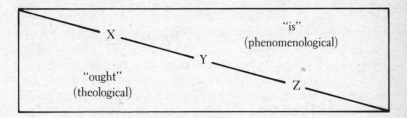

The "Ought"-"Is" Spectrum

Position X is mostly "ought" with little or no "is," while Position Z is the reverse. Position Y is a balanced view, the view that the Church Growth Movement strives to maintain.

In order to do this, however, it may have been necessary in recent years to allow the pendulum to swing slightly toward Position Z. One reason is that most contemporary Christian leaders have been professionally trained in seminary and Bible school around Position X. As a result they are somewhat uncomfortable with the phenomenological approach to reality. The tools of the social sciences seem at best strange and at worst a threat. Absolutes are more comfortable to work with than relatives. Graduate programs are based on library research rather than on field research. Schools of theology are suspicious of the academic integrity of schools of missiology. Philosophy enjoys a more hallowed tradition in the world of scholarship than the upstart, sociology. Is not theology the "queen of the sciences?" Apologetics prefers dogma to hypothesis. Findings are more normative than descriptive.

Adding Phenomenology to Theology

A growing number of practicing ministers are raising questions as to whether this kind of Position X training has maximally equipped them for ministry. They comment that their professors seemed to be training them to be professional scholars rather than professional ministers. They have found, somewhat to their consternation, that the people in the pews were not much interested in some of the term paper topics they had slaved over in seminary.

The Church Growth Movement recognizes this situation both on the mission field (where not only missionaries but many national leaders trained by missionaries are at Position X), and in North American churches. The Church Growth Movement is making an effort to help Christian leaders move from X to Y. This is why church growth has asked for and received help from the social sciences, mainly cultural anthropology. Many who have been firmly rooted in theology have been helped to combine new phenomenological insights and increase their effectiveness both in reaching unbelievers with the gospel and in nurturing Christian people. It has helped them to be goal-oriented rather than exclusively process-oriented and to move from a proclaimer-centered message to a listener-centered message. Thus it has introduced a humanizing dimension into ministry. The minister, rather than approaching people with preconceived ideas of what their needs ought to be, finds it more fruitful to make the effort to discover what their *felt* needs really are. This involves, in part, getting away from preaching repentance of sins that happen to be on the preacher's agenda and instead preaching repentance of sins that the Holy Spirit has placed on the hearer's agenda.

If it is true that, in the effort to stimulate a shift from Position X to Position Y, some church growth leaders have gone too far toward Position Z, this should not be interpreted as *advocating* Position Z. It may *seem* to some Position X advocates that any move from Position X toward the more balanced Position Y is a move further toward Position Z than it in fact is. I hear many critics accusing church growth of espousing Position Z, while their criticism really springs from a fear of any move at all from Position X.[8] Since those at Position X typically have little sense of goal-orientation and feel an aversion to what we have called "consecrated pragmatism," they might well find themselves saying, "It may work in practice, but it's no good in theory."

In any case, it is the clear intention of the Church Growth Movement to combine the "ought" and the "is," the theological and the phenomenological, the normative and the descriptive in a balanced way that does justice both to God's revelation in Scripture and God's working in the hearts and lives of people in concrete historical situations.

Some theologically oriented leaders postulate that Christian action emerges from previous theologizing. There is some validity in this, of course. To know theologically that men and women without Jesus Christ will spend eternity apart from God helps stimulate Christian people to fulfill the evangelistic mandate. Knowing that God is a God of justice and that he wants the social conditions of the poor and oppressed to be improved helps stimulate action in the area of the cultural mandate. But it also must be recognized that theology is dynamic, not static. Theology attempts to make God's eternal, absolute, supracultural revelation in the Scriptures meaningful to human beings in a certain place at a certain time. That is the phenomenological dimension of meaningful theologizing. Missiologists are calling this "contextualization of theology."

The Christian movement itself was not theologized from the beginning. Jesus never wrote a theology. Perhaps the most theologically oriented book in the Bible is Romans, which was written some 30 years after gospel preaching began. The Reformation began before Luther, Calvin, Kuyper, Barth, Henry, and others theologized it. The modern missionary movement began as a spontaneous working of the Holy Spirit, not from a study of the works of Luther and Calvin. Third World theologies are just now beginning to emerge, in some cases a century after Christianity was first introduced. Latin American theologians disdain theology that is divorced from "praxis" or concrete action in a historical situation. Christian theology often emerges from the work of the Holy Spirit in the world. It is an attempt to discern and to articulate what God is actually doing. Some of this theologizing turns out to be biblical and some not. The biblical theology makes Scripture the norm; the nonbiblical theology makes history the norm. Some contemporary theologies of liberation, for example, fall short at this point. They are so praxeological that biblical authority is bypassed. While the Church Growth Movement refuses to divorce phenomenology from theologizing, it affirms that the ultimate bedrock of all theologizing is God's holy Word, the Bible. It strives for a theology that is both contextualized and biblical.

Is Functionalism an Adequate Model?

Cultural anthropology has been the social science most influential on the Church Growth Movement. Particularly as it has touched the field of missiology, it has brought an orientation toward the anthropological school of thought called "functionalism." This has come under some strong criticism, particularly from Latin Americans and from counter-culturally inclined Americans.

The subject of functionalism is highly technical and has only recently come under discussion in the missiological literature. My colleagues Paul Hiebert and Charles Kraft, who are both professional anthropologists, are giving considerable attention to it. I raise the issue here, not because I have either the inclination or the expertise to discuss it thoroughly, but because it has a direct bearing on how the Church Growth Movement views society, social change, and social issues in general. Orlando Costas remarks, "it seems to me that church growth theory suffers from an 'anthropological-functionalistic syndrome.' "[9]

What is functionalism? Paul Hiebert traces the movement to anthropologists Bronislaw Malinowski and A. R. Radcliffe-Brown, each of whom published an influential book in 1922. They argued that "cultural traits were explained in terms of their social significance, by the functions they served within the society." The basic function of cultural traits was "to weld society together into an organic whole" and, as this was done, "all cultural practices contributed to the maintenance of a social order."[10] These early functionalists were intensely interested in social stability, and at times even opposed to social change. This is one of the reasons why some Latin Americans, who strongly favor social change, see a threat in a functionalist approach. Costas fears that because of functionalism the Church Growth Movement is unable to "look at change as social phenomenon that brings about blessings and difficulties and to which the church must address herself in the formulation of her theology and in the fulfillment of her mission to the world."[11] Escobar argues that "American functionalism . . . tends to make societies as they now exist an almost static standard of what society should be."[12]

Cultural anthropology has come a long way since 1922. Hardly an anthropologist alive would uncritically accept Malinowski and Radcliffe-Brown. Hiebert describes many modifications that have been introduced into cultural anthropology precisely because early functionalism could not adequately deal with culture change. He points out that "what is functionally useful for one part of a society may be disruptive for another part or for the whole of the society."[13] He uses the example of segregated housing, which, while it may serve the interests of the rich members of society, is at the same time detrimental to the well-being of the poor.

Church growth teaching not only recognizes that the theory of culture change is an important part of current anthropology, but, because it is committed to fulfilling the evangelistic mandate, it constantly *promotes* culture change. Every time the gospel is introduced into a new culture, change occurs. Sometimes the change is abrupt and fundamental. For example, the homosexual subculture in the United States could not remain intact after the introduction of biblical Christianity because that particular subculture has developed around a blatantly immoral behavior pattern. For the same reason a Ku Klux Klan community could not remain intact.

But missiologists have discovered that most of the world's cultures are not this way. When Christianity is introduced, change occurs to varying degrees, usually short of destroying the fundamental set of values and behavior patterns which knit the culture together. Kraft points out that the inherent ability of Christianity to take on the configuration of almost any culture is in a profound theological sense a reflection of the incarnation itself. God learned our human language, he did not make us learn his.[14]

Church Growth and Socio-Cultural Change

Thus, the criticism that either the Church Growth Movement or the cultural anthropology which informs it is against change is spurious. The real issue is *how much* and *what kind* of change is to be advocated. In the field of evangelical missiology some would argue that the introduction of Christianity should produce a minimum of cultural change, while others favor a more radical change, particularly when unjust social structures are involved. Since those advocating minimal change are already being called "functionalists" it may be well to continue using that label. The opponents of functionalism might then be designated "social engineers."[15]

The Church Growth Movement, which leans toward the functionalist camp, advocates minimal cultural change and concentrates mostly on religious change. It believes that changes which come about after the gospel is introduced should be generated primarily from within the particular culture by the ministry of the Holy Spirit. Because it is receptor-oriented it is very cautious, if not suspicious, of social change introduced from the outside. Outside evangelists who think they know "what is right" for a particular people often know nothing of the sort.

I recall with embarrassment, how, as a new American missionary to
Bolivia, I was not prepared for a culture that used domestic servants.
I thought that Christian families whose servants ate in the kitchen
were not practicing Christian love. So my wife and I had our maid eat
at the family table in order to introduce what we innocently thought
was healthy, Christian culture change. We soon realized that the
Bolivian people (including our maid) did not interpret our action as
noble, generous, antiracist, or a mark of radical Christian discipleship
—just uncouth. We learned that we were not very good social engineers.[16]

Social engineers tend to concentrate on socio-economic changes.
They see cultures as containing "perpetual conflict between social
classes," as Tito Paredes says.[17] They feel enough confidence in their
analysis of the socio-economic conditions in a given society to recommend radical structural changes as part of the Christianity they are
introducing. They want to overthrow, in the name of Christ, dominant
elites who are exploiting the lower classes.

The difference between these two approaches was described by Paul
Hiebert in the terms of landscape architecture on college campuses. One
school of architects draws plans for where the sidewalks "ought" to be
and locates and installs them accordingly. They are equivalent to the
social engineers. The other school of architects builds the buildings and
then lets at least one year elapse before installing the sidewalks. They
put the sidewalks where the students have already made paths. They
would be equivalent to the functionalists. It may take longer, but they
believe that the results are superior.

Social engineers tend to take a low view of culture and feel that
biblical Christianity will necessarily oppose a great deal in the ordinary
culture. Functionalists have a higher view of culture and feel that while
Christianity demands some changes, it tends leave culture mostly intact.
They believe that much valuable information comes from observing how
God, in fact, works through those who are disciples of Jesus Christ in
a given context. They attempt to combine the phenomenological with
the theological in a balanced way. They are patient. Charles Kraft
recognizes that when Christianity enters a culture, the worldview
changes, but that "this changing of worldview, while radical, often takes
a long time."[18] Social engineers often want more radical change, and
now.

Civilization Before Evangelization?

Functionalists have become very skeptical of social engineering as they have observed it in the past. They have seen too many missionaries preach American cultural values as part of the Christian Gospel. "Civilization before evangelization" is an obnoxious slogan. The old idea that monogamy should be a prerequisite for baptism is now widely questioned in missiological circles. Making pacifism a part of the gospel is open to much debate. Advocating planned economies or socialism as a Christian socio-economic design is extra-biblical at best. Contemporary liberation theologians may be excessively self-confident in promoting "consciousness raising" as a Christian activity. As Peter Berger points out, a crucial assumption of such ideologists is that "lower-class people do not understand their own situation, that they are in need of enlightenment on the matter, and that this service can be provided by selected higher-class individuals."[19] Functionalists are not sure that higher-class people always do know what is best for lower-class people, or that Russians know what is best for the Polish, or Americans for Viet Nam.

This discussion relates directly to some issues discussed in other chapters. Church growth people refuse to allow the cultural mandate to be given priority above the evangelistic mandate. They stress a minimum of ethical content in the discipling phase and a maximum in the perfecting stage of Christianization. They believe in receptor-oriented communication of the Christian faith. They attempt to balance the "ought" with the "is."

The Church Growth Movement affirms the cultural mandate and promotes the values of the kingdom of God. But it holds that the most beneficial and long-lasting social change is usually generated from within a culture by men and women who have become disciples of Jesus Christ through the free grace of God. Donald McGavran, who has spent a lifetime in India, recognizes that the highest Hindu scripture, the Bhagavad Gita, "consciously sanctifies the caste system" by declaring that "the superiority of the classes and the inferiority of the masses are rooted in the divine order."[20] If the Bhagavad Gita were accepted at face value, all efforts to change the social order from within or without would be considered wicked. McGavran, with whatever functionalism he might claim, is strongly in favor of change and justice for the masses.

Methodologically, however, he does not suggest that breaking caste become a requirement of accepting the gospel. More Indian people, who in the future will promote more biblical social change, will be introduced into the kingdom of God while yet in the caste structure.[21] After this happens, when they are discipled, power will be released from "God the Father Almighty who hates injustice." When people become Christian, they develop a worldview "which irresistibly, though often slowly, creates equality of opportunity and undergirds all strivings against entrenched privilege."[22]

Church Growth has never been a defender of the caste system with its blatant injustices. It favors social change toward love, harmony, and equality of all peoples. But it does not agree that Christian social engineering or making radical social change a part of the Good News itself is either biblical or practical.

Thinking About Conversion: Bounded and Centered Sets

The Church Growth Movement is indebted to Paul Hiebert for some valuable work examining how we think about about who is a Christian and who is not. If we understand this, we come to understand much of what is at the root of the methodological assumptions of church growth teaching.

Hiebert describes two alternate approaches to thinking about who is a Christian: the bounded set approach and the centered set approach. His point is that our mind tends to form the set first, then see where people fit into it. Our idea of who is a Christian and who is not will be largely determined by the way we form our sets.

The *bounded set,* as the name implies, starts with a boundary. To illustrate, look around at any object you see. Here is a pencil. A pencil is a writing instrument that contains lead. There are other writing instruments around me, such as a pen, a Flair, a typewriter, a print-out calculator, and a magic marker. But none of those is a pencil because it has no lead. Lead is the *boundary* which separates pencils from other writing instruments. It can be a mechanical pencil, a wooden pencil, a carpenter's pencil, a broken pencil, a hard-lead or soft-lead pencil, a long pencil—but it is still all pencil.

The same with a Christian. To decide who is a Christian, a bounded-set approach determines certain characteristics of belief or behavior or both and postulates that if you think such-and-such or do such-and-such, you are a Christian. For some the boundary might be the Trinity. If you believe in the Trinity you are a Christian, but if you deny the Trinity you are not a Christian. For some it is baptism by immersion. For some it is monogamy as against polygamy. For some it is brotherhood as against racism. For some it is sobriety as against drunkenness. In every case the boundary is the principal determinant.

The *centered set* is different. According to Hiebert, "It is created by defining a center and the relationship of things to that center. Some things may be far from the center, but they are moving *towards* the center; therefore they are part of the centered set."[23] While it is easy for me to illustrate a bounded set with a pencil, it is not so easy for me to do it for a centered set because my English language forces me to "see the world largely in terms of bounded sets."[24] Most of us with a Western orientation prefer to see the whole world in bounded-set categories.

In a centered set designed to define what a Christian is, the center is established before the boundary. The center is Jesus Christ. Everyone headed toward Christ is part of the set—a Christian. Everyone not headed toward Christ is not a part of the set until they turn around toward Christ. Notice that the boundary is drawn, so there is a difference between Christians and non-Christians. But the boundary is not drawn *first.* It is drawn *after* the person's direction is determined. The most important thing about being a Christian is neither consent to a doctrinal creed nor conformity to an ethical code, but one's relationship to a person, Jesus Christ. The most important act is conversion—the turning around toward Jesus.

Epistemologically, the Church Growth Movement has operated largely from a centered-set perspective, although it was unaware of it until Hiebert pointed it out. The centered-set perspective, for example, is consistent with the view of conversion, salvation, discipling, and perfecting set forth in the last chapter. Paul Hiebert argues that a centered-set approach "avoids the dilemma of offering a cheap grace," making it possible for even "the ignorant" or "the gross sinners" to become Christians "without lengthy periods of training and testing." This is what is called discipling. It means, simply, that "the person has turned around." He or she has "left another center of god and has made Christ his center."[25]

But this is not the end. A centered set, unlike a bounded set, is dynamic. There is always motion *toward* the center. This is what church growth calls "perfecting." Hiebert says that "we need evangelism to bring people to Christ" but that is only the beginning. "Growth after conversion is an intrinsic part of what it means to be a Christian."[26]

Fundamentalists and Radical Christians

Illustrations of bounded-set thinking are abundant in American Christianity. Two contemporary groups that clearly use bounded sets are fundamentalists and radical Christians. This may sound like a strange combination, but it is strange only because they start with different boundaries. Fundamentalists usually start with doctrinal beliefs and personal ethical codes. Radical Christians usually start with social ethical codes. "You can't be a Christian if you drink or smoke" and "you can't be a Christian and be a racist" are both declarations based on bounded sets.

Those who establish bounded sets find afterwards, as Paul Hiebert says, that they "need to play boundary games."[27] Reading Jim Wallis' *Agenda for Biblical People,* for example, I find a book-length boundary game. Boundaries between biblical Christians and others include such things as "the consumptive mentality," "the will to power and domination," "oppression of race, sex and class," "arrogance of national destiny," "economic imperialism," and "military aggression." Christians who have different social views are frequently accused of "idolatry," and it must be assumed that Wallis believes that idolaters will not inherit the kingdom of God (1 Cor. 6:9–10). His boundaries have excluded his opponents.

One further illustration of bounded-set mentality in a vocal church growth critic comes from René Padilla. At one point he criticizes the way the "consumer society" has caused many evangelicals to fall into an "obsession with numbers" which "mechanises the addition of people to the church" in order to "accompany a truncated gospel." He affirms (quoting Juan Luis Segundo) that "there are two ways to count Christians." The first way involves "the bare minimum," including baptism, some church attendance, and self-identity as a Christian. The second way is to count only those "who are ready to take their message to the rest of society . . . to commit themselves to a global transformation of society."[28]

The first way to count reflects a centered-set mentality. The second way is a bounded-set mentality. Padilla calls them "two conceptions of the Gospel." Those who choose the "bare minimum" of the centered set, Padilla says, "have not been able to escape from the conditioning of consumer society and, in their interest to find more converts, have accomodated their message to this society."[29]

Those who advocate what I called in Chapter 7 "exorbitant grace" raise their high boundaries because they are concerned about "cheap grace." In church growth terminology, they are concerned that people will be discipled, and fail to be perfected. Centered-set thinking, however, does not allow this. It accepts people as Christians with a minimum of change in belief or behavior so long as there has been a radical change in allegiance at the center of their life. Self is dethroned and Christ is enthroned. Fetishes are burned and Holy Spirit power takes their place. Jesus is both savior and Lord. Perfection begins at that point and continues through the lifetime. The centered-set understanding of Christianity is dynamic, and does not allow just turning around toward Christ and then sitting there. It demands a continual movement toward Christ, a growth in grace and in the knowledge of Jesus Christ.

While it is true, as Paul Hiebert argues, that a centered set approach "corresponds more closely to what we see happening in missions and church growth,"[30] some may wonder if the church growth people have not slipped in a boundary with their stress on responsible church membership. The Church Growth Movement measures the fulfillment of the Great Commission in terms of people who are disciples of Jesus Christ *and* responsible members of his church. However, responsible church membership is not considered a theological requirement for becoming a Christian. Repentance, faith, and conversion are the requirements, as was explained in Chapter 7. Responsible church membership is simply the most adequate tangible measuring device we have to help quantify evangelistic goals and monitor goal-attainment. In the final analysis, joining a church is a part of perfecting, not discipling. When people truly repent and become believers, their names are written in the Lamb's Book of Life. But since we do not have access to that volume, how can we tell if it has happened? The Church Growth Movement has chosen to use responsible church membership as the answer to that question. When understood in this way, it fits into centered-set thinking.

I like the way Bishop Newbigin expresses it in the question: "Can the oppressor and the oppressed share together at the Eucharist?" He refuses, although with hesitation, to require that the oppressor "disgorge his ill-gotten wealth" as a condition of being a communicant at the table of the Lord. Newbigin admits there might be individual cases of such blatant, overt oppression that excommunication is necessary. But in the broad sense, "in every society, in every nation, even in every family, there is an element of oppression," and the Eucharist is the place where "we acknowledge the fact that we are all in sin and that we are accepted only by grace."[31]

One thing that has amazed me about the biblical record is that the Apostle Paul recommended excommunication for only one member of the Corinthian church—the man who was overtly engaged in sexual relations with his stepmother. The rest of the Corinthians were hardly spiritual giants. Their lives were as messy and as far from Christ as practically any congregation that I am aware of today. Yet Paul was able to call them "saints." He apparently dealt with them from a centered-set approach.

As I have indicated, much more work needs to be done on the methodological aspects of the Church Growth Movement. I agree with Hiebert that these methodological questions must ultimately "be decided on theological, not pragmatic, principles."[32] This is just another of the many challenges for future research in the field of church growth.

Notes

1. Samuel Escobar, "Comment on the Social Status of Early Christianity," *Gospel in Context* 2, no. 1 (January 1979), p. 15.

2. David J. Hesselgrave, *Planting Churches Cross-Culturally: A Guide for Home and Foreign Missions* (Grand Rapids: Baker, 1980), p. 47.

3. Roger S. Greenway, "Winnable People," in *Theological Perspectives on Church Growth,* ed. Harvie M. Conn (Nutley, NJ: Presbyterian and Reformed, 1976), p. 46.

4. Orlando E. Costas, *The Church and Its Mission: A Shattering Critique from the Third World* (Wheaton, IL: Tyndale, 1974), p. 145.

5. Charles H. Kraft, *Christianity in Culture: A Study in Dynamic Biblical Theologizing in Cross-Cultural Perspective* (Maryknoll, NY: Orbis, 1979).

6. Arthur P. Johnston, "Church Growth Theology and World Evangelization," in *Theology and Mission: Papers Given at the Trinity Consultation No. 1,* ed. David J. Hesselgrave (Grand Rapids: Baker, 1978), p. 202.

7. Harvie M. Conn, "Church-Mission Relationships," in *Theological*

Perspectives on Church Growth, ed. Harvie M. Conn (Nutley, NJ: Presbyterian and Reformed, 1976), p. 108.

8. Of course, almost anyone on a continuum tends to see all others to the left or right of them as on "the other side." For example, in Africa the mission churches thought that the African Independent Churches were sub-Christian, while the African Independent Churches thought the Old Testament church movements were sub-Christian. Some of those at Position X perceive themselves to be at the correct, Christian center position, and any deviation from that can be considered sub-Christian. The attitude toward someone who introduces the social sciences, therefore, is frequently that they have sold out to the social sciences and that their view is sub-Christian.

9. Costas, *The Church and Its Mission,* p. 145.

10. Paul G. Hiebert, *Cultural Anthropology* (Philadelphia: Lippencott, 1976), p. 70.

11. Costas, *The Church and Its Mission,* p. 147.

12. Escobar, "Comment," p. 15.

13. Hiebert, *Cultural Anthropology,* p. 77.

14. See Kraft, *Christianity in Culture,* pp. 173–178.

15. Alfred Krass might prefer "structural-functionalists" as against "radical anthropologists"; see his "Contextualization for Today," *Gospel in Context,* July, 1979, p. 29. Ruben (Tito) Paredes labels the camps "functionalist-relativist" and "conflictive-dependency"; see his "Different Views of Socio-Cultural Change: Towards an Awareness of our Own Socio-anthropological Presuppositions in Mission and Church Growth Studies," unpublished paper, September 1980.

16. For detailed missiological discussions of what change actually occurs when Christianity is introduced into a culture, see Donald R. Jacobs, "Conversion and Culture—An Anthropological Perspective with Reference to East Africa," in *Down to Earth: Studies in Christianity and Culture,* eds. John R. W. Stott and Robert Coote (Grand Rapids: Eerdmans, 1980), pp. 131–146; and Kraft, *Christianity in Culture,* especially Chapters 18 and 19.

17. Paredes, "Different Views of Socio-Cultural Change," p. 6.

18. Kraft, *Christianity in Culture,* p. 344. Kraft's chapter, "Christian Conversion as a Dynamic Process," as well as numerous other passages in his book, provides an extensive discussion of these issues.

Kraft, along with Paul Hiebert, is continuing to explore the social-scientific methodological assumptions of missiology and church growth. Besides functionalism they are drawing on ethnohistory, cognitive anthropology, symbolic anthropology, and other methodologies. Kraft is working on linguistic methodology and ethnoscience. Hiebert is working on symbolic theory and cognitive structures and worldviews.

19. Peter L. Berger, "The False Consciousness of 'Consciousness Raising,' " in *Mission Trends No. 4,* ed. Gerald H. Anderson and Thomas F. Stransky (New York: Paulist Press; Grand Rapids: Eerdmans, 1979), p. 98.

20. Donald A. McGavran, *Understanding Church Growth,* rev. (Grand Rapids: Eerdmans, 1980), p. 286.

21. A book-length discussion of this principle is Donald A. McGavran, *Ethnic Realities and the Church: Lessons from India* (Pasadena: William Carey Library, 1979), pp. 256–257 and elsewhere.

22. McGavran, *Understanding Church Growth*, p. 288.

23. Paul G. Hiebert, "Conversion in Cross-Cultural Perspective," in *Conversion: Doorway to Discipleship,* ed. Henry J. Schmidt (Hillsboro, Kansas: Board of Christian Literature, Mennonite Brethren, 1980), p. 95. This is the most mature of Hiebert's essays on the subject to date. He previously published the concept of sets in "Conversion, Culture and Cognitive Categories," *Gospel in Context,* October, 1978; and in "Sets and Structures: A Study of Church Patterns," in *New Horizons in World Mission: Evangelicals and the Christian Mission: Papers Given at Trinity Consultation No. 2,* ed. David J. Hesselgrave (Grand Rapids: Baker, 1979), pp. 217–227.

24. Hiebert, "Conversion in Cross-Cultural Perspective," p. 96.

25. Ibid., p. 97. I am surprised that Alfred Krass reviews Hiebert's set theory and comes to the conclusion that it justifies thinking of evangelism and nurture as describing the same activity. He says, "We must evangelize each other all our lives" and "the goal of evangelism is this: that we all might come to maturity in our knowledge of the Lord. . . ." He fails to see that the point of turning brings a person from outside the set to inside the set and that this turning is what happens when a disciple is made—evangelism. From that point, nurture or perfecting begins, and lasts a lifetime. See Alfred Krass, "Maybe the Problem Is in Our Heads," *The Other Side* 16, no. 5 (May 1980), p. 45.

26. Hiebert, "Conversion in Cross-Cultural Perspective," p. 97.
27. Ibid.
28. C. René Padilla, "Spiritual Conflict," in *The New Face of Evangelicalism: An International Symposium on the Lausanne Covenant,* ed. C. René Padilla (Downers Grove, IL: InterVarsity Press, 1976), p. 217
29. Ibid., pp. 217–218.
30. Hiebert, "Conversion in Cross-Cultural Perspective," p. 98.
31. Lesslie Newbigin, *The Open Secret* (Grand Rapids: Eerdmans, 1978), pp. 123–124.
32. Hiebert, "Conversion in Cross-Cultural Perspective," p. 98.

CHAPTER 9

The Homogeneous Unit Principle
as an Ethical Issue

The "homogeneous unit principle" is by far the most controversial of
all church growth principles. Because it relates directly to socio-cultural
issues, it cannot be omitted from this book. My treatment of it, however,
will be highly selective for two reasons: (1) An expansive treatment
would dominate the book and overshadow other issues, and (2) two
book-length discussions of the homogeneous unit principle have recently
been published. They are Donald McGavran's *Ethnic Realities and
the Church*,[1] which uses India as a case study, and my *Our Kind of
People*[2] using America as a case study. Both have been quite strongly
attacked. One reviewer from India accuses McGavran of advocating
"psychological tricks to swell the numbers by taking crowds unawares
and to carry away in one swoop a whole tribe by cajolery or material
inducement."[3] One American review of my book is pointedly titled,
"Evangelism Without the Gospel."[4]

While these books have received criticism, they have also been
praised. So the discussion—or, more properly, the debate—continues.
Over the past decade, each side has learned a good deal from the other.
The first international consultation sponsored by the Theology Working
Group of the Lausanne Committee for World Evangelization was a
consultation on the homogeneous unit principle in 1977.[5] It helped
significantly to clarify the issues. What I most regret about the matter
is that, in the minds of some people, the homogeneous unit principle
has assumed such proportions that it is considered the sum and substance of the Church Growth Movement. This is far from the case.

What the Homogeneous Unit Principle Really Is

The homogeneous unit principle should be seen at the very beginning for what it really is: a tool which many have found helpful in implementing the evangelistic mandate. But it is nothing more or less than a tool. It is not an eleventh commandment or a sixty-seventh book of the Bible or a footnote to the Apostles' Creed. If it is found to be a useful tool for a given time and place, it should be used to the glory of God. But if some alternate way of implementing the evangelistic mandate is deemed superior in a given time and place, by all means that one should be used to the glory of God. The essential purpose of the Church Growth Movement is not to fulfill the homogeneous unit principle, but to fulfill the evangelistic mandate. The evangelistic mandate relates directly to the lifestyle of the kingdom of God; the homogeneous unit principle may or may not (according to which side of the debate you select).

The classic formulation of the principle comes from McGavran's *Understanding Church Growth:* "Men like to become Christians without crossing racial, linguistic, or class barriers."[6] Notice two significant things about that statement.

In the first place, McGavran's statement is descriptive, not normative. It is phenomenological, not theological. He does not say, "Men *ought to* become Christians" but rather "men *like to* become Christians." Many who have been trained at Position X on the Ought-Is Spectrum described in Chapter 8 have failed to see that. Some, alas, do not even believe there can be a difference between the two statements. As a phenomenological observation, however, McGavran's claim that "this principle states an undeniable fact"[7] is valid. For over two decades critics have attempted to find empirical evidence which would refute it, but to no avail. It has become quite clear that there is little or no evidence to the contrary. By this I do not mean that there are no exceptions to the rule. Of course there are. But they remain just that —exceptions—and thereby do not modify the rule.

Secondly, McGavran's statement relates to discipling, not perfecting. It is a principle of evangelism, not Christian nurture. The "men" of the statement refers to men (and, of course, women) who are *unbelievers.* They are not in the kingdom of God. Jesus is not their Lord. They know nothing of the fruit of the Holy Spirit. If the gospel is presented in such a way that it carries racial overtones, and if becoming a Christian involves a social rather than a religious or spiritual decision, most of them will not even hear it. They will choose to remain with their people, in their sins, and outside the kingdom of God. This is the central thrust of the homogeneous unit principle. It should not be interpreted as expounding the ideal way that *Christians* should relate to one another, but the way in which unbelievers become followers of Jesus Christ and responsible members of his church.

The homogeneous unit principle should be regarded as a *penultimate* spiritual dynamic. The *ultimate* is that believers are all one in the body of Christ, and the more this is manifested in a tangible way, the better. For example, Gerald Palmer of the Southern Baptist Home Mission Board feels that the heterogeneous unit, not the homogeneous unit is the ideal. "But," he argues, "we must not stop starting churches because groups of people fail to meet our standards of ideal heterogeneity." He says that our goal should be starting churches, not necessarily *homogeneous* churches. "But," Palmer adds, "we must be willing to start churches that are homogeneous in nature if this is the best way to reach people and help them begin the journey in fellowship with other believers." He frankly recognizes that "the homogeneous unit is a spiritual and effective way of beginning and moving a group of people toward a heterogeneous scriptural ideal."[8] McGavran and Wagner and any church growth advocate I know would join Palmer in describing the homogeneous unit principle as a *penultimate dynamic*, not an *ultimate ideal*.

The Principle Is Risky

I intentionally postponed discussing the homogeneous unit principle in this book until after I presented the perspectives on discipling and perfecting (Chapter 7), and bounded sets versus centered sets (Chapter 8). It is very important to see the homogeneous unit principle as part of the discipling stage and as "Christian" in the centered-set sense. Generally speaking, those who have theological and/or epistemological reasons for rejecting discipling-perfecting and centered-set theory will find themselves uncomfortable with the homogeneous unit principle. Their boundary game usually involves something along the line of "oneness in Christ" and an insistence that part of being a Christian is to attach such a low value to the integrity of peoplehood and culture[9] that all true Christians will freely mix in primary group relationships with those of other racial, linguistic and class identities. Anything short of this seems, to the critics, to be another case of "cheap grace" or "easy believism."

It appears to some that encouraging the formation of homogeneous unit churches is implicitly placing a seal of approval on segregation, discrimination, racism, the caste system, and apartheid. Much to the dismay of church growth leaders, it has, at times, been used for those ends. In the Lausanne Congress on World Evangelization in 1974 Ralph D. Winter made a plenary session presentation which incorporated the homogeneous unit principle. A few weeks later we heard that some white South African participants had played tapes of Winter's address on the radio to prove that Lausanne had endorsed apartheid. Winter was shocked. Approving apartheid was so far from Winter's mind that the whole affair seemed ludicrous. But just as a knife can be used as an instrument of mercy in a surgical operation or as an instrument of horror in a murder, the homogeneous unit principle can be used for good or for bad. Properly applied, it can be an effective force to reduce racism; wrongly applied, it can support racism. It must be admitted that the principle carries with it an element of risk.

The Dilemma of the Two Mandates

The lifestyle of the kingdom of God involves participating in both the evangelistic mandate and the cultural mandate. Each has its objectives and its demands. When both are related to the issues raised by the homogeneous unit principle a kind of dilemma occurs. Let me describe it.

The evangelistic mandate, for its most effective implementation, requires the multiplication of homogeneous unit churches. I will not bother marshalling evidence here to support that affirmation since, (1) research sources now abound—mostly in case study form—to support it,[10] and (2) even critics of the homogeneous unit principle now concede the point. For example, Martin Marty, in a piece with the provocative title, "Is the homogeneous unit principle of church growth Christian?" admits that "Wagner, McGavran and company win hands down on the pragmatic issue."[11] But while the critics agree that the easiest, most natural, and most effective way to evangelize unbelievers is to gather the converts into congregations which they perceive to be "our kind of people," they question whether the result of such a procedure really glorifies God.

This question arises from an underlying concern for the cultural mandate. One of the blights on Planet Earth is the pervasive racism which infects every region of the world. Another is the ruthless oppression of powerless and disadvantaged classes for economic gain by the rich and powerful. Christian people, concerned for the values of the kingdom of God, abhor these conditions and strive to see them overcome. One way to do this is to make it quite evident to the world that in the kingdom of God there is no Jew or Gentile, no Scythian or Barbarian, no slave or free, no male or female—the middle walls of partition have been broken down. The desire to do this comes from the Holy Spirit who dwells in each believer and whose presence is evidenced by the fruit of the Spirit. "By this shall all men know that ye are my disciples," said Jesus, "if ye have love one to another" (John 13:35). The love Jesus talked about is meaningless unless and until it is manifested clearly to the world in white Christians loving black Christians, rich Christians loving poor Christians, powerful Christians loving powerless Christians, and Western Christians loving Third World Christians. Only through bringing Christians of all kinds together can this demand of the cultural mandate adequately be fulfilled.

So here is the dilemma. Homogeneity aids the evangelistic mandate, heterogeneity aids the cultural mandate. The question for biblical Christians is how to do them both?

My first answer to the question is this: *Evangelize strenuously.* If strenuous evangelism means to multiply homogeneous churches, multiply them. The rationale for this suggestion, as I argued in Chapter 5, is that the evangelistic mandate is more important than the cultural mandate. The Lausanne Covenant is correct in stating that in the total mission of the church, evangelism is is primary. This is also basically what Gerald Palmer was saying. No one involved wants to sacrifice the cultural mandate, but if it is necessary to settle for something short of the ideal in order to bring new people into the kingdom of God, then it is proper to make the sacrifice.

Simply from the mathematical point of view, it seems that the more people in the world who turn to Jesus Christ, orient their lives around him, and agree to obey him as Lord, the more potential there will be for implementing Christian social concerns.

My second answer is: *Teach believers that God's people are all one in*

Christ. Make every effort to relate Christians of different homogeneous units to each other *on appropriate structural levels.* In the church system, certain structures are appropriate for primary (heart-to-heart) group relationships and other structures for secondary (face-to-face) group relationships. The more the structure reflects primary groups, the more homogeneous we would expect it to be. The more it reflects secondary group relationships, the more heterogeneous it ought to be. I have made the first of these sentences descriptive and the second normative for the reason that primary group relationships cannot be legislated by either ecclesiastical or political powers. It is not possible to coerce people to marry outside their primary group without dehumanizing them, nor is it possible to dictate for any length of time who will or will not be close personal friends. In a free society it is not acceptable to manipulate people into choosing doctors, dentists, lawyers, or pastors outside their own identity group. All these—family, close personal friends, and professionals with intimate access to the person—are primary group relationships. Violating the integrity of primary group relationships can be a form of psycho-social oppression as serious as the economic oppression of Latin American *latifundistas.*

The second sentence was normative because secondary relationships can and *should be* legislated. Employment, entertainment, public schooling, restaurants and hotels, libraries, beaches, transportation, public buildings, hospitals, and other such social institutions bring people together in secondary social relationships. In a pluralistic society some of these relationships take shape naturally, but where they do not they should be encouraged by government action. I personally believe in mandatory busing (where feasible) and in affirmative action. I live in an integrated neighborhood and send my children to integrated public schools. But while I vote for mandatory busing to keep a racial balance in our schools (there are more blacks than whites in Pasadena schools), I cannot and would not vote to legislate who the kids eat lunch with, walk home with, or go on dates with. As the Japanese learned after thirty-five years of intense effort to force the Koreans to learn the Japanese language, marry Japanese spouses, and adopt the Japanese culture, primary group relationships cannot be legislated.

What does this have to do with the evangelistic mandate?

Building boundaries over which unbelievers must leap if they are to become Christians is a type of spiritual legislation. To suggest that part of becoming a Christian is to renounce loyalty to one's primary group is a form of exorbitant grace. It is what the judaizers in New Testament times attempted to do and what the Council of Jerusalem condemned. People happen to love those in their primary group more than those outside it, and I know of nothing in the gospel that condemns that. Almost all of Jesus' primary relationships (eleven of the twelve disciples, his mother and her friends, the family of Lazarus) were with Galilean Jews. I cannot think of Gentiles or Samaritans or even Hellenistic Jews to whom Jesus related in a socially primary way, although there may have been a scattered few. When the Gaderene wanted to join his group, Jesus turned him down flat (Mark 5:18–19). I do not think that reduced group loyalty is either a price tag for saving grace or a fruit of the Holy Spirit. A fruit of the Holy Spirit is a changed *attitude* toward other primary groups and a reduction of prejudice, discrimination, exploitation, and oppression.

One collective fruit of the Holy Spirit would be a kind of spiritual legislation making contact between Christians of different homogeneous units more frequent and meaningful than we have seen in American Christianity to date. What this spiritual legislation might look like I do not know specifically. But I do feel that American congregations, which are mostly homogeneous, are too self-sufficient. Practical answers need to be explored, and they will somehow have to take into account the different nature of primary and secondary group relationships and how they fit into appropriate church structures. I have found the following model helpful in understanding this:

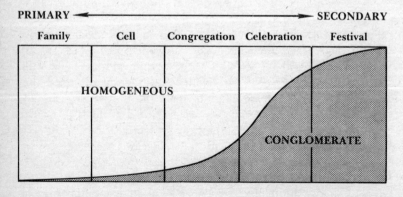

Church Structures and Homogeneity

Church structures move from primary to secondary relationships, from the family (the nuclear family in America) to the cell (a small, intimate sharing group of 8–12), to the congregation (a fellowship group of 40–120), to the celebration (all the church membership in worship), to the festival (large conventions, crusades, camp meetings, or convocations). The more the relationships become secondary, the more appropriate is a conglomerate or heterogeneous mixture.

To repeat, on the left side of the scale we should not legislate how people group together. As we move toward the right, legislation becomes more appropriate. If this is properly done, the way is open for the maximum implementation of both the evangelistic and cultural mandates. Some churches and denominations are doing this now. Probably the Southern Baptists have the lead in America, but much is also being done among Assemblies of God, Church of the Nazarene, Christian and Missionary Alliance, Church of God (Cleveland) and other denominations. United Methodists have the desire to do more, but they are still debating whether to legislate spiritual primary groups. In any case, it is my hope and expectation that models of a positive and simultaneous fulfillment of both mandates in the area of group relationships will be multiplied among American Christians in the decade to come.

With this as a background, I would like to devote the remainder of this chapter to discussing the most acute charge leveled against the homogeneous unit principle, that of promoting racism, and to introduce some material that does not overlap too much with *Our Kind of People*.

Homogeneous Units in the Kingdom of God

The basic orientation of the kingdom of God is eschatological, as explained in Chapter 1. It will only be realized in its fullness in the age to come. In the present age, those of us who are part of the community of the king are obligated to display through our lives, to the greatest extent possible, the values of the coming kingdom.

What relationships do groups of people have to each other in the coming kingdom? Or to repeat an earlier question: are there groups at all in the kingdom? Will Peter still be a Jew? Will the eunuch still be an Ethiopian? Will Cornelius still be a Gentile? Will the woman at the well still be a Samaritan? Or will group identity be wiped out?

I know of no sure and final answer to this question. But it is clear that certain theological assumptions can lead to certain conclusions. For example, if it is assumed that the existence of different human groups is intrinsically evil, or if they, like disease and birth pains and social injustice, are the result of sin, then it can logically be concluded that in the eschatological kingdom of God they will disappear with everything else evil. A corollary to this position is that part of today's cultural mandate is to do everything possible in this age to obliterate human group distinctions.

While many Christians hold this view, it is not at all a necessary conclusion from biblical data. An alternate interpretation of biblical data, at least equally reasonable, is to assume that human differences were part of God's creative intention for the human race. Probing of the social dynamics behind the Tower of Babel incident (Gen. 11: 1–9) can lead to the conclusion that God's intention for the human race was that they become diversified, but that humans rebelled and tried to thwart God's plan by consolidating themselves in a city. God then intervened and, instead of a gradual differentiation, made it instantaneous.[12] It is my own position that socio-cultural pluralism was intended by God to be good for humans. There is no question that it can be and has been grossly abused throughout history. God's institution of marriage is analogous. It was created for good, but has been grossly abused. Nevertheless, on balance, both marriage and socio-cultural pluralism have been beneficial to human beings. A corollary to this position is not that human differences should be obliterated, but that we should do all possible to ameliorate the abuses and to enjoy the blessings of cultural pluralism.

One other indication of the presence of people groups in the coming kingdom is a passage in Revelation which describes the variety of peoples singing the praises of the Lamb on the throne. It says that there will be a great multitude divided into "nations, and kindreds, and people, and tongues" (Rev. 7:9). Again, the proof is not conclusive, but one reasonable way of understanding the biblical data is that, yes, people groups do and will continue to exist in the kingdom of God.

The second question, then, is what will be their relationships to each other? The answer to this is much clearer. In the kingdom of God, a kingdom of *shalom,* there is no war, no hatred, no oppression, no exploitation, no racism, no xenophobia, no greed, no militarism, no segregation, no discrimination, no redlining, no unfair housing practices. Kingdom people respect the integrity of cultures other than their own and relate to people in other cultures in love, mutual concern, and interdependence. They know how to share without either subservience or paternalism. They enjoy each other's differences while affirming a basic human unity. They promote human rights. They work diligently toward an open society where people are free to make their own choices without coercion.

Toward an Open Society

As I perceive the world situation, there have been seven basic social designs that large groups have used to relate to other groups in geographical proximity: genocide, deportation, apartheid, structural racism, assimilationist racism, open society, and secession. I have listed them in the order in which I feel they approach the ideals of the kingdom of God.

Before dealing with each one individually, I want to suggest that a very helpful way of understanding group relationships is to conceptualize some groups as powerful and some as powerless. As Jim Wallis says, "The divisions of the world today are less along the lines of ideology than they are along the lines of powerful and powerless, rich and poor, strong and weak, those who benefit and those who are victimized."[13] The division of the world into political units called nation-states is itself in many cases an oppressive and discriminatory act, executed somewhat arbitrarily by the powerful to exploit the powerless. While abuses of human relationships do occur between nations, that should not mask the tensions between the powerful groups and the powerless groups within national boundaries.[14]

What, then, are the principal ways that powerful human groups relate to powerless groups coexisting in geographical proximity?

Genocide. In the practice of genocide, the powerful group decides to kill the powerless group. This is a simple and uncomplicated way of resolving tensions between groups. If one group is exterminated, there will be no future problem. During World War I the Turks practiced genocide on the Armenians. It happened during World War II when Hitler attempted to wipe out the Jews and killed six million in the process. A more recent case of genocide has been witnessed in Kampuchea (Cambodia).

America has not been free from tendencies toward genocide. In the minds of many people on the American frontier, the best way to deal with the "Indian problem" was to kill the Indians. The slogan that "the only good Indian is a dead Indian" even now surfaces in some of our Western movies. The current practice of killing some 1.5 million unborn babies every year in America is also a form of genocide. Certainly there are very few human groups more powerless than unborn babies in the wombs of selfish mothers and in the hands of unscrupulous doctors.

Deportation.   A more humane, and in some cases more profitable, way of eliminating an entire group is for a national government to deport them. In Uganda, for example, Idi Amin deported all the East Indians, even those who were Ugandan citizens. He could have killed them as he did black Ugandans from other tribes, but it was more efficient to deport them. More recently the government of Viet Nam has been deporting ethnic Chinese, including those born in Viet Nam. In both cases the groups had accrued some commercial and economic power, but they were politically powerless and susceptible to being banished from their own homeland by tyrannical, totalitarian regimes which then appropriated their economic holdings.

Some Americans today advocate deportation to help solve problems that exist between human groups. The Ku Klux Klan believes that "all civilizations were the result of the creativity of the white race" and that civilizations have fallen in the past "because of the decline of the racial purity of the culture-creating race—the white race." They, therefore, argue that "the total voluntary separation of the races is in the best interest of the American Republic," and to attain that goal, they "will seek the resettlement of the black race in their homeland on the continent of Africa."[15] Fortunately for the American Republic, the Ku Klux Klan does not have enough political power to carry out their Idi Amin-like threat.

Apartheid.   In apartheid, the powerless group is allowed to coexist with the powerful group, but legal barriers are constructed to prevent social contact. In this case, group contact is illegal. The Indian caste system, when decreed by law, was a form of apartheid. The best known use of apartheid today occurs in South Africa where the powerful white minority population has chosen to protect its power by outlawing social contact with the non-white majority, mostly blacks and coloreds (those of East Indian descent). Such behavior is so far from the ideal of the kingdom of God that it is difficult to understand how white South African leaders, many of whom are Christians, can persist in supporting it.

It is only within the last two or three decades that America has ended apartheid. Before the Civil Rights Movement, running from the mid 1950s to the early 1970s, several states had Jim Crow laws which prohibited blacks and whites from eating in the same restaurants, staying in the same hotels, using the same public toilet and drinking water facilities, going to the same schools, working in the same factories, living in the same neighborhoods, sitting together in buses and many other similar prohibitions.

Structural Racism.   Structural racism is similar to apartheid in that group contact is disallowed, but in this case it functions through social pressures rather than written laws. Up to 1947, for example, American blacks were excluded from playing major league baseball. There was no law against it, but the structure had been closed by the powerful whites to the powerless blacks. A substantial social upheaval occurred when Jackie Robinson began playing for the Brooklyn Dodgers in 1947.

Structural racism is still very much a part of contemporary American life, although the national trend is to reduce or eliminate it. Integrated housing, schools, restaurants, hotels, factories, and public transportation are commonplace. But in the centers of power such as government, the judiciary, management in business and industry, and many others, there is still underrepresentation of the groups less powerful than the dominant Anglo-Americans.

Assimilationist Racism.   Assimilationist racism takes a more subtle approach to resolving the differences between the powerful and the powerless. In assimilationist racism, the powerful group attempts to absorb the powerless group. "If you abandon your group," the powerful person says, "and become a member of my group, I will accept you." If enough social pressure can be brought to bear, powerless groups can be eliminated through assimilation. Some have recognized it as an effective form of "ethnocide," because it attempts to do away with a sociocultural unit. It does not kill *people,* it only kills *cultures.*

The Japanese vigorously tried assimilationist racism on the Koreans between World War I and World War II. But thirty-five years of bitter and dehumanizing experience taught both the Japanese and the Koreans that ethnocide is an extremely difficult and unpleasant way to resolve group problems. The United States tried this for long periods of time with American Indians. They tried to erase "tribalism" by coercing Indians to give up their cultures and become Anglo-American. The goal was to make "red white men," or as they are currently called, "apples" —red on the outside and white on the inside. Indian children were severely punished if caught speaking their tribal languages in the government boarding school designed by the powerful group to deculturate them. This has not worked, however. Over 100 American Indian languages are still living, and there is a growing trend for English-speaking Indians to learn their tribal languages.

During the early 1960s, when the Civil Rights Movement was just gaining momentum, assimilation seemed to many to be the ideal solution to America's racial problems. By the end of the decade, however, most leaders were realizing that assimilation might be an ideal solution for the powerful, but far less than ideal for the powerless. The more they assimilated, the less power they had. In the early 1960s, for example, black theologian Joseph Washington was advocating that blacks should "close their houses of worship" and "enter white congregations." He felt that the black congregations were "inadequate and lacked vital leadership."[16] But this assimilationist approach was changed before the decade was over. Washington sees that assimilation is "the wiping out of black culture and blood"[17] and that it appeals to few whites or blacks. He says that the best model is "equal partnership in a pluralistic society."[18]

Assimilationist racism is as oppressive as other kinds, but it may be more dangerous because it is so subtle. It is the most pervasive kind of racism in America today, practiced by those who attempt to legislate, both inside and outside the church, primary group relationships.

Open Society. In an open society, powerful groups respect the identity and integrity of powerless groups. Social structures provide free and open access to both groups. On a voluntary basis individuals or families can choose to leave one socio-cultural group and join another. This kind of a society most nearly approaches the values of the kingdom of God, as I understand it.

Secession. Secession is a corollary of an open society. If a society is truly open it will place the integrity of the groups within that society even ahead of national self-interest. It believes in the principle of self-determination. It affirms that the powerless ought to have power if they so desire. The United States' policy toward Puerto Rico reflects to a degree that of an open society. Puerto Ricans themselves can decide whether they want independence, statehood, or to remain in commonwealth status. Whether a petition from the Navajos to become a separate Navajo nation would be approved is doubtful, although it would be if the ideal values of the kingdom of God were reflected in American national policy. Canada did well to allow Quebec to decide by referendum on their own political future. The ultimate political gesture on the part of the powerful is to extend to the powerless the right of secession.

The Open Society and the Homogeneous Unit

In discussing the continuum from the oppression of genocide to the justice of an open society, I purposely avoided as much as possible mentioning the church. Most Christian people I know would agree that the place on the continuum they want to be is the open society, although some might have second thoughts about secession. The homogeneous unit principle, when rightly understood and applied, is an open society position. To understand it properly, however, two things must be borne in mind:

The Homogeneous Unit Principle Rejects Structural Racism. There is no room in the thinking of church growth people for a church that is racist or segregationist. It would strike me as odd to see that David Bosch accuses McGavran of recommending "racially segregated churches"[19] except that Bosch is a South African and would read the literature from the point of view of a society which still supports apartheid (although Bosch himself does not). Furthermore, perhaps Bosch understands the term "segregationist" differently. A racist or segregationist church in my definition is one which excludes people from worship and/or membership because of their skin color or the socio-cultural group to which they belong. Former President Carter's Plains Baptist Church, for example, is a racist church to all intents and purposes, because it excluded a black from membership (although other reasons were alleged). This is not the kind of church that the Church Growth Movement has ever recommended. In a local congregation, worship, membership, and the Lord's Table must be open to all.

The Homogeneous Unit Principle Rejects Assimilationist Racism. The Church Growth Movement refuses to say, by word or by deed, that "in order to become a Christian, you must become like me." It respects the right of people to form congregations that are socio-culturally specific if that is their desire. Most Koreans in Los Angeles, for example, prefer to worship in Korean congregations. Is there some theological principle that says they would be more pleasing to God if, rather than starting new churches in their own homogeneous unit, they joined already existing Anglo or Hispanic or black or Japanese churches? Such a thing would be sheer exploitation of the powerless, a type of theological imperialism. The existence of new Korean churches in Los Angeles is not contrary to the biblical doctrine of the unity of the body of Christ. However, there is a theological principle which says that if a Korean family wants to join a black church but is turned away because they are Korean, it is displeasing to God. The homogeneous unit principle attempts in every way to avoid both structural and assimilationist racism and promote the open society principle in churches.

No denomination in the United States has more consistently applied the homogeneous unit principle and or seen such a fruitful ministry among the multitudinous pieces of America's ethnic mosaic than the Southern Baptists. Their key executive for ethnic ministries, Oscar Romo, recognizes the need "to allow culture to set the agenda for our sharing the love of Jesus Christ for all people." He does not call for assimilation or integration in the sense of "Americanizing" or "acculturating" the ethnic. He refuses "to squeeze from him his last drop of ethnic identity" or to "distill from him his last ounce of ethnic pride." He recommends that Anglo church facilities be made available for other ethnic congregations to develop "side by side . . . each using his or her own unique characteristics" within the broader context of "the wholeness of Jesus Christ."[20]

Ironically, the Southern Baptist open society attitude was recently tested by an event similar to secession. The Southern Baptist principle has been to form homogeneous unit ethnic congregations of local churches, but to unite these congregations in heterogeneous associations and conventions on a geographical basis. In the California Baptist Convention, churches have been started among thirty-seven different ethnic groups. But leaders of the twenty-two Hispanic churches and missions in the Los Angeles area felt that in order better to evangelize the vast Southern California Hispanic community, it would be better to have an entirely Hispanic Association. So in March 1979, the Hispanics "seceded" from the mixed Los Angeles Association and started the *Asociación Bautista,* much to the consternation of the Anglo leadership of the State Convention. The leader of the new *Asociación,* Alfonso García, claims that separately the Hispanics can "evangelize, educate potential leaders, and achieve better recognition" than with the mixed association.[21]

The homogeneous unit principle would support the formation of such an association, but only under the condition that meaningful relationships with churches of the other thirty-six ethnic groups in California be cultivated and that Baptists manifest visibly to the world that they are "one in Christ." As I consider such events, I often wonder if and when the National Baptist Convention, now virtually all black, will start an aggressive program of planting white and Hispanic and Korean National Baptist churches. Primary church structures (congregations) should be accepted as they naturally form, but secondary church structures (inter-congregational) need to be planned and developed so as to give tangible witness of the unity of all peoples in the body of Christ.

The homogeneous unit principle, though it is a penultimate not an ultimate, characteristic of the kingdom of God, does provide a useful tool not only for the effective implementation of the evangelistic mandate, but also for helping people of differing human groups to live together in greater love and harmony.

Notes

1. Donald A. McGavran, *Ethnic Realities and the Church: Lessons from India* (Pasadena: William Carey Library, 1979).
2. C. Peter Wagner, *Our Kind of People: The Ethical Dimensions of Church Growth in America* (Atlanta: John Knox Press, 1979).
3. A. C. Dharmaraj, "Book Review of *Ethnic Realities and the Church,*" *The North India Churchman* 10, no. 11 (November 1979), pp. 6–10.
4. Tom Nees, "Evangelism Without the Gospel: Church Growth in *Our Kind of People,*" *Sojourners* 9, no. 2 (February 1980), pp. 27–29.
5. John R. W. Stott, ed., "The Pasadena Consultation—Homogeneous Unit," *Lausanne Occasional Papers No. 1,* (Wheaton, IL: Lausanne Committee for World Evangelization, 1978).
6. Donald A. McGavran, *Understanding Church Growth,* rev. ed. (Grand Rapids: Eerdmans, 1980), p. 223.
7. Ibid.
8. Gerald Palmer, "An Unqualified, 'It Depends . . . ' " *Home Missions Notebook* (Southern Baptist), Summer 1980, p. 8.
9. A homogeneous unit, according to the most general definition of McGavran, is: "Simply a section of society in which all the members have some characteristic in common," *Understanding Church Growth,* p. 95. A refinement of this, now used as the definition of "people group" or homogeneous unit by the Strategy Working

Group of the Lausanne Committee for World Evangelization is: "A significantly large sociological grouping of individuals who perceive themselves to have a common affinity for one another," Edward R. Dayton, *That Everyone May Hear: Reaching the Unreached,* 2nd ed. (Monrovia, CA: Missions Advanced Research and Communications, 1980), p. 25.

10. See McGavran, *Ethnic Realities;* and Wagner, *Our Kind of People.*
11. Martin E. Marty, "Is the Homogeneous Unit Principle of Church Growth Christian?" *Context,* March 15, 1978. Among other references to the empirical validity of the homogeneous unit principle see Jackson W. Carroll, Douglas W. Johnson and Martin E. Marty, *Religion in America: 1950 to the Present* (San Francisco: Harper & Row, 1979), p. 44; Lyle E. Schaller, *Assimilating New Members* (Nashville: Abingdon, 1978), pp. 65–66, 87–90; and David J. Hesselgrave, *Planting Chruches Cross-Culturally; A Guide for Home and Foreign Missions* (Grand Rapids: Baker, 1980), pp. 163–164. Many of the more than 350 graduate theses and dissertations in the Fuller School of World Mission Research Library add to the evidence.
12. I developed this theme in some detail in *Our Kind of People*, pp. 110–113, and later discovered an essay which takes the same viewpoint, written by Princeton Old Testament scholar, Bernhard Anderson, "The Babel Story: Paradigm of Human Unity and Diversity," in *Ethnicity,* ed. Andrew M. Greeley and Gregory Baum, (New York: Seabury, 1977), pp. 63–70.
13. Jim Wallis, *Agenda for Biblical People* (San Francisco: Harper & Row, 1976), p. 78.
14. I am struck by the relative underemphasis on, or even absence of references to, the social abuses of modern nationalism in the literature of the radical discipleship camp. My hunch is that this "people blindness" is caused by a low view of culture, a lack of missiological insight, and an inherent unwillingness to appreciate the socio-cultural benefits which can accrue from using the homogeneous unit paradigm.
15. "Introduction to the Klan," *The Klansman,* June 1977, p. 8.
16. Joseph R. Washington, Jr., *Black Religion: The Negro and Christianity in the United States* (Boston: Beacon Press, 1964), p. 258.
17. Joseph R. Washington, Jr., *Marriage in Black and White* (Boston: Beacon Press, 1970), p. 16.

18. Joseph R. Washington, Jr., *Black and White Power Subreption* (Boston: Beacon Press, 1969), p. 8.

19. David J. Bosch, *Witness to the World: The Christian Mission in Theological Perspective* (Atlanta: John Knox Press, 1980), p. 208.

20. Oscar Romo, "Lest We Forget," *Home Missions*, (Southern Baptist Home Mission Board), 1979, p. 14.

21. John Dart, "Hispanic Baptist Churches Break Away," *Los Angeles Times*, June 2, 1979.

CHAPTER 10

Structuring for Christian Social Ministry

I hope Christians agree that one essential aspect of living a kingdom lifestyle is participation in fulfilling the cultural mandate. Believing that, however, is only the starting point. Faith without works is dead. Desire must become doing. This chapter will present some practical guidelines on how to get involved in Christian social ministry. The major key to effectiveness in this area of service, as I see it, is to employ the appropriate structure.

Many raise the pointed question: Should the church get involved in politics? My answer is yes, at least when the church is located in a democratic society and where the size of the Christian community can make a difference. But in order for this to be effective, the structure must match the issue. Some church structures are appropriate for some issues, and others are not. If the issue is matched to the wrong structure the predictable result will be a loss of effectiveness in implementing both the cultural and the evangelistic mandates. In other words, churches have *lost* members by going about their social ministries in the wrong way.

Choosing Political Options

Let us assume that attaining the greatest degree of social justice is a common Christian objective. In our present world, political events largely determine the degree of social justice prevailing at a given time and place. The defeat of Japan in World War II, for example, brought more social justice to Korea. The replacement of rule of a white minority by a black majority brought more social justice to Zimbabwe. The land reform of the social revolution of 1952 brought more social justice to Bolivia. All these were political events.

With some exceptions, citizens of most nations of the world are called upon to participate in national politics. Several political options are usually open to them. Almost every political party justifies its existence and its platform on the premise that if they are given power they will improve social justice in their nation. And social dynamics are such that all citizens, including Christians, have to make political choices. There is no avoiding it. Instead of choosing one of the political parties, a person may act as an individual. But it must be understood that it is a choice, and a choice with political repercussions. The choice not to get involved in the political process is a vote for the status quo, and should be recognized as such. Some may choose not to endorse any of the political options that the system offers, but to move outside the system and either start a counterculture or join the revolution. That is clearly a political decision.

In the free world, the ballot box is the place where political opinion is most frequently registered. But a given individual in the voting booth makes very little political difference. More difference is made if that person joins a political party or other political action group. Groups are more important in the political process than individuals. How does a Christian choose which group to belong to?

First it must be discovered how the political group defines the issue or issues which it feels will promote social justice. Americans generally agree for example, that equal educational opportunity for all citizens is a part of social justice. In Pasadena, California, where I live, providing equal educational opportunity has been a prominent political issue. While all agree on the objective, not all agree on the means that should be used to provide the best public education for all. Because Pasadena's schools have mostly minority enrollment (whites are less than 30 percent) the issue of whether mandatory busing should be used came up. Some thought busing was the best way to provide educational opportunities. Others thought strengthening neighborhood schools was the best way. Choosing the means, then, is an important step.

As to specific political options, at one point the school board favored neighborhood schools. Those who favored busing drew up a petition to recall the school board members and elect new ones who would agree.

There were three political options: recall, pro-board, or silence. Recall was a vote for busing, but both pro-board and silence were votes for neighborhood schools.

Which option was the Christian option? Was one closer to the values of the kingdom of God than the others? In fact, there were Christians on both sides of the issue. (As a matter of record, busing has been practiced in Pasadena since 1970, with very good results, on the whole.) Questions like this need to be thought through before choosing political options. While individual choices by church members do not have much effect on the growth or decline of churches, when Christians join together to generate more political strength the structure they choose can have a significant influence on church growth.

One Church: Two Structures

In thinking about the involvement of the church in mission, it is helpful to recognize two basic and complementary structures. Over the past decade or so, Ralph Winter has led the way in elucidating these two structures in the field of evangelical missiology.[1] They are not new; they have existed since New Testament times; nor is Winter the first to notice them. But Winter's unique contribution has been to legitimize the two structures biblically, and to show how they are both needed for God's purposes in the world to be carried out effectively.

Most of Winter's work has focused on showing how these two structures are useful in fulfilling the evangelistic mandate, particularly in the area of foreign missions. My purpose here is to show how they can be equally useful in implementing the cultural mandate.

The first structure is what most people think of by "church." Winter calls it a "modality." In the secular sphere a modality is the government structure of a city or state. Members are born into it, and they all have a vote. The obligations of members are few, and the discipline is low. Few actually go to jail. Its purpose is to promote harmony, peace, and justice among the members. Applied to the church it might be better to use the term "congregational structure" instead of modality. This refers either to the one local congregation or a cluster of congregations in a judicatory or denomination. The congregation is people-oriented. New members are socialized into the group as children of existing members, or they come as transfers or converts. Discipline is relatively low, and there are few obligations to retain membership. Excommunication is rare. Government is largely by consensus. If the people don't like their pastor they can usually take steps to get rid of him or her.

The second structure Winter calls a "sodality." It chiefly differs from the modality in being task-oriented rather than people-oriented. The only members are people who have applied to join and are accepted because they can contribute to the task. The organization is more important than the people, and the people can be and are fired for incompetence without trial by jury. In the secular sphere, sodalities would be organizations such as grocery stores, motion picture theaters, the police department, or factories. They are not governed through consensus, but management is by objective. In the church it might be better to call this a "mission structure" rather than a sodality. Some refer to it as a para-church organization. It requires a second decision to become a member, the first being to join the congregational structure. It is not designed so much to produce harmony and brotherhood as to accomplish a specific task. Nominality is not tolerated in the mission structure as it usually is in the congregational structure. Examples of the mission structure would include the American Bible Society, Wycliffe Bible Translators, Campus Crusade for Christ, the Sudan Interior Mission, the Billy Graham Evangelistic Association, the Southern Baptist Home Mission Board, an Evangelism Explosion team in a local church, or Gordon-Conwell Theological Seminary.

Both the congregational and mission structures are, in the broad sense of the word, church structures. They are formalized gatherings of God's people. They have different styles and different purposes but each is a manifestation of the community of the King. Most members of mission structures are also members of congregational structures, but not vice versa. Mission structures are too demanding for the run-of-the-mill Christian.

Are Mission Structures Legitimate?

While all observers agree that the two structures exist, many are not sure that they *ought* to exist. For example, G. W. Peters regards mission structures as an "unfortunate and abnormal historic development" which, he laments, has "produced autonomous, missionless churches on the one hand, and autonomous, churchless missionary societies on the other hand."[2] Orlando Costas argues that the "existence of missionary societies apart from church bodies" in reality represents "God's judgment upon the church." He finds "no ground in the New Testament for a concept of mission apart from the church," and feels that, at best, mission structures are temporary and should be taken over by the congregation as soon as the congregations recognize their legitimate responsibilities in mission.[3] Harvie Conn adds that the church growth school's analysis of church-mission structures is "a failure," based on his opinion that the sodality or mission structure is "less than ideal."[4]

Ralph Winter, of course, disagrees. He finds the two structures in the New Testament. Whereas the local congregations in the New Testament took over the already existing Jewish synagogue structure and adapted it to their use, Paul's mission band took over the already existing Jewish proselytizing band structure and adapted it to Christian service.[5] The argument that Paul and his co-workers were sent out by the church at Antioch is far from conclusive, as Harold Cook has shown. Cook argues, "There is absolutely no indication in the text that these men were acting on behalf of the church."[6] They had cordial relationships with the church, they kept the church informed as to their activities, and undoubtedly the church prayed for them. But, for example, when, after his first term, Paul fired John Mark and hired Silas to take his place, there is no reason to think that the leaders of the church at Antioch were the ones who made the decision.

I agree with Howard Snyder, who finds that "these two structures are justified biblically" and that there are "numerous precedents throughout the history of the church."[7] What is most needed, is not for the congregational structures to criticize or write off the mission or parachurch structures, but rather for them to understand them and their nature better so that God's purposes can be fulfilled in our day.

Understanding Each Other Better

In order to further this mutual understanding and attempt to get past mutual recrimination, let me voice three propositions:

Both structures are ordained of God. While blueprints for neither congregational nor mission structures were sent down from heaven, they are both described in the New Testament and were found useful there. Both took over existing cultural forms, and God blessed them.

Both structures bind together the people of God. I believe that both congregational and mission structures are kingdom structures. They are not ends in themselves, but they enable God's people to serve him and to bring glory to him.

Both structures need each other. Congregational and mission structures ought to exist in a symbiotic relationship. They should not be competing with each other, but helping one another. Too many churches feel threatened by parachurch organizations, and too many parachurch organizations pay scant attention to churches. Mission structures become irritated because congregational structures "can't get anything done," while congregational structures become irritated because mission structures "bypass the local church," or worse, because they are "parasites on the church." I believe that this kind of irritation is caused primarily by a failure on the part of each to understand and appreciate the nature of the other structure.

It is the responsibility of the congregational structure to maintain a broad vision. The mayor of a city should make sure that all the pieces fit together. If another restaurant or gas station is needed, he or she sees that it happens, but the mayor does not do the job personally. Likewise the congregation. The congregation should make sure that God's work gets done, and that when necessary, mission structures get started and are supported with personnel, prayer, and finances. Pastors do well not to try to do everything. They should encourage the formation of mission structures both within and without the church and delegate responsbility. One reason that Garden Grove Community Church can sustain such a variety of ministries, for example, is that Pastor Robert Schuller understands and practices this principle. He has encouraged the formation of between twenty and thirty local mission structures which are separate from the congregation itself, with their own leadership, programs, and budget.

Mission structures, at least the better ones, do not have a broad vision. They are single-minded and concentrate on one task. Their narrow vision is part of their very nature, not something to be criticized. The better mission structure leaders frequently exhibit three characteristics which broader-minded pastors need to understand and appreciate (although at times it is difficult to do so).

The better mission structure leaders are convinced that their task is the most important task in the kingdom of God. Whether it is Bible translation, church planting, relief and development, evangelistic crusades, church renewal, leadership training, or what have you, the leader of the group doing it had better think that it is the most important thing in the world. Those who don't can still lead mission structures, but not as well.

The better mission structure leaders are convinced that their particular organization is going about the task better than any other similar organization. They would never say this overtly, since it would be considered immodest. They try to get along with other parachurch leaders, they pass out compliments to others at times. But deep down, if they suspect that they might not be doing the job better than others, they initiate the action necessary to improve.

Because of these two characteristics, mission structure leaders often find that they irritate both congregational structure leaders and other mission structure leaders. Since they operate with a narrow vision, this is to be expected. Pastors and other congregational leaders, however, should rise above the temptation to let parachurch leaders disturb them, because pastors are expected to have a much broader vision.

The better mission structure leaders have a low need for people and a high dedication to the task. People are useful in mission structures to the extent that they can help get the job done. When they cease to be useful they are dismissed. This is quite unlike congregational structures which are people-oriented, not task-oriented. The maimed, the lame, and the blind are welcomed by the congregational structure, but not by the mission structure unless their handicap is overcome. The two missions I served with, for example, required strict medical exams for membership. No congregation that I have ever joined has asked me for my medical history. Each procedure is appropriate for the structure.

Structures and the Cultural Mandate

Historical research has shown that the spread of the Christian faith worldwide has usually been most effectively accomplished by mission structures. I will not stop to rehearse the evidence here, except to mention the little-observed fact that the principal reason why the churches of the Reformation did not become active missionary churches for over two centuries was in all probability that Luther had rejected Catholic orders—the mission structures.[8]

Returning to the question, "Should the church be involved in politics?" we are faced with the need to answer it in the context of what we now know about structures. Some of the social ministry of the church is appropriately done by the congregational structure and some is more appropriately left to the mission structure. In order to make this clear, I will use a graphic model:

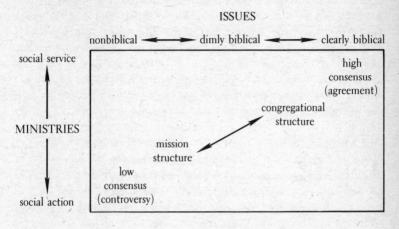

Christian Social Ministries Matrix

The most important feature on the Christian social ministries matrix is the high consensus vs. low consensus, or agreement vs. controversy scale. When there is high consensus among a population of Christians that a certain social ministry should be undertaken in the name of Christ, the congregational structure is a good vehicle for it. On the other hand when the particular issue is controversial, the mission structure, not the congregational structure, should be used to promote it. There is no clear borderline between the two on the model. More frequently than not, the decision whether to use a congregational or mission structure is complex, subjective, and ambiguous. But the consequences of the wrong decision may well involve decline in church membership.

Notice that two sets of factors, issues and ministries, impact the consensus that a particular kind of social involvement will enjoy. They need to be considered one at a time.

Issues. The horizontal axis is a continuum from nonbiblical, through dimly biblical, to clearly biblical issues. The more clearly a particular social issue can be justified by the Bible, the more appropriate is the congregational structure. The actual process of locating an issue on the continuum is not always objective. One congregation might agree that an issue is clearly biblical while others would read the Bible differently. The crucial factor is that the particular congregation *perceives* the issue to be biblical. For example, in Dade County, Florida, a recent political issue revolved around whether homosexuals would be allowed to teach in public schools. Most objective Bible scholars would agree that it is not an issue that any part of the Bible deals with forthrightly and clearly. Yet many Christian congregations in Dade County *perceived* it as a clear biblical issue, and many of them were used—as congregational structures—to promote a political option. Although I have not seen a specific study on it, my impression is that this decision did not hinder the growth of those congregations. It may even have helped.

It apparently did help growth in Los Gatos Christian Church of Los Gatos, California. The church, a large, growing congregation of 5,000, south of San Francisco, decided to go public with their opposition to homosexuals teaching in public schools. The media picked it up and gave it wide publicity. They threatened to vote out of office any local politician who disagreed. The pastor, Marvin Rickard, said, "We don't want legalism and a judgmental spirit, but if we are committed to the Bible as the Word of God, we have to take a stand." Since they went public, Rickard says, "attendance has increased."[9]

Ministries. The technical difference between social service and social action was described in detail in Chapter 2. I indicated there that churches which specialize in social service (meeting immediate human needs) tend to grow better than those which specialize in social action (changing social structures). The vertical axis of the above matrix describes a similar thing, pointing out that the more a type of ministry approaches social service the more consensus can be anticipated, but the more it approaches social action the more controversial it will likely become. Congregational structures are more suited to social service, while mission structures are more suited to social action.

Many congregations in America, for example, took up special offerings and sent emergency relief aid to the victims of the devastating earthquake that recently hit Guatemala. This was clearly a social service type of ministry, and it enjoyed virtually unanimous consensus among Christians. The congregational structure was appropriate. However, there is another issue in Central America that is potentially even more destructive than an earthquake: the oppression of peasants by a few wealthy, powerful landowners. But, since overthrowing governments and promoting land reform require social action types of ministry, the mission structure is a much more appropriate way to deal with this in the name of Christ than the congregational structure.

There are some cases, such as homosexuals teaching in Dade County schools, that are social action ministries, yet can enjoy high consensus in the congregational structure because of the perceived weight of biblical issues. On the other hand, a church sponsoring a Boy Scout troop is a nonbiblical matter. But it is so definitely a noncontroversial social service ministry that the congregational structure can handle it well.

To illustrate further, in 1977 President Carter halted production of the B-1 bomber. It was a controversial, highly politicized process. National leaders agree that one of the major factors in the decision was the pressure brought to bear by Christians. Mission structures, appropriately, were used for this social action venture. A group called Clergy and Laity Concerned (CALC) together with the American Friends Service Committee (AFSC) "were instrumental in bringing down the B-1," according to a report in *The Christian Century*.[10]

Why Social Action Hinders Growth

Why is it that congregational structures, whether local churches, judicatories, denominations, or councils of churches are not appropriate structures for social action? The answer to this question is complex, but I believe there are at least six reasons, which I will list as dangers:

The Danger of Elitism. The leaders of the congregation or denomination lose touch with the grass roots, the people in the pews who are sincere about serving God, but whose convictions about Christian involvement in social issues are not reflected in the attitudes and actions of the leaders. Several recent studies have documented the elitist tendency of clergy leadership.[11]

The Danger of Divisiveness. Social action is controversial. Predictably it will introduce seeds of division in a church except when the congregation becomes convinced that the issue is clearly biblical. For example, if my church in Pasadena had taken a stand one way or another on the busing issue, it would have had a devastating effect on the congregation. Honest disagreement was present at high levels: the senior pastor was against busing and the associate was for it.

The Danger of Dehumanization. It is not frequently recognized that by using a congregation as an instrument of political power, some members of the congregation can be oppressed. They join a church for spiritual reasons and then find that they and their money are being used for political ends. Anthropologist Margaret Mead warns that "the church is an instrument of God, not of somebody else's political program."[12] When a congregation or denomination takes a political stand, it does so in the name of its members whether its members agree or not. This can be dehumanizing.

The Danger of Social Impotence.   From Durkheim to Dean Kelley, sociologists have told us that the basic social nature of churches is conservative. As Ivan Illich says, the specific function of the church "must be a contribution to development which could not be made by any other institution. I believe that this contribution is faith in Christ."[13] This is disturbing to many social action advocates who would like to use congregational structures to further their political views, but congregations that allow themselves to get involved in controversial social action affairs, for the most part, end up losing social strength. Kelley argues that we should not expect congregational structures to be "social action barracks where the troops of militant reform are kept in readiness to charge forth at the alarums and excursions of social change." A more realistic view is that they are "conservatories where the hurts of life are healed."[14]

The Danger of Bungling.   The track record of congregational structures that have insisted on becoming involved in social action ministries has not always been the best. One reason political scientist Paul Henry concludes that "the institutional church should show great restraint in becoming politically involved," is that many resolutions and pronouncements of denominations and church councils "are in effect little more than hot air."[15] Social problems are extremely complex and difficult even for specialists to deal with. Rarely do the leaders of congregational structures have the expertise to come to intelligent decisions. Both Carl McIntyre and the World Council of Churches have demonstrated this, although they usually come to opposite conclusions on a given social issue. In offering advice to pastors on how to make use of their local newspaper's religion page, journalsit Tom Minnery says: "By all means stick to the Bible. If you strike out into the social gospel or into political commentary, you'll get nowhere."[16]

The Danger of Constantinism.   Suppose the congregational structures take political positions and win? Is it the goal of the churches to control politics or society? It seems to me this could only be considered a viable option by those who have not read history. As mentioned in

Chapter 2, this is not a commendable goal. When the church controls the world, it tends to lose prophetic power.

Social Issues in the United Presbyterian Church

In Chapter 6, I argued that the major cause of the decline in membership of the mainline denominations since 1965 was a national institutional factor I called "The Great Priority Shift." In the 1960s, mainline denominational bureaucracies elevated the cultural mandate to a higher priority position than the evangelistic mandate. One thing that surprised me after I developed the hypothesis was the finding of a United Presbyterian study on membership trends concluding that "the frequently argued theory that church involvement in social action has caused membership loss has at best very limited validity."[17]

Previous to that I had been under the impression that some controversial social stands taken by the leaders of the United Presbyterian Church had deeply offended large numbers of its members. One was the decision of the Presbyterian Council on Church and Race to donate $10,000 of their mission offerings to the defense fund of Angela Davis in 1971. As John Fry observes, the news "hit the General Assembly like lightning" and resulted in what he calls "The Great Offering Plate Boycott." Fry calculates that between 1965 and 1973, a total of $18 million was withheld from the General Mission giving because of the "alarming gap" between the position of the bureaucrats and that of the people in the pews on socio-political issues.[18] This seemed to tie in closely with research reports such as that of Stanford's Harold Quinley, who found that the "new breed activists" in the clergy of the 1960s "met with considerable resistance from their congregational members . . . and many lost members and finances."[19]

The Hartford consortium, which reported its results in *Understanding Church Growth and Decline 1950–1978*,[20] brought further light to the United Presbyterian study. It turns out that the original study used the term "social action" loosely. It did not make the important distinction between social service and social action. Further investigation showed that social ministries such as "organizing for the disadvantaged" or "financial support for activities customarily associated with churches— Scouts, rehabilitation for example" were positively related to growth. But on the other hand, the "use of congregational facilities by groups concerned with social action" and "explicit efforts at changing society" tended to be negatively related to growth.[21] The former, in my terminology, is social service and the latter social action. A second finding was that, not the social ministry itself, but rather "the congregational tension and disunity" was crucial. As I indicated on the Christian social ministries matrix, high or low consensus is the major key to understanding how social ministries affect growth in the congregational structure. This report concurs by saying: "Social action that does not create disharmony is unlikely to have a negative effect on growth."[22]

My reading of the evidence, therefore, is that the decisions made by United Presbyterian leaders to donate to the Angela Davis fund and to support equally controversial socio-political movements were decisions inappropriate for congregational structures. If, for example, someone had created a mission structure called "Presbyterians for the Support of Angela Davis" and solicited contributions on a free-will basis, they would probably have raised more than $10,000 *without* alienating individuals, losing some $2 million per year in mission funds, and triggering declines in membership. The problem came when they used the funds contributed by members for such a controversial social action project without their consent. They paid the price in a serious loss of members.

As I see it, the United Presbyterian leadership did not adequately take into account three factors: (1) the difference between social service and social action, (2) the potential symbiotic relationship between congregational structures and mission structures, and (3) the inherent and persistent conservative nature of church members. As Dean Hoge discovered, the main opposition to congregational involvement in social action is "the argument against social reform."[23] In other words, Christian people in general are usually more in favor of the status quo than of social change. Whether they *ought* to be or not is another question.

The conservative nature of religion would incline us to think that liberalism has a negative correlation with church growth. This has been confirmed in some recent studies. Dean Hoge, for example, has done a study correlating several institutional factors with denominational growth. Theological liberalism showed the highest negative correlation with growth.[24] Also, in a study of United Church of Christ growth patterns, William McKinney found that "theological conservatism is associated with membership growth."[25] Although there are some notable exceptions, it seems to be a fact of life that theological conservatism is attached to socio-political conservatism, and that theological liberalism is attached to socio-political liberalism. As far as church growth is concerned, congregations that maintain a conservative stance generally seem to be those most relevant to the unbelievers in society. This is probably because they have more accurately discerned, both from theological and from phenomenological sources, the important functions of the church.

The Rise of the New Right

I debated whether to include a section on the New Right because for all I know it might fizzle and be forgotten in a short period of time. However, I feel that the participation of evangelical Christians in the Presidential election of 1980 revealed some important issues that are highly relevant to the matter of matching church structures to social issues. Whether it fizzles or not, the New Right illustrates some important principles of church growth and social issues.

One of the most dramatic changes in the American religious scene occurred in 1980 when what Martin Marty calls "private Protestants" went public. The private Protestants are the evangelicals who "accentuated individual salvation out of the world, personal moral life congruent with the ideals of the saved," and other things such as revivalism. The public Protestants, on the other hand, "gradually lost faith in revivalism and worked instead with the techniques and processes which strove for some transformation of the world."[26] When Marty wrote this in 1970, the Great Reversal, as Moberg and others call it, had not come to an end. But the accelerating deterioration of the moral life of America during the 1970s brought evangelicals out of their socio-political closet.

Several mission structure organizations were formed in 1979 and 1980, including Jerry Falwell's Moral Majority, which became the most prominent, Christian Voice, Religious Roundtable, and other such coalitions. In the 1980 election, although some of them denied in theory that they would endorse specific candidates, they did in practice, and contributed to Ronald Reagan's victory. It is also reported that in the thirty-eight congressional races the New Right entered, twenty-five of their candidates were elected. It was obviously a substantial involvement in social action on the part of Christians.

The initial, rather stunned, reaction of the public Protestants was: What do you think you're doing in the public arena? We are the ones who represent Christians here. Go back to your prayer meetings and your altar rails and your evangelistic crusades and your Sunday School bus routes where you belong. What do you know about women's rights and nuclear energy and capital punishment and defense spending? One wrote editorially in *The Christian Century,* that the "frightening thing" about the "gospel of rightwing politics" is "that they have baptized a particular ideological perspective and identified it with the Christian proclamation."[27]

Is this not a classic case of beholding a mote in thy brother's eye, but not considering the beam in thine own? Although the views of liberal social activists are more balanced at this writing, some are still raising the question of separation of church and state which the same individuals never mentioned when they were marching, lobbying, and petitioning in the 1960s and early 1970s. Martin Luther King was not accused of blurring the separation of church and state, even by evangelicals. It will undoubtedly take a while to get used to private Protestants going public.

Wallis and Falwell

In the final analysis, Jim Wallis of Sojourners and Jerry Falwell of Moral Majority have much more in common than not. Both are committed Christians, both obey Jesus as their Lord, and both have dedicated their lives to serve him. Worldwide, those qualities put them both in a very tiny minority. But tinier yet, both are white, Anglo-American males, both think that there is something frighteningly wrong with American society, and both think that unless something radical is done and done quickly, America will come under the severe judgment of God. Furthermore, both believe that it is the duty of Christians to speak out in the name of Christ on important social issues, calling publicly for Americans to repent and get back to living a lifestyle which reflects the values of the kingdom of God.

What, then, is the difference? The basic difference is the social agenda of each. What do Americans need to repent *of?*

Wallis' agenda includes such issues as "the consumptive mentality," "the will to power and domination," "the oppression of race, sex, and class," "the arrogance of national destiny," "the efficacy of violence," "the victims of the various systems of the world," "economic and cultural imperialism," and the like.[28] Jerry Falwell's agenda includes such issues as abortion, homosexuality, pornography, humanism, and the fractured family, which he lists as "the five major problems that have political consequences, political implications, that moral Americans need to be ready to face."[29]

It is not helpful to say, as some have done, that Wallis is dealing with social ethics while Falwell is dealing with personal ethics. Both are dealing with social ethics, but of a different nature. Wallis is horrified that "the government is able to kill a million Indochinese and justify it with 'saving them from Communism.' "[30] Falwell is horrified that "last year more than 1.5 million little babies were murdered in America,"[31] deaths justified by the theory that mothers should have the right to choose whether their infants live or die. Since the permission to kill babies was granted by the Supreme Court in 1973, abortion can scarcely be relegated to "personal ethics." Yet the liberal press accuses the evangelicals of "exploiting abortion," which is a "religious issue," as "a front for what is in reality a right-wing political campaign."[32] But abortion can hardly be perceived as a "religious" issue while issues such as opposing war or nuclear energy or capital punishment are seen as something other than religious. All are defending the integrity of human life, a Christian moral principle. I myself wonder why Christians have not yet picked up smoking as a social issue when, despite the persistent warnings of the Surgeon General, more Americans die each year of lung cancer than died in the whole Viet Nam war. On what grounds does a society outlaw Laetrile, which may save lives, but not cigarettes which are proven to take lives? The tobacco industry has killed many more humans than nuclear energy.

Structures and the New Right

The apparent political success of the New Right in the 1980 election took many Americans by surprise. At this writing it is impossible to say what effect private Protestants' going public will have on the growth of evangelical churches. However, I do have some observations for the New Right based on the thesis of this chapter, that unless social issues are properly matched to appropriate church structures, church growth can be negatively affected.

Mission structures are stronger than congregational structures in promoting social action causes. The Moral Majority, for example, is a mission structure. It has wisely chosen to incorporate as a political lobby and not claim religious tax-exemption. This is one reason it is a stronger structure in socio-political affairs than the National Council of Churches or the National Association of Evangelicals or Fourth Presbyterian Church of Washington. The Moral Majority represents only those Christians who volunteer to identify with its goals and contribute funds to its program. It is an evangelical group, but it does not represent all evangelicals. In my own church, for example, many members support Moral Majority and many do not. Some choose to support Sojourners and the Jubilee Fellowship. Thus the Moral Majority, like any mission structure, can gather strength without coercion, produce identity without division, and allow for cooperation without compromise.

Congregational structures can be damaged if they are improperly involved in social action issues. Jeffrey Hadden's question, addressed to the clergy who are leading the New Right, should be taken seriously: "Will their constituents follow them? Or, like the liberal Protestant clergy of the 1960s, will they get too far out in front of their flocks?"[33] While social issues are important, the cultural mandate must never take priority over the evangelistic mandate. *Moody Monthly* warns: "History demonstrates that the marriage of Christian groups with political partisans produces discord, disillusionments, and frequently dishonor to God's name."[34] I would add that this danger is much more threatening to congregational structures than to mission structures.

Jerry Falwell is Senior Pastor of Thomas Road Baptist Church, Lynchburg, Virginia, obviously a congregational structure. He is aware that the congregational structure is not appropriate to the kind of Christian social action that Moral Majority is involved in. I have heard Falwell say, "Our church never mentions politics from the pulpit. Our church has no political action committee." I have my own doubts whether such a distinction can really be sustained. Falwell cannot at the same time both be the pastor of Thomas Road and not be the pastor. Wherever he goes he is the chief spokesperson for that congregational structure, as is any senior pastor. Like it or not, Thomas Road Baptist Church is, through its pastor, involved in Christian political action.

But the key to growth is still consensus. As long as Falwell can persuade the congregation that the issues he and Moral Majority are dealing with are *biblical* issues, the vitality of the congregational structure can be sustained.

I am not as concerned about Jerry Falwell as I am about thousands of evangelical pastors around the country who are likely to try to imitate him, but who will not be able to pull it off without causing serious growth problems in their congregations. It may become the "in" thing for evangelical preachers to make socio-political pronouncements from their pulpits in the 1980s, as it was for the liberals in the 1960s. Getting involved in the cultural mandate might become so heady that the evangelistic mandate is neglected. If so, evangelicals can expect a decline both in membership and in social strength.

If the proper structures are employed, however, both the evangelistic mandate and the cultural mandate can be effectively implemented by the people of God who are serving him in the community of the king.

Notes

1. Ralph D. Winter's basic document is "The Two Structures of God's Redemptive Mission," *Missiology: An International Review* 2, no. 1 (January 1974), pp. 121–139. See also his "Ghana: Preparation for Marriage," *International Review of Mission*, July, 1978, pp. 338–353; and for his latest thinking, "Protestant Mission Societies: The American Experience," *Missiology: An International Review*, April, 1979, pp. 139–178. The latter was his Presidential address to the American Society of Missiology in 1978.

2. G. W. Peters, *A Biblical Theology of Missions*, (Chicago: Moody Press, 1972), p. 214.

3. Orlando E. Costas, *The Church and Its Mission: A Shattering Critique from the Third World* (Wheaton, IL: Tyndale, 1974), pp. 168–169.

4. Harvie M. Conn, "Church-Mission Relationships," in *Theological Perspectives on Church Growth*, ed. Harvie M. Conn (Nutley, NJ: Presbyterian and Reformed, 1976), pp. 115, 122.

5. See Winter, "The Two Structures," pp. 122–123.

6. Harold R. Cook, "Who Really Sent the Missionaries?" *Evangelical Missions Quarterly* 11, no. 4 (October 1975), p. 234.

7. Howard Snyder, *The Community of the King* (Downers Grove, IL: InterVarsity Press, 1977), p. 153. Snyder gives five excellent reasons why mission structures should be encouraged within the context of the local church on pp. 155–156.

8. See Jarislav Pelikan, *Spirit Versus Structure: Luther and the Institutions of the Church* (New York: Harper & Row, 1968), pp. 53–56; Kenneth Scott Latourette, *A History of Christianity* (New York:

Harper & Brothers, 1953); and the works by Ralph D. Winter previously cited.

9. Marvin Rickard, *Los Gatos Christian Church Bulletin*, April 17, 1978.

10. James Robison, "How the B-1 Bomber Was Brought Down," *Christian Century*, August 17–24, 1977, p. 711.

11. See especially Jeffrey K. Hadden, *The Gathering Storm in the Churches* (Garden City, NY: Doubleday & Co., 1969); and Douglas W. Johnson and George W. Cornell, *Punctured Preconceptions: What North American Christians Think About the Church* (New York: Friendship Press, 1972).

12. Margaret Mead, *To Love or to Perish: The Technological Crisis and the Churches*, edited with J. Edward Carothers, Daniel D. McCracken and Roger L. Shinn (New York: Friendship Press, 1972), p. 130.

13. Ivan Illich, *The Church, Change and Development* (Freiburg, West Germany: Herder and Herder, 1970), p. 17.

14. Dean M. Kelley, *Why Conservative Churches Are Growing* (New York: Harper & Row, 1972), p. 151.

15. Paul B. Henry, *Politics for Evangelicals* (Valley Forge, PA: Judson Press, 1974) pp. 112, 96.

16. Tom Minnery, "Good News about the Religion Page," *Leadership* 1, no. 3 (Summer 1980), p. 47.

17. C. Edward Brubaker, Dean R. Hoge, Margaret Thomas, and John E. Dyble, *A Summary Report of the Committee on Membership Trends* (New York: United Presbyterian Church, 1976), p. 16.

18. John R. Fry, *The Trivialization of the United Presbyterian Church* (New York: Harper & Row, 1975), pp. 40, 44, 51.

19. Harold E. Quinley, "The Dilemma of an Activist Church: Protestant Religion in the Sixties and Seventies," *Journal for the Scientific Study of Religion* 13, no. 1 (March 1974), p. 1.

20. Dean R. Hoge and David A. Roozen, eds., *Understanding Church Growth and Decline: 1950–1978* (New York: Pilgrim, 1979).

21. Wade Clark Roof, Dean R. Hoge, John E. Dyble and C. Kirk Hadaway, "Factors Producing Growth or Decline in United Presbyterian Congregations," in *Understanding Church Growth and Decline*, ed. Hoge and Roozen, p. 216.

22. Ibid. The report further says: "Involvement in controversial actions can lead to congregational division and disharmony, and if so, it will

likely lead to membership decline; yet, some types of social action attract newcomers and offer members a sense of religious and social responsibility," p. 222.

23. Dean R. Hoge, *Division in the Protestant House* (Philadelphia: Westminster, 1976), p. 87.
24. Dean R. Hoge, "A Test of Theories of Denominational Growth and Decline," in *Understanding Church Growth and Decline,* ed. Hoge and Roozen, p. 191. See also p. 366, which explains how the degree of liberalism was determined.
25. William J. McKinney, Jr., "Performance of United Church of Christ Congregations in Massachusetts and Pennsylvania," in *Understanding Church Growth and Decline*, ed. Hoge and Roozen, p. 241.
26. Martin E. Marty, *Righteous Empire: The Protestant Experience in America* (New York: Dial Press, 1970), p. 179.
27. Robert E. McKeown, " 'Christian Voice:' The Gospel of Right Wing Politics," *The Christian Century*, August 15–22, 1979, p. 782.
28. Jim Wallis, *Agenda for Biblical People* (San Francisco: Harper & Row, 1976), pp. 2, 15, 60.
29. Jerry Falwell, *Listen, America!* (Garden City, NY: Doubleday, 1980), pp. 252–253.
30. Wallis, *Agenda for Biblical People,* p. 62.
31. Falwell, *Listen, America!,* p. 165. It might be mentioned that it appears the Sojourners and Jim Wallis are accepting Falwell's agenda item on abortion, although for years one of the factors that kept them from doing it was their aversion to right-wing political positions in general and their support of the feminist movement in particular. They now "see abortion as yet another form of violence against women." See Jim Wallis, "Coming Together on the Sanctity of Life," *Sojourners* 9, no. 11 (November 1980), p. 3. Falwell and others would stress that babies are the victims and mothers the oppressors.
32. James M. Wall, "The New Right Exploits Abortion," *The Christian Century*, July 30–August 6, 1980, p. 747.
33. Jeffrey K. Hadden, "Soul Saving via Video," *The Christian Century* 97, no. 20 (May 28, 1980), p. 612.
34. Ted Miller, "Shall We Join the New 'Christian Crusade?' " *Moody Monthly* 81, no. 1 (September 1980), p. 20.

Index

"Great Reversal," 2–4, 27, 89–90, 115, 197
Green, Michael, 139
Greenway, Roger, 150
Grimmer, Amanda, *xi*

Hadaway, C. Kirk, 202
Hadden, Jeffrey, 122, 200
Hartford Consortium, 123, 195
Hartford Seminary, 119
Hartman, Warren, 122
Hatch, Nathan O., 24, 126
Henry, Carl F. H., 3, 39, 96, 103, 143
Henry, Paul, 194
Hesselgrave, David, 54, 65, 92, 150, 182
Heterogeneous unit, 168
Hiebert, Paul G., *xiii, xv,* 33, 150, 154, 156, 158–62, 164
Hocking, William E., 89
Hoekstra, Harvey, 88
Hogan, Philip, 8
Holy Spirit, *xiv*
Hoge, Dean, 120, 196, 202
Hohensee, Donald, 142
Holistic evangelism, 87–106
Holistic growth, 82
Holistic mission, 87–106
Holy Spirit, 142–43
Homogeneous unit principle, 166–81
Hopkins, Charles Howard, 126
Hubbard, David, 103
Hudnut, Robert K., 79–80, 82, 119
Hunter, George G. III, *xv,* 77, 85, 107, 122, 125–26
Hutcheson, Richard, 74, 122

Illich, Ivan, 194
Incarnational growth, 14–15
Integration, 171
International Review of Mission, 89
InterVarsity Christian Fellowship, 118

Jacobs, Donald R., 163
Jesus Christ, Lordship of, *xiv,* 4
Johnson, Douglas W., 182, 202
Johnston, Arthur, 26, 90, 92, 97, 104, 118, 123, 150
Jones, Jim, 81
Jubilee Fellowship, 70, 200

Kasdorf, Hans, 141
Kelley, Dean M., 120, 121, 194
King, Martin Luther, 198

Kingdom of God, *xiv,* 1–23, 50, 101, 170, 173–75
Kingdom of God, biblical teaching, 4–7
Kingdom of God, signs of, 15–23, 37
Kingston, Georgia, 23
Kirk, Andrew, 9, 61
Korea, 177
Korean-Americans, 179–80
Kraft, Charles H., *xv,* 147, 150, 154, 155, 156, 163
Krass, Al, 57, 95, 98, 103, 164
Ku Klux Klan, 155, 176

Ladd, George Eldon, 2, 4, 9, 20
La Salle Street Church, Chicago, 70
Latin American Theology, xiii
Lausanne Committee, 53–54, 56–57, 70, 77, 92, 97, 166, 181
Lausanne Congress on World Evangelization, 9, 90–93, 98, 115, 169
Lausanne Covenant, 14, 37, 45, 61, 91, 92, 95, 96, 98, 104, 170
Lewis, Ron, 85
Liberalism, 196–97
Liefield, Walter L., 65
Local contextual factors, 119–20
Local institutional factors, 120
Los Gatos Christian Church, 192
Luther, Martin, 190
Lyles, Jean Caffey, 82

McGavran, Donald A., *xi,* 8, 12, 14, 29, 30, 42–43, 53, 57, 62, 69, 71, 72, 75, 78, 82, 83, 105–6, 107, 111, 115, 123, 127, 130–33, 145, 149, 157–58, 164, 166–68, 179
McIntyre, Carl, 194
McKeown, Robert E., 203
McKinney, William, 196
Malinowski, Bronislaw, 154
MARC, 77
Martin, Ralph P., 82
Marty, Martin, 79, 113, 169, 182, 197
Matthew 28:19–20, 134–36
May, Henry F., 126
Mead, Margaret, 194
Mead, Sydney, 89, 118
Michaelson, Wes, 3, 61
Mickey, Paul, 122, 124
Miller, Ted, 203
Miller, William, 3
Minnery, Tom, 194
Miracles, 17